SCOTTISH LITERATURE INTERNATIONAL

The Space of Fiction

Voices from Scotland in a post-devolution age

MARIE-ODILE PITTIN-HEDON

Association for Scottish Literary Studies

Published by
Scottish Literature International
Scottish Literature
7 University Gardens
University of Glasgow
Glasgow G12 8QH

Scottish Literature International is an imprint of
the Association for Scottish Literary Studies

www.asls.org.uk

ASLS is a registered charity no. SC006535

First published 2015

Copyright © Marie-Odile Pittin-Hedon, 2015

All rights reserved. No part of this book may be
reproduced, stored in a retrieval system, or
transmitted in any form or means, electronic,
mechanical, photocopying, recording or otherwise,
without the prior permission of the
Association for Scottish Literary Studies.

A CIP catalogue for this title
is available from the British Library

ISBN 978-1-908980-09-0

ALBA | CHRUTHACHAIL

ASLS acknowledges the support of Creative Scotland
towards the publication of this book

Contents

Acknowledgements		v
Introduction		vii
One	Millennium Babes: Female Urban Voices after James Kelman and Irvine Welsh: Laura Hird, Anne Donovan, Zoë Strachan and Alison Miller	1
Two	Female Crime Fiction: The Space of Transgression	33
Three	James Robertson: The Contagion of History	56
Four	Suhayl Saadi: The Third Space of Fiction	81
Five	Ewan Morrison: The Non-Place of Fiction	117
Six	The Confines of the Human: Shorter Fiction by Michel Faber, Des Dillon, Suhayl Saadi, Ewan Morrison and *Scotland Into The New Era*	150
Seven	Conclusion	182
Bibliography		191
List of abbreviations		203
Index		204

Sections of Chapter Two, **Female Crime Fiction: The Space of Transgression**, first appeared in Abouddahab, Rédouane and Josiane Paccaud-Huguet (eds). 2011. *Fiction, Crime and the Feminine* (Newcastle: Cambridge Scholars Publishing). Published with the permission of Cambridge Scholars Publishing.

Acknowledgements

I would like to thank Ian Brown for reading several chapters of this book in its early stages and giving me precious advice on them, and for helping me throughout this project. Many thanks also to Scott Lyall and Duncan Jones for their close reading, for all their suggestions and their help.

I also want to thank the team, Romain and Marie-Thé first, my parents, for the logistical backup they gave me, and for their huge support in all circumstances; my brothers, Vince and Christophe, who have carried my books around so often that they feel there are far too many books being written in Scotland. And of course, my love to my children Juliette, Amaury and Louis. I want to thank them for putting up with the hectic lifestyle we sometimes have, and for repeating the same thing many times when they know I'm only pretending to be listening. Thanks team, for those and for so many other reasons.

Introduction

Writing about Scottish culture in the 1980s and 1990s, Cairns Craig developed the concept of a 'national imagination' to describe what Scottish literature was most in need of. Faced with a situation of 'historylessness', 'a world where history has no meaning',[1] artists in Scotland were described as needing to create a connection between individuals' personal lives, and 'the larger trajectory of the life of the community from which they [drew] their significance'.[2] This concept of a national imagination captures the essential nature of late twentieth century Scottish literature, because it intertwines nationalism, politics, the idea of the nation and of representation as well as an underlying goal of increased cultural visibility. The extent and intricacy of the interdependence of the political and the literary, going back, in recent history, to Tom Nairn's 1977 book *The Break-up of Britain*, have led to the argument by a majority of commentators that where the political process failed in Scotland, the arts have led the way, showing a possible avenue for Scottish identity, sometimes Scottish nationalism, indeed for the very existence of Scotland as a culture *and* a nation. The argument has historically been up against quite a lot of passive, or even sometimes overtly active negation or opposition, both inside and outside Scotland, as testified for example by Richard Bradford's very assertive rejection of the notion of a Scottish renaissance in his 2007 book, *The Novel Now: Contemporary British Fiction*, which dismisses Irvine Welsh's *Trainspotting* claiming provocatively, but rather arbitrarily, that the characters in this novel 'bespeak Scotland's virtual extinction'.[3]

Five years after *The Modern Scottish Novel*, another volume, *Scotland in Theory: Reflections on Culture and Literature,* edited by Eleanor Bell and Gavin Miller, gathers contributions from significant commentators on Scottish history, politics and culture, such as Tom Nairn, Cairns Craig, and Christopher Harvie. Many of its chapters theorise the link between politics and the arts in Scotland. Harvie emphasises the fundamental role of Scottish writers in the crucial period from the renaissance of Scottish culture through the years leading up to devolution by taking up the argument that in the absence of political democracy during the period, it was left to literature to explore the interconnections of power in a devolved Scotland. The assumption that writers have created or in any event underwritten devolution, an idea summed up in the somewhat proactive title of one of Craig's papers, 'No Nationality Without Literature',[4] surfaces in many other publications to the extent that it has now become a critical commonplace. For instance Angus Calder, in *Scotlands of the Mind*, states that many political victories in Scotland in the late years of the twentieth century (such as the demise of the conservative party) can be attributed to actors of the literary world,[5] and writers themselves acknowledge this interaction by stating, in the words of Duncan McLean speaking in the wake of the setting up of the Scottish Parliament, that 'there's been a parliament of novels for years'.[6] Tom Leonard even more categorically states the artists' role in bringing about a parliament for Scotland in the 1999 issue of the *Edinburgh Review*:

> What influence will the Scottish Parliament have on Scottish Writing? Very little. The influence will be the other way around. After all, hasn't Scottish writing been one of the major causes in bringing the Scottish Parliament into existence?[7]

And indeed, the context for such assertions has been one of creative explosion in Scotland in the last thirty years. The literary scene in particular has come a long way from the days not so long ago when Iain Banks was reduced to using a sort of arithmetical formula to bear witness to the very existence of Scotland as a valid and valuable place for fiction to come from.[8] But this is not to say that literature can (or indeed should) be substituted for politics, or that literature took over in Scotland in the absence of political will. There is very little hard evidence to justify the claim, and many writers are equally impatient with this assertion. Janice Galloway, for instance, makes this clear:

> Cross-fertilised soil is always richer, and it might help get us off some of the rather tedious single-track roads this country's writers are often expected to go down. Who wants to write about *nation* all the bloody time? To write through it, take it for granted – dear me yes.[9]

INTRODUCTION

Alex Thomson considers that this dilemma in the appraisal of the role of literature for the constitution of our idea of the nation leads us back to the distinction drawn by René Welleck and Austin Warren in their classic study *Theory of Literature* (1949) between two types of literary histories, a distinction which can be extended to literary analysis more generally between the 'intrinsic' and 'extrinsic' approaches to literature. The intrinsic approach 'seeks to explain particular works of art as autonomous artifact', whereas extrinsic criticism 'seeks to explain particular works, or the development of series of works, in relation to social, political or historical events'.[10] Thomson uses this distinction to make a case against the current trend in literary criticism in Scotland, claiming that:

> [t]he revival of historicism in literary studies has tended [...] to dissolve literary history into something more like anthropology or cultural studies, in which the nation becomes an object of analysis rather than a causal or explanatory principle and the literary artwork becomes an index to a particular configuration of social forces.[11]

This may be an exaggeration, but the fact remains that the concept of 'writing Scotland' is today a sum of sometimes conflicting ideas: it covers writing about and through Scotland, as indicated by Galloway, but also writing for Scotland, to Scotland, or even quite simply in Scotland, a fact which leads the writer, as well as the critic, back to the dilemma summarised by Thomson. It is certainly obvious that creative artists have increasingly come to see their homeland as a place where the arts are at last a real and viable proposition as is indicated for example by Alasdair Gray's confidence at a conference at the University of Avignon in 2009:

> [C]ertainly there's less pessimism in Scotland nowadays, about the prospect of being an artist there, partly because undoubtedly things have improved. There are art dealers working in Glasgow now with international connections, and in the 1950s and 60s there weren't any at all. And from the point of view of individual writings, one of the things I find quite cheery about the Scottish situation nowadays is that it would once have been unthinkable to have a private eye

crime fiction with a Scottish setting and a Scottish detective and Ian Rankin has shown that possible. People have accepted that Scotland is as possible a place to have what is called genre fiction as anywhere else in Britain.[12]

Gray has good reasons to show such confidence. There has been, over the last ten years, a remarkable increase in the number of novels and books of short stories – not to mention poetry and drama – published in Scotland or by Scottish writers, as is showcased by the Edinburgh Book Festival every summer. Scottish universities throughout the country now offer a variety of very prolific creative writing courses, with – over the years and looking only at the University of Glasgow as an example – tutors such as Gray, James Kelman and Tom Leonard, but also Zoë Strachan, herself a former student of the course, and Louise Welsh. This vitality, as Ali Smith indicates in a 2009 interview, shows an increased confidence in an opening up of Scotland's literature, with all the diversity that this openness suggests. Smith indeed claims that 'Literary Scotland is a collective, immensely versatile, often cosmopolitan consciousness, or a vital, wide-open book'.[13]

Nevertheless, this confidence begs the question of the kind of issues that are addressed by contemporary writers, and of their own theoretical, stylistic and even thematic and political agenda. What will be adopted in this monograph is precisely an approach that mixes intrinsic and extrinsic characteristics. Starting from an extrinsic point of view, the study will follow works which travel back and forth between social or political issues and very idiosyncratic theoretical or stylistic issues far removed from political or historical events. Glaswegians Louise Welsh, Zoë Strachan or Anne Donovan, whose first novel *Buddha Da* (2003) was shortlisted both for the Orange Prize and the Whitbread first novel prize, show, in their own separate ways, how personal relationships and even the sense of one's identity can be endangered by traumatic or extraordinary events. Alison Miller, whose first novel *Demo* (2005) takes her characters from the anti Iraq-war demonstrations in Glasgow to London and Italy, shows an interest in class issues that goes beyond the Scottish borders. Ewan Morrison's novels *Swung* (2007), *Distance* (2008), and collection of short stories *The Last Book You Read* (2005), set in Scotland and in the US, convey a sense of disaffection with the bland universalism of the world in a global, consumerist age. Suhayl Saadi, a Glaswegian writer of Afghan and Pakistani descent, author of landmark novels *Psychoraag* (2004) and *Joseph's Box* (2009) is described by Willy Maley as one of the many Scottish writers who crosses borders.[14] All these novelists testify to the wealth and diversity of contemporary Scottish writing and stretch in their own ways the geographical and artistic boundaries of Scotland.

Ian Brown and Colin Nicholson contextualise this tendency of Scottish writers to work across boundaries by showing how poets and dramatists, as well as prose fiction writers, began to cross geographical, linguistic and generic borders in the mid-twentieth century. They account for this phenomenon in terms of its peculiar artistic, ideological and political relevance in a Scottish context, stressing that it enables artists to assert a different, multiple and complex identity, to 'reconfigur[e] [...] the possible':[15]

> As the 'United' Kingdom's nature is questioned, so writers who cross genre, language and art-form boundaries reflect that enquiry. Interrogating artistic borders, they interrogate the national idea. (2007: 263)[16]

By stressing the evolution of the link between artistic and political borders to take into account the paradigm-changing nature of the Scottish Independence Referendum of 2014, Brown and Nicholson acknowledge the shift in contemporary Scottish literature from the first generation of writers – Gray, Kelman, Galloway, Welsh, Kennedy – who opened up a space for Scottish fiction and Scottish identity in a British context, to the present generation, represented by writers as diverse as Morrison, Saadi, Donovan, Strachan, Faber, Robertson, but also Alan Bissett, Rodge Glass or Alan Warner, whose task it has been to occupy and transform the literary scene in Scotland. But Brown and Nicholson's assessment, while keeping the national idea in view, also makes use of the intrinsic approach, when they discuss the challenging of both artistic and national boundaries. The connection between the two, however, needs to be discussed, as there is no simple, 'natural' or organic correspondence between them. All the writers whose novels and short stories are examined in this book interrogate artistic borders in their own specific ways, while their connection to the national idea is not necessarily a straightforward one. They project what can be called a new space of fiction, a polymorphous space for fiction, as do more recently published artists such as Jenni Fagan, whose first novel *The Panopticon* (2013) follows the life of fifteen-year-old Anais Hendricks in the stark universe of institutions, homes for the young offenders and housing schemes, or Jason Donald and Andrea McNicoll, recent graduates of the University of Glasgow creative writing course, and the authors respectively of *Choke Chain* (2009) set in South Africa, where the author lived as a child for a period of fourteen years, and *Moonshine in the Morning* (2008) set in Thailand where McNicoll spent many years of her young adult life. Together with other, sometimes very famous border crossers, such as Edinburgh-based J. K. Rowling, whose Harry Potter series is included in studies of genre fiction in Scotland, they evidence a prolixity and diversity which raises the issue of Scottish identity and Scottish art in a manner widely different from what it was in the early 1980s. They tackle the question of space in Scottish fiction in a way that ties in with the theoretical shift of the last thirty years, from identity politics to creativity, from postmodernism and language politics to post-nationalism, from devolutionary writing to post-devolution writing, from nationalism to globalisation and cosmopolitanism. *The Space of Fiction* aims at following this shift, to try and explore the changed territory it has uncovered.

Nationalism, globalism, cosmopolitanism and the Scottish novel

In *Scotland in Theory*, Miller and Bell describe the contemporary period as a 'post-national age'. Bell, starting from the theoretical thinking of Richard Kearney, contends that a European identity is developing because of the way power is restructured at a European level, with the emergence of countries as super-nation-states, which are gradually prevailing over nation states. 'This focus on the postnational', she argues, 'encourages a re-thinking of the traditional concept of "Scotland"'[17] In *Literature as Intervention*, Jürgen Neubauer, opposing those he calls 'the nationalist critics', argues that the concept of national identity itself is problematic, as is the link established by critics between literature and national identity. He borrows instead Habermas's concept of the 'postnational constellation' to show that with the collapse of national boundaries there has been, in European countries, a move which he describes as transnational as well as local. This analysis, Neubauer insists, applies to both macroeconomic issues and to culture and the arts: 'Scottish writers are beginning to imagine life in postnational constellations in which interactions and relationships are both more local and more global than the nation.'[18]

This concept of a post-national identity, and therefore of a – possibly problematic – post-national literature, raises the issue of the interconnections of art, ideology and politics, which are precisely the crossroads the Scottish novel is standing at. It problematises the notions of space, identity and writing, and therefore implies a re-examination of formal and generic issues, therefore inviting the circulation between the intrinsic and extrinsic treatments. This book aims to be an examination of this concept of contemporary Scotland that is created in fiction – which has segued into many inter-related notions such as the post-national, the post-devolution or the cosmopolitan – through a critical analysis of some of the emerging voices of the literary scene, or of authors who have come to prominence in the period since the setting up of the Scottish Parliament. It will focus on the shift from the postmodern – 'the postworld of our postmodernity' (Craig, 1996: 218) – and the problematic delineation and creation of a 'national identity', to an integration of some of the strategic aspects of the postmodern into the present context, represented by a post-devolution (Schoene), post-national (Bell, Miller), hybrid, globalised (Crawford), cosmopolitan (Schoene) or even mongrelised (Calder, Bissett) aesthetics. It therefore aims to focus on a specific yet diverse sense of place and space, and examines fiction produced in the first decade of the twenty-first century with that particular angle.

In *Scotland's Books,* Robert Crawford contends that 'literature has operated in advance of political structures, to signal the need to pay attention to the conventionally excluded, then to focus attention on a global community and Scotland's relationship to it',[19] once again linking novelistic and political discourses while putting the emphasis on an enlarged, 'globalised' context. Marc Lambert speaks of 'compensatory stories' which 'function as surrogates for the missing story of power',[20] while Crawford speaks of contemporary Scotland as 'a land whose writers may be more ready than its politicians to explore the consequences of globalisation' (2007: 727). The idea of globalisation itself is, however, an ambiguous one, especially in terms of its connotations, which, as is indicated by Berthold Schoene, suggest homogenisation and ultimately Americanisation.[21] Tom Nairn is particularly vocal in describing Britain as undergoing 'indirect rule' or 'elective subjection' at the hands of the US, with 'self colonisation' as its inescapable result,[22] while Irvine Welsh, in *Glue*, has his own economical way of pointing to the fact when his character states that 'We're [...] the fifty-first US state'.[23]

Globalisation in the shape of Americanisation is indeed an issue that is present in many contemporary novels, among which Morrison's *Distance* (2008), or James Kelman's very critical *You Have to be Careful in the Land of the Free* (2004). It will be the focus of the fifth chapter of this book, entitled 'The Non-Place of Fiction', which examines the failure of the idea of a global space as presented in Morrison's work. But globalisation, with its tendency to invade all realms of public and private life, with the increasing ubiquity and therefore vagueness of the term, is a concept fraught with contradictions. Schoene's conceptual thinking will therefore be useful, particularly his desire to avoid what he describes as the regulatory, almost neo-imperialistic connotation of the term 'globalisation', by using the term 'cosmopolitanism' as a more assertive position which in addition manages to encompass the local:

> Cosmopolitanism must not be cultivated at the expense of a people's cultural difference or national self-expression; in fact, it is crucial to understand that, as Pheng Cheah explains, cosmopolitan's 'antonym is not *nationalism* but statism'. Cosmopolitanism repudiates reductions of 'society' and 'the public' to what inhabits or evolves within a neatly staked-out homogeneous realm. [...] In fact, cosmopolitanism's greatest strength lies in defusing the undesirable side-effects of globalisation by working to deconstruct neo-imperial hegemonies, champion transnational partnership, and project the world as a network of interdependencies. [...] One of the chief attractions of a cosmopolitan outlook for literary creativity is that without detracting from a writer's cultural extraction or sense of belonging, it loosens the nation's grip on the individual talent. (2008: 75–76)

In that sense, cosmopolitanism precisely enables writers to accept their heritage and identity as such, without the absurdity of somehow having to work from a sort of generic identity kit that would justify their creations, an idea which Janice Galloway sums up as writing *through*, rather than *about* the nation. What is underlined here is the symbolic effect of the setting up of the Scottish Parliament, resulting in a freeing of literature which is allowed to be just that, rather than an expression of the nationalist movement or at the very least of the sense of the nation's identity, a liberation Schoene captures under the heading 'post-devolution literature'.[24] Douglas Gifford and Dorothy McMillan address the opening up of the space of fiction in the run up to devolution, speaking of a 'new spectrum of possibility [which] is based on a new willingness to allow a multi-faceted Scotland no longer demanding allegiance to a single MacDiarmid agenda, but recognising other people's right to perceive Scotland differently also'.[25]

The idea of multiple perceptions as well as that of cross-fertilisation in addition points to the idea of a 'multi-faceted Scotland', which sometimes reads as multicultural, or quite simply, but very importantly, diverse. Angus Calder takes up the idea of Scotland being 'a mongrel nation', aired by William McIlvanney to define how nationalism can be understood within a context of diversity, therefore announcing the link made by Schoene between cosmopolitanism and a brand of nationalism in Scotland devoid of ethnic connotations. For Calder (2002: xiii), 'the concept of mongrelism also makes it easier to affirm diversity as, paradoxically, a basis for our unity.' Brown and Nicholson (2007: 271) go even further by insisting on the sheer necessity of mongrelism, when they claim that '[B]order crossers [...] celebrate alterity. Their work welcomes and embraces the hybridity of cultures and of Scotland and recognises the fecundity of impurity and the necessity of intermingling.'

The new context has given birth to a new concentration of the novel on the diversity of human experience as well as to a new aesthetics, or rather, a plurality of aesthetics. To borrow Schoene's words again (2008: 76), the writer, rather than straining to write to establish a sense of a specific identity 'again becomes an ambassador of human experience'. Galloway also expresses this idea when she insists on her interest in the notions of nation, gender or class from the point of view of 'how they affect an individual consciousness'.[26] Ewan Morrison describes his interest in relationships between individuals, in the way they connect or fail to connect in a context in which, he explains, globalisation has been imported into our everyday lives in the shape of consumerism. Gerry Hassan, in the *Scotland 2020* volume which he edited in 2005, also insists on this back-to-basics approach which, however, represents a huge leap forward for Scottish culture. For Hassan, '[w]hat Scotland requires is an ethic of living – a set of stories or narratives – that embodies and reflects the ways we live our lives'.[27] The stories envisaged by Hassan in order to create what he terms (2005: 33) – using a plural form – 'preferred futures for Scotland', need to devise and have been devising a new aesthetic which borrows at once from the local and the global, mixing as it does contemporary culture with the literary, the post-modern with the fantastic, the Kelmanesque voice with the defusing of realism, a sense of geographical expansion with a very peculiar sense of the here and now. Alan Bissett, for instance, has applied the DJing term of 'sampling' to describe Suhayl Saadi's or Anne Donovan's modes of novelistic composition.[28] Angus Peter Campbell describes the current period as 'post-post modernist' and elaborates, claiming that '[modernism and the folk tradition] now fit perfectly. You see, the contemporary world seems to me to be straight out of the Gaelic folk tradition: magical and fragmented, without any seeming "logic" weighing it down'.[29]

Another feature that defines contemporary literature in Scotland is its refusal to align itself with the conventional division into generic category, with the concept of 'genre fiction' as opposed to 'mainstream/literary fiction'. The codes that govern genres are often made to interact; they are displaced, distorted, parodied, pastiched, or simply transferred from one form of narrative to another. This constitutes a symptom of what A. L. Kennedy perceives as a propensity for Scottish writing to be 'non-aligned and anarchic and critical'.[30]

This book will attempt to follow the anarchic track presented by some post-devolution novels, trying to map out the way that they challenge and displace a variety of established borders. It will examine the tensions between the new, global economy, our market-driven world and its literary expression which favours a cosmopolitan approach. It will follow the current critical approach that has distanced itself from the notion of the genetically or linguistically 'pure Scot'[31] to consider, for instance, the input of novelists such as Michel Faber or Suhayl Saadi. It will also rely on the displacement of generic frontiers, which functions as a metaphorical echo of the displacement of geographical and maybe psychological borders, and will analyse the result of the undermining of genre, of language and of narration and therefore of the expected discourse carried by the novel, effectively uncovering what I have called a new space of fiction. What is interesting is ultimately the openness – to form, to discourse, to genre, to other artistic languages – of Scottish fiction in the last fifteen years, and an intrinsic approach will be used to describe this stylistic diversity, by looking at some of the artists who make up 'the wave of noughties' writers' (Bissett, 2007: 60). Seeking to examine this phenomenon from a position that avoids the concentration on proto-canonical writing,[32] and therefore focusing on writers who have up till now received comparatively less critical attention, I will examine novels which have been published after the opening of the Scottish Parliament, precisely for their capacity to add to the sense of place, to delimit and make sense of the ever-shifting, elusive space which, rather than being the national space, can best be described as the space of fiction.

The first chapter, entitled 'Millennium Babes', in keeping with the goal of tracing the shift from opening up a space to inhabiting and refashioning it, revisits urban spaces after James Kelman and Irvine Welsh, but also after the breakthrough of female fiction represented by the publication of Janice Galloway's and A. L. Kennedy's novels in the 1990s. It examines the novels of four women writers: Laura Hird, Anne Donovan, Zoë Strachan and Alison Miller. Starting from the depiction of the social and linguistic prison-house in which the four writers enclose their characters – a feature that links them to Galloway and Kennedy – and borrowing from Stephanie Lehner's use of the concept of the subaltern in literature, I will describe how the process of liberation is one of liberation of the voice, to constitute what Jeremy Scott calls an 'immanent voice'. This process implies an appropriation of discourse, a rewriting of traditions, as well as a creative process which is one of depicting identity as a void, in order to refashion this gap as a creative, communicative and imaginative discourse, an immanent voice in the sense of an immanent *and* cosmopolitan literary voice.

The second chapter, 'Female Crime Fiction: The Space of Transgression' brings the novels of Louise Welsh, which blur the border between genre fiction and literary fiction, together with the works of two novelists considered as writing from within the generic borderland of crime fiction, Val McDermid and Denise Mina. The goal is to describe the breakdown of the generic frontier. I will first focus on the way those writers operate – by applying revamped gothic formulae to the narration of crime for instance – in order to examine issues that concentrate on the depiction of violence and its status in society and in art, as seen from a feminine angle. I will show how crime, violence and abuse can involve the reader by foregrounding another boundary, that between fiction and the reader's reality. The 'literature of containment'[33], to borrow Gill Plain's characterisation of detective fiction, becomes a literature of contamination, of incrimination, a process which affects both the world of the fictional construct that is the novel and that of the reader.

Chapter three, 'James Robertson: The Contagion of History', explores a different, diachronic border. This chapter displaces the focus from fictional and generic space to historical space, and examines the space of the past with a view to showing how it seems to contaminate the present in a manner that is symmetrical to the way in which the present invades the past. The chapter, mostly devoted to the sprawling *And The Land Lay Still* (2010), which tackles both the recent past – the second half of the twentieth century – and the mythification of the Scottish past, will show how Robertson manages to fictionalise various discourses of the past, to embody the process of telling and writing history in order to de-mythify and re-mythify Scotland's past and present, and therefore to suggest a more dynamic vision of the Scottish literary and historical past in the post-devolution world.

Chapter four, 'Suhayl Saadi: The Third Space of Fiction', tackles the issue of cosmopolitanism, multiculturalism and the post-colonial narrative in a Scottish context. Starting from the novels of Suhayl Saadi, it focuses on the politics of identity in a context of multiculturalism and its fashionable appeal in novels throughout the world and particularly in Britain. Saadi's dismissal of what he terms 'safe multiculturalism', as well as the insertion of his fictions into a Scottish *and* cosmopolitan context, which he represents and problematises, reorganises the space of fiction as the space of ethical commitment, conveyed by a commitment to language which is a renewal of Kelman's politics of fiction.

Saadi's contribution to the delineation of the space of fiction suggests a careful, exacting use of multiculturalism to achieve a form of cosmopolitanism which can be linked to Morrison's indictment of globalisation. The fifth chapter, 'Ewan Morrison: The Non-Place of Fiction', discusses the three novels *Swung* (2007), *Distance* (2008) and *Ménage* (2009) to focus on the complex and interrelated notions of location and the individual, examining the forces of globalisation as they are expressed, parodied and dislocated. I will use Marc Augé's concept of the non-place, and Zygmunt

INTRODUCTION

Bauman's notions of emic and phagic places in connection not only with the shopping malls or airports Morrison uses as protagonists in tales where the human seems to be dissolved or overpowered, but also with the fragmentation of the sense of place which reflects the fragmentation of the self and the incommunicability between humans. Morrison's novels also examine identity through the prism of the mass-manufacturing of individuality, and the idea of newness and disposability imported from capitalism into the realm of the human.

Chapter six, 'The Confines of the Human', carries the logic depicted in chapter five to various fictional extremes by focusing on an increasingly virtual and therefore problematic space of communication. It is devoted to an examination of shorter fiction by Morrison, Saadi, Des Dillon and Michel Faber, among other writers, focusing on their inter-connected capacity to create, destroy and problematise worlds in which their characters do not seem to find a safe footing. The commodification of the human, the individual's crumbling sense of himself, are described as attempts by the narrators to achieve fictional resolution in an age of cybercommunication which results in the erasure of the human. This process is paralleled with an examination of the way in which the past, history and the nation are also commodified. This chapter takes up the conclusions of the preceding ones and conjures up a Brave New World that cannot shape the future.

The Space of Fiction therefore starts as a review of various spaces of fiction that have been opened in the wake the opening of the Scottish Parliament in 1999. However, it endeavours to map the interconnections between their various approaches to a post-national, cosmopolitan, multicultural or maybe even globalised Scotland, an approach which always leads us back to the literary. Between them, the chapters in this book follow Saadi's lead when the latter, writing about new Scottish writing, delineates three categories of writers:

> Simplistically, I perceive three dynamics:
> 1. Scottish writers gazing out and drawing on so-called 'other' societies or literary traditions and incorporating something of these into their own writing. What I call, 'looking out'.
> 2. Writers who hail from other cultures bringing something of their or their ancestors' experiences with them and those experiences

exerting themselves, either consciously or otherwise, in fresh contexts in their writing. I call this, 'moving in'.

3. Writers who dig deep into that which they perceive as being their own, indigenous Scottish culture(s) and who, in doing so, are able to hit the bedrock, as it were. This is what I refer to as, 'digging deep'.

By these processes – looking out, moving in, digging deep – writing becomes indigenised. It becomes perceived as mainstream. That which, in literary terms, was seen as being 'outside' or substratum becomes internalised, manifest.[34]

This book aims to look at writers looking in (Donovan), moving in (Saadi himself) and digging deep (Robertson) while including other contributors who might be described as zooming out (Mina or Welsh) or as aiming wide (Morrison). In short, it focuses on some of – but by no means all – the most significant contemporary contributors to the Scottish space of fiction.

INTRODUCTION

Notes

1. Craig, Cairns. 1996. *Out of History: Narrative Paradigms in Scottish and British Culture* (Edinburgh: Polygon), p. 49. Craig uses this phrase about Grassic Gibbon's *A Scots Quair*.
2. Craig, Cairns. 1999. *The Modern Scottish Novel: Narrative and the National Imagination* (Edinburgh: Edinburgh U.P.), p. 10.
3. Bradford, Richard. 2007. *The Novel Now* (Oxford: Blackwell Publishing), p. 167.
4. Craig, Cairns. 2006. 'No Nationality Without Literature', *GRAAT* no. 33, 79–98.
5. See Calder, Angus. 2002. *Scotland of the Mind* (Edinburgh: Luath Press), pp. xii–xiii.
6. 'Poets' Parliament', *Edinburgh Review* 100, (1999), p. 74.
7. Ibid., p. 73.
8. 'we're just ten per cent of the UK, but we've got more than ten per cent of the best writers'. 'A Quick Chat with Iain M. Banks', *The Richmond Review*, 1996, www.demon.co.uk/review/features/banksint.html [consulted January 1998].
9. Galloway, Janice. 1999. *Edinburgh Review* 100, p. 72.
10. Welleck, René and Austin Warren. [1949]. 1963. *Theory of Literature* (Harmondsworth: Penguin), quoted in Thomson, Alex. Autumn/Winter 2007. '"You can't get there from here": Devolution and Scottish literary history', in *International Journal of Scottish Literature*, Issue 3, www.ijsl.stir.ac.uk, [consulted April 2010], p. 2.
11. Ibid., p. 2.
12. Gray, Alasdair. 2010. *Alasdair Gray: La Littérature ou le refus de l'amnésie/Literature against Amnesia* (Avignon : Editions Universitaires d'Avignon), p. 49.
13. Ali Smith interview. 2009. *The Scottish Review of Books*, 5.2, May, p. 9.
14. Maley, Willy. n.d. *Discovering Scottish Literature: a Contemporary Overview*, www.scottishbooktrust.com/files/Border-crossing%20-%20New%20Scottish%20Writing%20by%20Willy%20Maley.pdf [consulted December 2008].
15. Brown, Ian and Colin Nicholson. 2007. 'The Border Crossers and Reconfiguration of the Possible: Poet-Playwright-Novelists from the Mid-Twentieth Century on', in Ian Brown (ed.). *The Edinburgh History of Scottish Literature*, vol. 3 (Edinburgh: Edinburgh U.P.), p. 262.
16. See also the artists who cross borders, among whom Brown and Nicholson include Iain Crichton Smith, Edwin Morgan, Jessie Kesson, Kenneth White or Jackie Kay, to name but a few. See for instance p. 266 for an analysis of Ian Hamilton Finlay's experiment with concrete poetry, Kenneth White's 'geopoetics' (268) or Edwin Morgan's project for a 'Republic of Letters' (268).
17. Bell, Eleanor, and Gavin Miller (eds). 2005. *Scotland in Theory: Reflections on Culture and Literature* (Amsterdam and New York: Rodopi), p. 84.
18. Neubauer, Jürgen. 1999. *Literature as Intervention: Struggles over Cultural Identity in Contemporary Scottish Fiction* (Marburg: Textum Verlag), p. 12. See also 'Introduction', pp. 9–19.
19. Crawford, Robert. 2007. *Scotland's Books* (London: Penguin), p. 661.
20. Lambert, Marc. 2005. 'The Age of Capitals: Edinburgh as Culture City', in Gerry Hassan, Eddie Gibb and Lydia Howland (eds), *Scotland 2020, Hopeful Stories for A Northern Nation* (London: Demos), p. 127.
21. See Schoene, Berthold. 2008. 'Cosmopolitan Scots', in *The Scottish Studies Review*, 9, 2, Autumn, pp. 71–92.
22. Nairn, Tom. 2005. 'Break-Up: Twenty-Five Years On', in Eleanor Bell and Gavin Miller (eds), p. 27

23 Welsh, Irvine. 2001. *Glue* (London: Jonathan Cape), p. 413.
24 See Schoene 'Introduction', in Schoene, Berthold, (ed.). 2007. *The Edinburgh Companion to Contemporary Scottish Literature* (Edinburgh: Edinburgh U. P.), pp. 1–4.
25 Gifford, Douglas and Dorothy McMillan (eds). 1997. *A History of Scottish Women's Writing* (Edinburgh: Edinburgh U.P.), p. 597.
26 Galloway, Janice, in *Edinburgh Review* 100, p. 71.
27 Hassan, Gerry. 2005. 'That was Then and This is Now', in Hassan, Gibb and Howland (eds), p. 33.
28 See Bissett, Alan. 2007. 'The "New Weegies": The Glasgow Novel in the Twenty-First Century', in Berthold Schoene (ed.), p. 63.
29 Campbell, Angus Peter. 2009. *Scottish Review of Books*, 5.1, p. 16.
30 Kennedy, A. L., *Edinburgh Review* 100, p. 73.
31 Angus Calder critically takes up the idea, by pointing out that 'there is no such thing as a 'pure' Scot, linguistically or genetically' (2002: xiv).
32 Stuart Kelly outlines what he calls a proto-canon of contemporary Scottish writing, which is composed of Edwin Morgan, Liz Lochhead, Alasdair Gray, James Kelman, Andrew Greig, Christopher Whyte, Iain (M.) Banks, Janice Galloway, Jackie Kay, Irvine Welsh, Kathleen Jamie, Don Paterson, Alan Warner and A. L. Kennedy. See Kelly, Stuart. 2009. 'How Tartan is Your Text?', *International Journal of Scottish Literature*, Issue 5, Autumn/Winter, www.ijsl.stir.ac.uk [consulted April 2010].
33 Plain, Gill. 2001. *Twentieth Century Crime Fiction: Gender, Sexuality and the Body* (Edinburgh: Edinburgh U. P.), p. 3.
34 Saadi, Suhayl. 2000. 'Infinite Diversity in New Scottish Writing', asls.arts.gla.ac.uk/SSaadi.html [consulted 28 February 2011].

1. Millennium Babes: Female Urban Voices after James Kelman and Irvine Welsh: Laura Hird, Anne Donovan, Zoë Strachan and Alison Miller

With the coming to prominence of two great voices in the 1990s, Janice Galloway and A. L. Kennedy, the all-male focus in Scottish writing, or at least the male domination over fiction-writing since the 1970s which, though not absolute, was very hegemonic, came to an end.[1] Two major critical works published in the late 1990s and early 2000s, Gifford and McMillan's *A History of Scottish Women's Writing* (1997) and Christianson and Lumsden's *Contemporary Scottish Women Writers* (2000), noted the advent of a new diversity for Scottish writing, and although Christianson and Lumsden deal in their introduction with the difficulties inherent in trying to interpret a work of art according to the gender of its author (all the more so as the authors themselves resist being classified either in terms of their gender or, for that matter, their nationality), they identify and describe the creation of a new voice for women in the last two decades, the voice of writers who 'interrogate the "space" of Scotland in their own way'.[2] While Gifford (1997: 609) warns that 'the real concerns and the real voices of contemporary women should genuinely be heard in Scottish society, and not just paid condescending lip service', Kirstin Innes even more pointedly insists on the stumbling-block represented by an all-male literary tradition, in a way that refuses qualification and nuances:

> The much fêted new visibility of Scottish culture, which coincides with the working-class male's literary enfranchisement, appears to be won at the expense of women, gay men and ethnic minorities whose voices are silenced by the new literature's blatant misogyny, homophobia and racism.[3]

Innes goes on to contend that female experience in Scotland is dislocated by a national language which is both male and androcentric, an issue which is certainly tackled by both Kennedy and Galloway in their novels *Looking for the Possible Dance* (1993) and *The Trick Is to Keep Breathing* (1989). This chapter focuses on a generation of women writers in Scotland whose books were published at the turn of the millennium, in the wake of Galloway and Kennedy, while also being linked to the urban fiction of Welsh and Kelman, with its particular concentration on the urban working-class or underclass and their specific idiom. Donovan, Hird, Strachan and even more recently Alison Miller can all claim the ambiguous epithet of 'Renton's bairns' bestowed on them (and on other writers such as, notably, Suhayl Saadi) by Innes. Of Renton's bairns, none can claim kinship with Welsh as much as Hird who was first associated with him, Duncan McLean, Gordon Legge and James Meek in Kevin Williamson's project *Children of Albion Rovers* in 1996, succeeded by the mockingly threatening *Rovers Return* in 1998.[4] Hird's first novel's title, *Born Free* (1999), reads like a statement of purpose, as well as an affirmation of liberation from the constraints commented upon by her predecessors, for an author who does not feel as if her gender or any other aspect of herself might have stood in the way of publication. The novel itself, a domestic comedy of a dark and bitter kind, like Hird's shorter fiction published in *Hope and other Urban Tales* (2006), presents the reader with a voice which, as in Donovan's and Miller's fiction, makes great use of the vernacular, and with a focus upon the lower classes of society, in the case of Hird's 'Welshian novel', the upper levels of the working classes.[5]

Like Welsh in *Glue*, she shifts points of views in her alternate chapters, but unlike Welsh, who almost exclusively uses male focalisers and narrators, she presents the reader with the points of view of all family members, male and female, as do Donovan in *Buddha Da* – though in a more sympathetic way – and Alison Miller, who uses two female narrators in *Demo* (2005). All these voices, together with those of Strachan's female protagonists in *Spin Cycle* (2004) and *Negative Space* (2002), because they articulate a depiction of space dependent on the treatment of voice, both vernacular and narrative voice, and share Kelman's preoccupation with the representation of the working classes, can be described not only as demotic voices, but, to borrow Jeremy Scott's concept, as 'immanent voices', namely voices rooted to their location. Scott notes:

> the enormous difficulty of the task faced by any piece of writing which attempts to invest its narrative discourse with the 'spirit of the place' – to make the voice immanent to its location, in other

words to its urban context, and immanent to the people who speak with that voice.[6]

Strachan, whose use of dialect is more limited but by no means absent, and whose narrative is also fragmented into spaces controlled by the distinct and distinctive voices of her various protagonists, presents a vision of how the past and the present are inextricably linked in the psyche of an individual, and in the projection of one individual story of the past onto the present, while Donovan, Miller and Hird focus on the immediacy of the characters' present. All of them, however, present immanent voices that shape post-Kelman and post-Welsh urban spaces.

The social and linguistic prison-house

In keeping with Moira Burgess's 1998 identification of Glasgow as a 'kaleidoscope city',[7] Donovan, Hird, Miller and Strachan all present a kaleidoscopic vision of the urban space they concentrate on, which is informed by multiculturalism as two of the novels' plots hinge on cultural diversity. Bissett also points out that the novels comprise ideological spaces, which take into account not just Glaswegian-ness, or Edinburgh-ness, but also Buddhism, Islamism, youth culture and popular culture in the form of popular newspapers and music, therefore linking regionalism and globalism in a postnationalist fashion.[8] For all four writers, that kaleidoscopic urban space starts from a polyphonic basis: *Born Free*, *Buddha Da*, *Demo* and *Spin Cycle* all narrate their stories by using separate viewpoints and separate voices in alternate chapters. *Buddha Da*, a comedy of domestic crisis, like Hird's *Born Free*, a much more gritty and bitter version of the same general theme, alternates between the voices of the various family members, whereas Strachan's *Spin Cycle* uses the points of view of her four female protagonists.

Miller, who takes her characters from London and Glasgow to Florence, uses two focalisers, Clare and Laetitia. Indeed, in this coming of age novel Clare, a sixteen-year-old Glaswegian schoolgirl and her big brother Danny, attend an anti-globalisation demonstration in Florence as well as the anti-Iraq demo that took place in Glasgow in 2005. At the demo they meet Laetitia, an upper class English PhD student of literature, and her rich, smug boyfriend Julian, also a PhD student. With Julian, Clare undergoes sexual initiation

3

in Florence. Between the four characters, the separation is social, spatial (London vs. Glasgow) and political (Clare's father is a communist). The subplot also adds a religious and cultural divide with Clare's school friend Farkhanda, a Muslim whose family was originally from Pakistan. The text depicts the gradual estrangement of the two best friends as one becomes more and more involved in religion and the other is mired in a complicated relationship, or lack of one, with Julian. Farkhanda goes to university and is depicted as taking control of her life in the third part of the novel, whereas Clare does not sit her English exam and so cannot move on to university. She is left behind, a ghost in the house, whereas her brother has a job, and Laetitia and Julian have moved into the realm of adults and (unwittingly) become parents.

By alternating Clare's and Laetitia's viewpoints, the novel presents two voices, one Scottish, one English, and two visions with several dividing lines, as well as an overwhelmingly political focus, with both narratives pitting English and Scottish stereotypes against each other. However, what separates the characters most is their social background. Miller contrasts Clare's working-class Glasgow voice with Laetitia's upper class standard English, so that the voices in *Demo* become the main carriers of the confrontation of world views which is at its core. Working-class activism, combined with a lack of working-class prospects, as embodied by both Danny and Clare, and symbolised by the cleaving difference with the upper-class characters, is quite conventionally made explicit through a linguistic difference as well as a difference of schooling: both Laetitia and Julian are postgraduates, while the emphasis, for Danny and Clare, is put on their absence of a university education, as a sort of class fatalism. For Danny:

> Man, I don't know how yous can be bothered. Four years at university, then another five and six studying some deid writer. [...] what's it got to do with the price of mince? How's it gonny add to the sum of human happiness?
> Good question. Have you never thought of going to university?
> Nah. Didny stick in at school. Too busy runnin about the scheme wae my pals, getting into scrapes. Nay Highers, two poxy Standard Grades. My da went mental the day the results came out, did his Big Red Clydesider [...]: *Apart fae revolution, it's education that's gonny*

liberate the masses! There's nae room for a stumer in the struggle. He turned and smiled at her. So that was me. (*DE*, 193–94)

This is an unwitting statement of failure which is made even clearer in Clare's case:

> I'm dead jealous of Farkhanda being at uni. I could a been there with her if I hadny blew it, no sittin my Higher English. Why did I no? It's hard to remember now. I was on a real downer after the Glasgow demo and what happened wi Julian. And then the war started anyway and I thought, what's the point? What is the fuckin point? But when my da heard I'd dogged it, he was that disappointed, I thought he was gonny greet, so I sat the rest a them. At least that's something, he says. (*DE*, 309)

The conclusion is made in the personal realm, an inexorable one, drawn by Laetitia who rejects Clare as a partner for Julian on the grounds that 'He's all wrong for you' (*DE*, 100), aligning personal relationships with social issues in a fairly traditional way. Class antagonism may, however, be finding a new expression by taking stock of cultural diversity, as the introduction of Farkhanda as a major character in this novel indicates. This issue still remains very much on the forefront of Miller's preoccupations, in keeping with her interest in Kelman, which is linked both to his linguistic innovation and his enduring portrayal of that social class:

> I couldn't have written Clare's voice in 'Demo', for example, without Kelman and Leonard doing those linguistic experiments first. They made it possible for me to wrestle with the politics of dialect. Before them, narrative tended to be written in standard English and dialect restricted to dialogue. That immediately set up a power differential within the text, and often the effect was comic, even when it wasn't intended to be. Kelman showed that it is perfectly legitimate for his narrator to address the world in dialect. And he showed how it is much more the rhythm of the speech that characterises local dialect, and he created a more serious literary orthography of Glasgow dialect. In 'Demo' I'm trying to use similar techniques, but from a

female perspective. And it was writers like Liz Lochhead, Janice Galloway, Jackie Kay who first showed that, yes, you can write as a Scottish working class woman and make women characters central to your writing![9]

In a manner that would enable Miller to potentially claim the title of *Kelman's* bairn, in *Demo*, the dividing line, as social as it may be, is emphatically made to appear linguistic: Danny is linguistically rather than socially condemned by the narrative, by being endowed with a voice which does not seem to have any autonomous existence. Danny speaks in a language that appears extinct from the start, a mixture of cliché and stereotypes which, much more than his Scottish dialect, marks him out as a disappearing character, an endangered species. He gets bogged down in a language that offers no hope of individual and autonomous expression – 'Man, that is some day. It's chucking it down. Cats and dogs as the wee wumman says' (*DE*, 158). Julian or Laetitia on the other hand, the upper-class characters symbolically engaged in a creative and analytical project, the writing of PhD theses on literary icons, have at their disposal a literary, highly idiosyncratic therefore distinctive language that is used as a weapon against the lower-class characters. This takes the shape of offensive comments sometimes meant to go over their heads, as with Julian's condescending appraisal of some family anecdote of Danny's as 'family apocrypha. I love it' (*DE*, 67). In Miller's depiction of voice therefore, the Glasgow voice, in a way in fact quite at odds with Kelman's politics of dialect, is an encumbrance, or rather it remains locked in a fairly stereotypical dynamic with the English voice. Rather than being seen, as Donovan very matter-of-factly indicates, as the voice in which people speak and therefore the appropriate voice for the novel,[10] in other words a properly immanent voice, the voice in Miller's presentation of the characters conflates class and location in a manner which is in keeping with the militant outlook of the whole novel provided by its theme – the novel covering two protest marches used as a background against which the fates of the various characters are measured. This makes the destructive process at once inexorable (years of English hegemony still transpires from the easy superiority of the English characters) and, paradoxically, ultimately defeated, capitulating before the novel's construction of the necessity to abandon social and geographical prejudices. As Laetitia's diary records how Danny's parents help her take care of the child she is having with Julian, 'helping the lassie out till she gets on her feet' (*DE*, 301), she finally has to give up on social and geographical stereotypes, though not in a blind, angelic way:

> When I think of my hesitation in taking up their offer! I don't know *what* I expected that first day; some ghastly high rise with broken lifts and graffiti and used needles abandoned on the stairs. But their house is warm and comfortable – a good close, as Maeve said. There's plenty in the scheme not so good, but this stair's not bad. (*DE*, 296)

In that moment of played-down, subdued epiphany, which is both social and political, Laetitia's voice, doubly mediated by the fact that those words are written in her diary and are read by Clare, who stole the diary on a visit to her brother's flat and who therefore takes them up and broadcasts them, is strongly contrasted with her mother's words. The mother, like Danny, remains behind, stuck in her immutable social stereotyping that does not allow the freeing of her language:

> Not that [her mother would] mind terribly [her not being in Cambridge]; not if she knew her daughter was with Julian Legrozet, who, even with dreadlocks and *unfortunate political views*, came from the proper background. (*DE*, 199)

The stultifying characteristic of a language that is dead therefore displaces the English/Scottish demarcation line as well as the class line, in the process opening up for the female protagonists a fictional space situated in a future in which new identity markers will have to be devised.

The third part of the book, for all its weaknesses, in particular the way the Farkhanda/Muslim subplot is not developed in a convincing manner, but rather comes across as the author voicing her own multicultural politics, alternates the two voices at an increasingly rapid pace, displacing the confrontation from the social plane to that of language itself. As it shifts back and forth between two points of view, two voices, one dialect, the other one standard English, and two destinies, the book blurs the didactically established division of the first part, making it possible for the reader to go beyond the stereotyped voices and move forward. Ultimately, the two languages – which, at the beginning, are entrenched, and inextricably connected to their geographical and social point of origin – start to give, in a way which the realignment of characters along lines that have nothing to do with old prejudice indicate. Clare, whose voice concludes the novel, seems to open the narrative of the future for more than just herself:

> OK. Couple a weeks in Helensburgh. And that'll be me.
> Then back to Glasgow and
> who knows. (*DE*, 319)

The words of the young girl are an act of faith in the future held for her in Glasgow, in a manner that is also applicable to the other narrator, Laetitia, who chooses Glasgow over Cambridge. In that final expression of hope, the local/foreign division is blurred for the two characters linked throughout the novel by their pursuit of the same man,[11] blurred by a return to Glasgow, the place which can turn an immanent voice into a cosmopolitan sense of belonging provided by a synthesis of the two voices, and of the other voices of the narrative, not least of which is Farkhanda's. In the first part, the novel's voices classify the characters according to what, according to Schoene (2008: 75–76), are 'neatly staked-out homogeneous realm[s]',[12] and consequently part the novel along a central fault line which he would describe as a 'statist' line, thereby preventing the advent of the cosmopolitan voice the critic advocates. The eventual triumph of the cosmopolitan is not so much a triumph of the novelistic voice as an eventual sidelining of the local voice as a discriminating factor. To quote from Galloway, 'the voice is still there',[13] only it is gradually abandoning its discriminating, cleaving power.

This capacity of the Scottish voice finally to represent, to shoulder the responsibility for the artistic discourse, not specifically emphasised in *Demo*, is taken up in Donovan's *Being Emily*. This novel tells the story of Fiona O'Connell, an Irish girl first caught at the age of fifteen, her twin sisters Rona and Mona towards whom ever since her mother's death, she has played the part of the mother, her older brother Patrick and their alcoholic father. Her friend Jaswinder, or Jas, is a Sikh, and she also has an Aunt Janice, a lesbian who adopts a child with her partner in the early stages of the novel. The novel, mediated by Fiona, traces the stories of the family members, and started in Donovan's mind as the story of a girl connected to Emily Brontë, the author being fascinated by the whole family mythology. Fiona is an artist, a photographer who also makes installations. In this version of the portrait of the artist as a young woman, there is space for scathing bitterness, as, for example, when Fiona blames her father for burning down their flat, an event which, together with other traumatic events in her life, will in turn be integrated into her art. Indeed, she engages in a relationship with Jas's brother Amrik, a musician who, like Patrick, leaves Glasgow and makes it in London. Fiona gets pregnant with Amrik's baby, but has a miscarriage which spurs her, at her end-of-year art school show, to imagine an exhibit based on mutilated Barbie dolls and a dollhouse that catches fire.

In this novel Fiona, the artist, travels back and forth between her native Glasgow and a fairly stultified artistic London, only to discard old clichés and proclaim a sort of creative awakening of her city. This awakening reaches significance not just because of the artistic figures associated with it – namely Amrik the musician, Fiona herself and the other art school students – but also because of the faith Donovan, via her narrator, puts in the city's people, in their capacity to be truly transformed and transcended by art:

> The London audience loved Amrik, recognised his special quality, but they didnae need him the way Glaswegians did. London love was clean and manicured; after the gig they'd go off and have a lovely supper in an elegant restaurant [...]. But their souls werenae riven apart, their whole beings shattered and put back thegether in a new way. Mibbe they were incapable of it, or just didnae need it [...].
> (*BE*, 189)

For Fiona, the link between art and the people of the city has become organic. What she (re)discovers is the beauty of the city of Glasgow which was historically always present:

> My da was right about folk in Glasgow – we never see what's round us. So much of the beauty of the buildings is high up and we're scurrying about at ground level, looking intae shops, heiding tae work. Like insects. But the Victorians who built Glasgow were proud of their city, wanted all the fancy stuff – columns and capitals, statues and gold leaf. (*BE*, 231)

This realisation, itself an answer to Gray's 1981 'imagining a city' monologue in *Lanark*, in which Duncan Thaw, an artist like Fiona, points out that Glasgow does not exist as a place because 'nobody imagines living there',[14] points to a confidence that rests on the city's capacity to metamorphose through art as well as through the eyes of its beholders, and through an ability to move beyond static visions (the statist lines which Schoene sees as an obstacle to cosmopolitanism). The space of fiction can therefore be seen to be created 'live' for the characters as well as for the readers of Donovan's or Miller's novels. In keeping with Fiona's installations, it is a space which shifts and evolves, which integrates and destroys, which 'shatter[s]' and 'put[s] [things] back thegether in a new way' and links the intimate and the universal in a bid to question the very notion of borders.

Rewriting the subaltern

Donovan and Hird also explore a working-class context, but move beyond what Miller's fiction is still struggling with: the age-old English-Scottish rivalry. In both domestic tales, the voices and characters are all Scottish, and the difficult duality presented in Miller's book has been come to terms with. Hird's portrayal of a dysfunctional family in *Born Free* is much less hopeful than Donovan's due, as Dorothy Johnson puts it, to 'the narrative's descent into the squalid underbelly of Edinburgh'.[15] It nevertheless provides a particular angle for fiction, an immediacy conveyed by the sharing of the point of view between the four family members, which has prompted Kevin MacNeil to compare the novel to a TV docu-drama.[16] And indeed, the novel tells the story of an ordinary family who are all trying to escape from something and each other. The interactions between Jake, Joni, Angie, and Vic, all taking it in turns to focalise the story, reveal a cocktail of adolescent and mid-life crises, the problems of sibling rivalry, the failure of a marriage, and the unbridgeable gap between the generations. Joni, the daughter and main character, is obsessed with sex. When she is not masturbating, which she calls X2ing, she is discussing sex with her best friend Rosie, also her acolyte in thieving. Angie, the mother, works at a betting shop, sleeps with her boss, and starts drinking again though she has been sober for years. While Jake is just being the average offensive teenager, Vic, the father, in spite of his sometimes sarcastic comments, tries to pull the family together against all odds. It is a story of everyday life.

MILLENNIUM BABES: FEMALE URBAN VOICES

This realistic narrative moves beyond the principles of realism not by providing a modernist or post-modern type of fiction, but by using elements from the most prevalent form of popular culture, TV, in the process blurring the border between reality, the world external to the narrative, and the world of fiction. MacNeil's point is that the characters who people Laura Hird's book do not realistically resemble real-life people, but that they *are* real people, and therefore justify the range of themes covered in the book, with alcoholism, infidelity, working-class lack of freedom or familial claustrophobia all featuring as the 'reality' of their lives. This leads him to make the Kelmanesque statement that 'Hird shows us that there is fundamentally no difference between the ordinary and the extraordinary'.[17] The novel indeed shows that, as Kelman himself puts it, if we were to actually look at 'one day in the life of any individual [...] it [would] be horror'.[18] But unlike most of Kelman's novels, *Born Free*, like Donovan's *Buddha Da*, uses a female character as the main centre of consciousness, or at least the voice which, according to the author, the novel started from.[19] This leads Hird to an unconventional vision of women which enables her to delineate Angela in particular as a bully and a neglectful mother, a 'bitch'.[20]

Aside from this reversal of the dominant male focalisation in Scottish fiction, Hird differs from Kelman in the sense that she moves away from his circular fictions which refuse to allow the plot to progress. On the contrary, she borrows intertextually from several highly codified genres which put a premium on the structuring of their narrative into a recognisable plot pattern. Hird, who enjoys Kelman's early work but who also cites Alasdair Gray as her favourite writer, does not just follow her characters around in a manner that is suggested by the docu-drama comparison. Nor does she imagine an existential trap which makes all manner of plot line problematic. She has the confidence to let her characters walk on their own to create their own stories, however parodic the outcome. The novel can indeed be seen as a rewrite of several traditions, which can be associated with at least three of the narrative strands. It is the rewriting of those traditions that gives *Born Free* a reason to vindicate the title which cannot be found in the plot.[21]

Angie's narrative is the part of the novel that is most like Welsh's work, in the sense that she manages to be both offensive in her language and amoral in her behaviour.[22] The shock aesthetics that characterises most of

Welsh's writing can be found in particular in the language Angie uses, her crude depiction of sexual encounters and in her relentless spite for the world around her. But the portion of the narrative dedicated to Angie is more than a pastiche because of the twist Hird brings to the characterisation: Angie victimises her husband by her constant abuse; she verbally or mentally abuses her children, therefore providing a counter-model to the conventional part of the wife and mother. As such, she is the character who, with her daughter Joni, turns the table on the exploiting males of Welsh's fiction and lashes out at another archetype, the typical working-class hero. Indeed, Vic, the decent, well-meaning, caring character with high moral standards which prevent him from taking sexual advantage of the female lunatic (the typical victim) who offers herself to all the bus drivers of the company he works for, represents another twist Hird gives to another tradition: the Scottish working-class novel which is partly present in the tradition of the urban Kailyard and, closer to Hird, in the works of William McIlvanney.[23] Vic is an emasculated Big Man, in other words, a contradiction in terms.[24] As such, he defamiliarises the conventionally masculine archetype of working-class fiction to actually induce the reader to recover a form of perception of the situation. His constant association with the home and his attempts to keep the family together, which refer back to the role played by women characters in McIlvanney's fictions, is therefore a reversal which point to the inapplicability of previous narrative models. As an alternative model for the depiction of male characters in urban fiction, Vic can be contrasted with Hird's other masculine characters, who conform to the pattern of extreme misogynistic violence set by Welsh. In the story 'Castle Terrace Car Park'[25] for instance, the male narrator fantasises in very crude, chauvinistic terms about his boss's wife, Barbara, and ends up imagining that he is raping her while having sex with his own wife. By contrast, Vic's narrative therefore discards both Welsh's and McIlvanney's versions of the male voice in fiction, and questions the – diverging – underlying assumption on the kind of society to strive for made in those famous literary models.

Joni's narrative offers a re-examination of another, much more universal genre: the fairy tale. Joni in her own way dreams of prince charming (or rather repeatedly dwells on this moment of bliss 'when [she] finally get[s] a boyfriend' (*BF*, 5)), but instead of relying on the romantic, rather asexual way in which fairy tales operate, she presents a reality made of masturbation and dreams of 'romance' with Rosie's uncle John, a seedy character suspected of paedophilia and, in Joni's own words, 'a major spunk bucket' (*BF*, 2), only to finally lose her virginity to an unknown truck driver. The rather absent and finally inefficient father figure is unable to protect her from the figure of the step mother, whose words for her daughter ('little bitch' (*BF*, 128)) place the story in a context at odds with the fairy-tale romance of the generic model.[26] Joni therefore comes across as a Cinderella of the housing schemes, with myriad reflections of this motif in the various secondary female characters peppering the novel, from Joni's friend Rosie, whose dreams of romance finally come true in the shape of an Italian waiter who gets her to perform fellatio in a car park for money, or the even grosser figure of the retarded adolescent girl who, in surroundings of poverty and squalor at odds with the usual atemporal setting and spatial neutrality of fairy tales, frantically masturbates to a video showing a Hollywood actor. This distortion is actually one of the elements that can countenance Roderick Watson's assessment of Hird as working 'within a modern gothic genre'[27] in the sense that it exacerbates the dialectical relationship that the gothic has with the marvellous. Indeed, *Born Free* can be seen as 'gothic' not in the traditional historical sense of Matthew Lewis, author of *The Monk*, or Ann Radcliffe, but in a modern sense in which it appears as anti-marvellous. Alan Bissett's definition of the gothic in his introduction to the *Damage Land* anthology significantly rests on a conception of horror borrowed from Kelman's famous line on the horror of everyday reality, which he quotes as an epigraph. For Bissett, the gothic, which he sees as a 'way of *seeing*', hinges on 'that moment in which the familiar becomes unfamiliar', a moment of shocking realisation when reality barely hides the monstrous breakdown of familiarity and order:

> It is that which is going on beneath the world, that which we'd rather ignore [...] as if reality, life, survival, everything we take for granted, has come into sudden and shocking focus. Gothic is about breakdown, about terror, about the collapse of territory, structure, order, authority. [...] Its bible is written in the margins, its church is buried underground, its hymns praise taboo and its choir is the dead.[28]

In *Born Free*, the breakdown of traditional values, of structure and authority, as well as the defamiliarising effect of using the hypotexts as models against which this tale of the modern times can be set – the choice of hypotexts themselves, which provide an anchor into two Scottish literary models and a more magical, mythical form of literature turned horribly wrong – can all be seen as Hird's pert answer to the dilemma pertaining to the appeal of literature in general. This is articulated in a fatalistic way by one of the characters in 'Hope', a librarian and reader who regrets that 'Nobody's interested [in literature] these days if it's not about asylum seekers or talking dogs. Nobody wants real literature any more' (*HO*, 3). Hird, in her own exacerbated, paroxystic and parodic manner, does manage to give the reader both asylum seekers (in the shape of various seedy characters and the occasional excursion into the fringes of modern urban life) and the talking dog, with the rewrite of the conventional fairy tale or working-class fiction, as her stories morph into the monstrous, gothic endeavour to destabilise our vision of the 'real'. As A. L. Kennedy introduces Cyrano de Bergerac in modern Glasgow in *So I am Glad* (1995), so can Hird's novel ultimately be seen as moving away from social realism toward a 'new and non-essentialist use of the magical and the mythic'.[29] And as with *So I am Glad*, the result is a mixture of defamiliarisation and sarcastic humour, a reflection both on the society depicted and on the stories available or needing to be created to open up a space for it. It is the creation of an immanent voice that dismantles before it can reconstruct the space of fiction.

The particular reading of Joni's – and her reflectors' – story as a parodic rewrite of *Cinderella* also participates in what Stephanie Lehner, borrowing a term first coined by Marxist critic Antonio Gramsci and then used by postcolonial criticism, calls the 'subaltern' concern of many Scottish authors such as Janice Galloway, Brian McCabe or Alasdair Gray, namely their insistence on 'perceiving, registering and negotiating forms of marginalisation, oppression and disempowerment', and on observing 'the oppressive and disruptive effects that gendered institutional structures – such as work, the family, the wider community and the state – have on the individual'.[30] For Hird, this double bind is remarkably integrated into the novel thanks to the hypotexts for *Born Free*, which feature books by writers who have become emblematic of a 'Scottish tradition' (McIlvanney, Kelman and Welsh) and their combination with a literary tradition which she distorts by hovering between gritty rewrite and monstrous transformation. In a conflation of Bissett's very loose definition of the gothic and MacNeil's depiction of *Born*

Free as a docu-drama, one could therefore see *Born Free* as an anti-fairy tale set in the age of urban realism. In the same way that the two teenage girls Nisha and Anne Marie in *Buddha Da* who decide to form a girl band and 'cry themselves' the Millenium Babes,[31] create – or 'sample', to take up Bissett's appropriation of the DJing term – their music by mixing the Catholic tradition with the Buddhist one in order to invent their own popular and contemporary music, Hird, as a literary Millennium Babe, recycles cultural forms to present an urban voice that cannot be limited to the urban Scots that she uses, but that can at once synthesise, rewrite, remix, but also reverse. In short, she creates a voice that puts Lehner's goal of proposing an 'alternative history to the official one' (2011: 10) into fictional terms.[32] Like the girl's band in Donovan's novel, Hird offers an idiosyncratic, re-invented, distinctive voice for twenty-first century fiction. The subalternity located by Lehner in the voices of Galloway or McCabe is replaced by a voice which, in spite of its focus on Scottish urban working-class females, no longer simply registers oppression or the impact of gendered institutions on the female, but twists those in a dark discourse of parody *and* survival.

The negative space

Strachan, like Hird, focuses on the subaltern although in a different way. Writing about Kelman, she emphasises the major point of divergence between his work and her own writing as being directly linked with his depiction of female characters, stating that 'I did not see any point of reference between myself and his women characters, aside from the most obvious common denominators of Scottishness and femaleness'.[33] In order to offset this imbalance in the representation of a female Scottish psyche, Strachan set about to construct a fictional space which can be referred to as a gendered space or, to borrow Cristie March's words on Janice Galloway, a 'newly gendered vision'.[34] Strachan indeed focuses on the necessary shift in perspective in order to account for very specific, if related, problems, explaining that 'I was really taken with the idea of taking this existential angst that men have been having for years, from Camus right through the Beat generation, and exploring it through a young, female character'.[35]

And indeed, both *Spin Cycle* and *Negative Space* focus on the lives of women. In the former, Agnes, Myrna and Siobhan work in a Glasgow launderette, a workplace which rapidly becomes a sanctuary for the three characters. From it, they see the world as it comes to them in the shapes of the various customers using the facility, but also their own personal version of 'the outside world' as they carry it along with them. For Agnes, the world is contained in a frozen past moment, her cousin Vera's death twenty years before, when she had gone out to a club never to come home. For Myrna, it is a series of travel books which she uses to imagine a different life. Siobhan is the one who makes those carefully fenced in worlds collapse, as she engages in a career as an escort girl on top of her job at the launderette, a decision which will eventually involve all three women. *Negative Space* also focuses on exploring the world through a female character, as it starts in Glasgow on the most traumatic moment of Stella's life, the funeral of her beloved older brother Simon. The rest of the novel, mediated by Stella, is an account of her survival after the tragic event, from the solace she seeks in the arms of her brother's friend McCall, to her job as a model for the art school, and to the quiet relief she finds in an artist's residence in Orkney at the end of the story. The narrative injects an account of her life with her brother in short analeptic snippets which suggest the intensity of their connection.

For Strachan, the agenda in both these novels is a feminist one, of women's reclamation of their bodies (an aspect also present in Hird's novel, with its description of all aspects of female sexuality) and of an affirmation of lesbian relationships in both *Spin Cycle* and *Negative Space*. According to Innes (2007: 305), Strachan, like Hird, adopts 'a very different approach to creating a literary female space and corporeality, within which [...] the whole realm of woman's sexual pleasure, comes to be owned by the female characters themselves'.[36] This concentration on the female body as a locus of empowerment rests on the crude description of female sexuality and on an idiosyncratic, empowering re-appropriation of the language of abuse when connected with the female.[37] The two linked notions of agency and tradition, a dilemma which, as will be shown in chapter two, also occurs in many of the detective novels published by Scottish women in the years from the 1990s to the twenty-first century, is famously tackled by Janice Galloway in her first novel *The Trick is to Keep Breathing*.[38] *Negative Space* and *Spin Cycle*, which have in common their investigation of the private world of unhappy individuals in a context of urban loneliness, recall Galloway's own preoccupations summarised by Cristie March (2002: 128) when she states that '[t]he urban and domestic landscapes Galloway creates underlie the daily injustices her often bewildered characters suffer'.

Stella in *Negative Space* has much more in common with Galloway's Joy than the ironical choice of a luminous, optimistic first name. She is also a grieving woman mourning the loss of a brother, a character who, in a complication of the pattern set by Joy (who is trying to come to terms with the loss of her lover) by the suggestion of an incestuous relationship, presents the oppressive space of a woman walled into her own psyche. As with Joy, Stella's interior world, made even more hermetic by the novel's use of the first person and of an oppressive, suffocating internal focalisation, seems to be completely closed off – as the narrator herself puts it, 'I was on my own' (*NS*, 35). With its abysmal sense of lack, its free-floating isolation, this disconnected world is economically summarised by the ninth chapter's title – 'Nothing'. It is a void, an environment severed from an external world depicted as violently intrusive, either in the shape of an intolerance to anything extraneous to her interior world, as for example with people on the bus being fiercely resented, because Stella 'can't stand that invasion of space' (*NS*, 81), or by giving the invasion of her damaged interior space a violent, dislocated but above all ambivalent description, akin to sexual violation, as in this description of sexual intercourse with McCall:[39]

> Oh God I'm exhausted
>   all I want
>   is to
>
> Later he arrives, right on cue. This dream is graphic, more graphic than before. At first it's her, saying the familiar line, but you're dead, like she usually does. They embrace. This time though there's no abstract sexual atmosphere, this time it's full colour and close up, nought to sixty in 6.9 seconds. She doesn't even undress, her skirt is pushed up over her hips and her shirt ripped open and she's really into it as she feels his cock ramming into her. And suddenly it's not her, it's me, I feel the button of his trousers scraping my thigh, and his tongue squirming in my mouth and it's too much, it's suffocating.
> (*NS*, 125)

In this passage, the void, represented by the aborted initial sentence, and by the uneasy yet familiar proximity between existence and death, is finally further characterised by the offering of the victim/agent as an invaded, shattered space of femininity ('at first it's her'), grammatically rendered by the dislocation of pronouns into 'she', 'I', and 'you' which points, not just to a shattering of the self, but to the invalidity of language to depict it, as the barely semantic quality of the fourth sentence ('it's her [...] but you're dead') indicates. Yet the refusal of the victimhood trope as the easy way out for the narrator is integrated into this eruption of violence through the ambivalent indication that 'she's really into it', a statement which recalls the poised narrative structure of *Spin Cycle*, which balances Myrna's activity as an escort girl against the story of Vina's assassination, a sex crime which literally haunts the narrative by recurring in the shape of newspaper cuttings and scenes which can been seen either as reminiscences or projections of Vina's life through Agnes. Both novels project fictional spaces to represent that interiority and the necessary remapping of its constitutive features. In *Negative Space* this is represented by the artist's retreat in Orkney where Stella takes refuge with her friend Alex, a woman who makes her feel different and with whom she engages in a lesbian relationship; in typical non-Manichean fashion, it is both a refuge and a place of loneliness.[40] In *Spin Cycle*, the launderette, with its suggestion of interiority and circularity, is also repeatedly associated with the two notions of loneliness and protection, or at least with the idea of the launderette as a refuge for the characters: in the chapter entitled 'last wash', the three women repair to it after Myrna's near murder at the hands of a customer.[41] Significantly, this place of retreat, this spatial and functional equivalent of the interior space, is introduced into the novel as a sort of no-place, not in the utopian sense of the term, but rather as a functional counterpart of the depiction of the women's psyche in terms of a gap. It is a negative space in the sense of a space of negation, a space in-between:

> Next door, the plastic UNDER OFFER sign has yellowed with age, and the metal shutters are thoroughly fly-postered and graffitied; it used to be a newsagent and grocery, but there are plenty more of those nearby, well stocked with stale scones, fizzy juice and Rizlas. This old place, the launderette, only survives because of the area, its

transient student population, the abundance of bedsits, DSS B&Bs. Shiny new premises have opened on the main road, offering dry cleaning, ironing, vending machines full of cans and chocolate, and a good view of the passing talent. (*SC*, 2)

The launderette, wedged as it is between two worlds, functions as a deliberately localised counterpart to the retreat presented in *Negative Space*, where the choice of Orkney takes on, according to the author, a more universal value:

In taking the narrator, Stella, to the Orkney islands in the far north of Scotland I also wanted to put her in a situation where she could see the history of humankind – or more specifically of belief – laid out in the landscape all around her.[42]

As Stella sees the 'history of humankind' laid out before her in all its elemental starkness, she can gradually make sense of her own damaged identity. As a counterpart to that, Myrna, Agnes and Siobhan in *Spin Cycle* will first have to leave their unreal world behind in order to make sense of themselves, but also of the world. Myrna, who retreats into the travel books she brings to work, and Agnes, whose psychic world is made up of newspaper cuttings detailing her older cousin Vina's murder thirty years before as well as of her own dreamlike reminiscences of her time with her, immerse themselves in words which are alien to them. The gap, this intermediate space the characters occupy which, like the launderette itself, is stuck between other, more real existences, is at first signified by the heteroglossia which characterises the novel: Agnes's voice is delimited and impaired by Vina's own narrative, seeping into her own and distinguished from it by a smaller character size and a different font, telling its story backwards and in short, unchronological snippets from the moment of the murder. It is also covered by the lurid and stereotypical description of the murder and other murders by the popular press. This heteroglossia, which needs to be read as a desperate and ultimately unsuccessful attempt at covering the void, is echoed in *Negative Space* by Stella's equally doomed attempt to let the voice of medicine – a clinical description of aneurysm, the condition that took her brother from her – overlap with her own.[43] All those voices which interfere with the voices of the women and invade their retreat are as unsuccessful as Siobhan's attempt to live a vicarious life in Paris through her travel books. As Stella in the other novel realises about another discourse, conveyed by another artistic medium, the 'voice' of Simon's paintings of her, words do not speak *from* her, but rather about her; worse, they are sometimes very imperfectly connected to her:

> If every picture is worth a thousand words, I wonder what these pictures say. If they speak about me, about Simon, the relationship between us. On the surface there's only a representation of a body on a piece of paper, behind them there is so much more. (*NS*, 181)

In Agnes's world, Vina's voice, which speaks to her from the past, from a period of childhood innocence and hope, makes a connected point. As Vina is described at the end of the book as retreating into the recess bed, 'her den, her safe place', and telling Agnes 'of all her bright and shining hopes for the future' (*SC*, 299), the retreat is no longer a damaged, dangerous and alienating space; it performs the crucial, saving act of projecting existence forward in the shape of stories.[44] This scene gives a clue to the interpretation of all the vignettes in the novel, which describe a variety of characters from the point of view of the three launderette workers and therefore project a diversified, local but also cosmopolitan, familiar or strange, harmless or threatening world from a space of retreat and protection, from a gap, an interstice, a negative space which enables the narrators to focus on the 'so much more' hidden behind the flat representation of a body on the page. It is again Stella who, in *Negative Space*, discovers the type of voice that can suppress the heteroglossia which hides 'so much more', by once again using a non-verbal artistic simile:

> The tutor is speaking, talking about the gaps in the composition, between arm and body, leg and leg, the empty areas.
> —Always remember the importance of the negative space. You must capture the negative space. (*NS*, 173)

The negative space, no longer the space of negation, but rather the space where the outline of the subject becomes more real, more focused, maybe even more alive, could be equated with another artistic metaphor to describe a novel in which the main character turns to photography, that of the photographic negative. In the same way that Stella makes sense of herself, and maybe also of the history of humanity laid out before her in her retreat,[45] by simplifying her voice, by tackling her subject from the margin in order to show what is hidden behind the surface of herself and to let the voice speak *from* her, not *about* her, and therefore reach the end of the narrative 'still standing',[46] so the three protagonists in *Spin Cycle* can finally project their own stories, their own depictions of the world as it passes through the launderette. The numerous vignettes, distinct from the rest of the narrative because they are narrated in the present and convey an external point of view on a variety of characters – Jay, the young punk with his boyfriend, Sally the victim of unspecified abuse, Esther the little old lady who wears perfume 'for self respect', Ryan the Ned, and many others – all constitute between them the negative space for the novel as a whole, by managing to tell stories in an impressionistic, fragmentary way, resting on the domestic and the familiar as well as the foreign and cosmopolitan. In the process, the three characters/narrators take up the narrative – their own narrative as well as the narrative of contemporary Scotland, a fact which becomes clear at the conclusion of the novel, even though it is suggested all along by the haphazard distribution of the vignettes in the book. This freeing process, this capacity to tell is indicated by Vina's symbolical freeing from the heteroglossic discourse of the popular press or from that of the grieving memories which she is at first confined to, as those eventually join the main narrative. As her story, at the very end of the novel, appears in standard type, it is extracted from the discourse of grief delimited by the italics, and Vina herself is released and enabled to symbolically add her own voice to the various urban voices that make up the novel:

> And Vina? Vina is still dancing, her heels click-clickety-clicking as she moves lightly across the sprung dancefloor. Alone this time, but smiling, her ruby mouth open wide in joy, oh yes, she's smiling. (*SC*, 312)

Vina, another concurring voice that contributes to shape the negative space of these women's portrayal is, like Myrna, whose story is disturbingly made to appear like a re-enactment of her own, 'offered [...] a second chance' (*SC*, 310) to tell her story, to tell *the* story, *any* story in the same way that Stella, reunited with Simon after being finally able to cope with his death and symbolically to free herself from that story of the past, is able to re-interpret and therefore re-live her life with Simon as an enduring, if imaginary part of it. The negative space then becomes the positive space of imaginative construction in which Stella and Simon hold hands at the end of the novel. It is more importantly the positive space of stories constitutive not so much of the urban, but rather of the human space.[47]

The human space: communicability and language

Buddha Da, Anne Donovan's first novel, traces the story of a working-class Glaswegian painter and decorator, Jimmy McKenna, who discovers Buddhism, rejects old habits and seeks a more meaningful life, only to alienate his immediate family in the process. It is told from three points of view – those of Jimmy, his wife Liz, and their daughter Anne Marie. Liz and Anne Marie, who at first cannot understand why Jimmy – a staunch atheist – would suddenly want to become a Buddhist, eventually gain some insight into his motives, as well as into their own choices. Anne Marie is friends with Nisha, who, like her, is a fan of American pop music, and who helps her compose a song for the millennium, to be sung by their girl band of two which they call 'the Millennium Babes'.

In both this novel and her collection of short stories *Hieroglyphics*, and to a lesser extent in her second novel *Being Emily*, Donovan uses a Glaswegian demotic voice, the immanent voice specifically belonging to and constituting a fictional urban space. Jeremy Scott, in his analysis of the types of language used in *Hieroglyphics* notes that:

> It becomes abundantly clear to any reader of [Donovan's] work that one of her overriding concerns as a writer is to rescue Scots speech before it is unduly diluted or even drowned out by Standard English. (2009: 212)[48]

Donovan herself justifies her use of Glaswegian demotic in interviews simply by saying that 'that is the way people speak', noting that in her novel she did not know how to speak in Standard English.[49] In a manner that recalls issues raised in Kelman's fiction, this central concern raises political, colonial arguments but, as noted by Scott, her approach is less politicised and more humanistic than Kelman's. It is an approach that concentrates on the notion of communicability and its complex, paradoxical relationship with language. In his review of *Buddha Da*, David Moses emphasises the fact that the novel 'examines the way that an altered perspective can throw comfortable certainty into flux'.[50] In an approach that owes much to Bakhtin's concept of dialogism (therefore a resolution of heteroglossia), Donovan explains that her three protagonists all have Glasgow voices, but that she found it necessary to distinguish between the voices, in order to convey the idea of a shift in perspective from a linguistic point of view. The way to achieve that for Donovan is to associate each protagonist with a separate sense so that, for the author:

> I gave each character a dominant sense. So Jimmy is visual, Liz is much more sense of smell, and feel, and sensuality, and Anne Marie is voice. So when Jimmy sees things, he sees them, like when he describes Liz he describes what she looks like; when Liz describes Jimmy she describes what he smells like. […] So that helps as well to differentiate them, because I knew the voices were going to be similar.[51]

If one adds to this and to the ideological spaces which the novel inhabits the narrative's emphasis on multiculturalism, which Donovan simply acknowledges as being 'part of how things are',[52] one can describe Donovan's fiction as putting a premium on communicability and on the connections made between habitually distant discourses. As Moses points out (2004: 132), 'the dialogism of new perspective in established contexts lies at the heart of *Buddha Da*'. In *Hieroglyphics*, the eponymous short story depicts a dyslexic girl, situated on the wrong side of academic achievement, and makes the point of a necessary altering of perspective in order for communication to take place:

> *So, Mary, if hieroglyphics means Egyptian writing, why do you think I am referring to your script using that term?*
> Because you cannae ... can't read it, sur.

> *Precisely, Mary. And since the function of reading is to communicate, what point is there in writing something which is utterly unintelligible?*
> Ah jist sat there.
> *Well, Mary, I'm awaiting your answer.*
> *But if you were an Egyptian you could read hieroglyphics, sur.*
> *Are you trying to be funny, girl?*
> No, sur. (H, 6)

As this dialogue indicates, the enforced, common, far from immanent language spoken by the characters – Mary correcting herself and changing from the Scottish 'cannae' to the 'proper' 'can't' – is no guarantee of real, viable communication. This story points to the end of the supremacy of a dominant, monologic discourse, paving the way for *Buddha Da*'s examination of dialogism, in a way which is reinforced by the use defamiliarisation in another story, 'Virtual Pals'. Here, Siobhan, a Scottish schoolgirl, has as a pen friend Irina from Jupiter who, although she can understand Siobhan's language thanks to a translator called a 'transference tool', can no more fathom the idea of what she sees as an arbitrarily prioritised language policy as guess at the nature of a 'pet':[53]

> I am surprised that your teacher thinks that you can learn from my English. Surely the register, vocabulary and syntax of your language is culturally and socially appropriate to your environment and the only reason for using other forms of language is that they are more fitting in a given situation? I appreciate that there are different norms within complex social groupings. (On our planet we do have differences in vocabulary between areas, for example, and some differences between generations too.) However the idea that one form of language is better than the other is foreign to our culture. (H, 37)[54]

While Siobhan, in typical mindless teenager's fashion, casually turns her back on epistolary communication with this archetype of the displaced observer in order to attend to the much more pressing business of her newfound boyfriend, Mary, in 'Hieroglyphics', who ironically is the child discarded by the school system on account of not being bright, suggests, as

Being Emily also does, albeit with a different focus, a creative exit to the dilemma of communication and language. As Mary tells a story entirely in her own iconic language drawn from Egyptian hieroglyphics, thereby devising a literalised version of her Latin teacher's comment, itself resting on a stale metaphor, she creatively reverses the order of precedence between intelligible and unintelligible discourses, vindicating Irina and in the process injecting new life into the specialist of dead languages' dead metaphor. In this act of creation and liberation, this altering of perspective that makes the other children's papers, written in regular script, appear both foreign to her eyes and, more crucially, invalid vehicles of communication, she reverses the order of precedence by ascribing an entirely graphic purpose to 'aw they different kinds a haunwritin; squinty, straight, big or wee, different sizes and shapes on the page' (*H*, 10). When Mary puts her essay on top of the pile on the teacher's desk, the short story proclaims the triumph of a language that formerly appeared as inarticulate and unfit for communication. With the help of Irina's detached comments, the rehabilitated hieroglyphics clamour for the adoption of a new perspective on the very notion of communication.

Buddha Da, in keeping with the humorous tone of 'Virtual Pals', adopts a comic angle to tackle the notion of communicability, as the description of the novel as a domestic comedy indicates. Janice Galloway's definition of the comic points to a feature that can be seen as a fundamental element in Donovan's foregrounding of communicability:

> One of the things about comedy that is important is that it points out the division between what we are and what we aspire to. [...] The gap between aspiration and comic human reality is absurd, but also heroic.[55]

This underlining of a gap as both absurd and heroic finds its manifestation in the plot of *Buddha Da*, which depicts how Jimmy is looking for a meaning to his life in Buddhism, a culture entirely foreign to his own, just like David, Liz's student lover, turns to the discourse of philosophy with the even more ambitious project of discovering the meaning of life (*BD*, 216). It is also present in the number of religious and spiritual epiphanies which do not take place, itself a major source of comedy. As Jimmy goes on a

Buddhist retreat in order to experience that cultural and spiritual eureka, the emphasis is instead comically placed on the cultural gap:

> We filed in, efter takin aff wer shoes in the cloakroom, and took up wer places. Ah thought ah wis getting a loat better wi this sittin cross-legged but at the Centre it was only fur twenty minutes at a time. And ah don't know if it wis bein tired efter a day's work, or the drivin or whit, but ah couldnae sit still. Vishana talked us through the mindfulness a breathin meditation but ah couldnae settle. Ah kept fidgetin, and every time ah made the slightest wee movement ah felt as if everybuddy could hear it, cos it wis dead quiet except fur some guy ower tae ma right somewhere who sounded as if he wis on a life-support system.
>
> And as fur ma mind. Mindfulness aye, but no the way Vishana meant. Ma mind wis full aw right – thoughts fleein aboot lik [sic] motors on a racin track. Vroom, vroom, wan eftir anither. And the main wan that kept comin up wis, whit the fuck are you daein here? (*BD*, 28)

The last comment is a vivid reminder of the underlying preoccupation with possible, valid communication, and with the inherent weakness of all language when the narrator finds himself in a displaced position. Emphatically, the novel reminds the reader that the familiar is also a source of displacement, as with the drifting apart of Liz and Jimmy, or of Jimmy and his family, by using the commonplace metaphor of the 'other planet': Jimmy may well be rationalising his failure to understand his fellow would-be – or even confirmed – Buddhists by optimistically stating that 'it's good tae mix wi folk fae another planet' (*BD*, 27); he equally reflects on the combination of proximity and distance of the familiar: 'it's a funny place, Edinburgh. An hour away fae Glesga and you might as well be in another country. Another planet even' (*BD*, 53). The parallel comparisons bridge the gap in their own, idiosyncratic way, providing an extended perspective on the local. In doing so, they point to the necessity of inventing a new method of communication that can speak to both Glasgow and Edinburgh, to both Liz and Jimmy, or again to both Jimmy and the Buddhist Rinpoche, therefore to both Jimmy and the world. Jimmy's experience, and by extension the experience of his whole family, reflects upon the destabilisation of identity once the familiar has been displaced. Donovan keeps decentring language in order to problematise the notion of locality and belonging, in a context which, as her use of Buddhism as well as multiculturalism indicates, is both localised and globalised, or at least placed in an increasingly global context. From that point of view, Buddhism is an excellent vehicle, representing as it does extremes of geographical, linguistic and cultural difference.

Donovan uses Anne Marie's simple, matter-of-fact expression to mark the gap. In the initial, comic situation depicting a group of Buddhist monks thrown into Glasgow to tell parents that their newborn baby is the next lama, Anne Marie captures the communication hiatus by playing on the functional gap between the metaphorical and the literal:

> Three of them, staundin on the doorstep on a Saturday efternoon and the way the neighbours were lookin at these guys they might as well have been llamas with humphy backs insteidy lamas. (*BD*, 6)

In that linguistic equivalent of cultural decentring, in which linguistic polysemy equals cultural diversity, the lamas become the symbols of a perspective which redistributes notions of foreignness and separateness, of similarity and belonging. The baby is discovered not to be the new lama after all, on account of it being a baby girl, a fact which prompts the comment 'is that no a bit sexist?' from Anne Marie (*BD*, 14). The scene, however, finds a counterpart in another scene of spiritual epiphany, involving Liz and her Catholic faith. Liz, though equally unsuccessful in her spiritual quest and therefore equally poised on the brink of a gap as Jimmy, goes to church only to discover, in her one moment of intense enlightenment, that she wants a baby, in a way, as is suggested by the particular occasion in which she undergoes this revelation, a Christmas Catholic mass, that comically mirrors the search for a saviour of the world of the first chapter, only in a different culture. In a sort of structural epanalepsis, the baby with whom she is pregnant at the end of the novel becomes the novel's baby lama of the beginning, endowing the narrative with a capacity to conflate the cultures that are consistently and comically described as separate. As in Buddhist philosophy, where something that cannot happen in one world can happen in another, Donovan makes the novel communicate with itself. Communication, or the lack thereof, requires more than one language, it is irrespective of language, but rather depends on the 'transference tool' that each narrative, each voice, be it immanent or not, manages to create for itself. Nisha and Anne Marie, ignoring the local/global division in their everyday lives as well as in their art when they realise that neither Tibet's nor Scotland's flag can be found in their world atlas, create their own cosmopolitan urban voice. It is the international voice of pop music which they see as an accumulative language with possibilities of transference, as Anne Marie explains the method of composition of the song: '*Salve Regina* could be the main part, but we'd need tae build up loads a different layers' (*BD*, 238). The voice of communication therefore necessitates the adoption of a language that can conflate, mix and that can above all circulate between layers, a transference tool that does not need to choose, that does not give one single equivalent but that is happy to provide a polyphonic, multicultural answer. At the end of the novel, the not at all virtual pals Nisha and Anne Marie answer in their own way Jimmy's objection, in another chapter, to the presence of a translator to mediate the words of the lama on the ground that communication should be fluid, 'enlightened' (*BD*, 167), by creating their own transference tool, their song, in which communication is not lost, but rather found in translation. Their song is the perfect vehicle for the expression of Angus Calder's concept of the 'mongrel nation', which he sees as the path to a renewed sense of Scottish identity. Anne Marie and Nisha's mongrel song truly captures the new voice of Scotland because it captures and embraces the very process of change, an aspect which will be taken up again in chapter four with the examination of Saadi's novel *Psychoraag*, which also uses music and its composition as a metaphor of communication or non-communication. As Donovan herself puts it, the motif of Buddhism is important in her novel for its capacity to usher in a new voice, a new culture:

> Buddhism [...] teaches about the process of change, the wheel of change, and I think that was quite an underlying [topic] as well. [...] In order to get something new, you've got to some extent destroy something, because that is never going to be the same. So you've got to lose something to gain something.[56]

For Donovan, the space of fiction is not, as in Strachan, a negative space, a space that can be captured by resting on the ex-centric position in order to actually delineate the subject and capture an immanent but also universal voice. It is a space of change and renewal which, contrary to the idea of a cramped and confined space, happily embraces and translates, 'transfers' the voices of the various individuals that make up the mongrel, i.e. Scottish, nation. It is a space that is complementary to that created by Strachan, Hird or Miller, a space of fiction which, for all fours writers, turns a void into a necessary vacuum, which they fill with voices, narrative, fictional voices rather than simply Scottish or female voices. In their own separate ways, by creating their own versions of the transference tool and placing it at the heart of their novel's communicative process, those writers create a space of dialogue with the self and the other, a space of fiction as a space of multiple discourses rather than simply voices.

Notes

1. In drama, the usual date identified for the rise in women's writing is around 1980, though Ena Lamont Stewart's major pieces are from the 1940s; Liz Lochhead and Marion Angus were two of the great twentieth-century women poets; Lorna Moon or Willa Muir's novels were from the 1930s, and one can think of Margaret Oliphant as a great nineteenth-century writer, or of Joanna Baillie as an important eighteenth century playwright. The reason why Galloway or Kennedy were hailed as putting an end to male hegemony therefore has more to do with the fact that in the 1970s and 1980s, prose fiction in particular was mostly a man's world.
2. Christianson, Aileen and Alison Lumsden (eds). 2000. *Contemporary Scottish Women Writing* (Edinburgh: Edinburgh U.P.), p. 3. Laura Hird, is certainly a writer to have done that, with the creation of her own website, which showcases new Scottish writing, as well as providing a space where new voices can brush with more established writers.
3. Innes, Kirstin. 2007. 'Mark Renton's Bairns: Identity and Language in the Post-*Trainspotting* Novel', in Berthold Schoene (ed.), p. 303.
4. See Adams, Jill. 2003. 'Interview with Laura Hird', www.barcelonareview.com/35/e_int_lh.htm, April, [consulted November 2011]. In this interview, Hird stresses that Welsh's writing 'was very accessible in a way that writing had never seemed before. The ethos was that everyone should have a go'.
5. Michael Gardiner writes that 'Laura Hird [...] is perhaps the only writer from these circles successfully to pull off a novel in something comparable to Welsh's abrasive Edinburgh idiom, in her compelling *Born Free*'. Gardiner, Michael. 2009. 'Arcades – the 1980s and 1990s', in Brown, Ian and Alan Riach (eds), *The Edinburgh Companion to Twentieth-century Scottish Literature* (Edinburgh: Edinburgh U.P.), p. 188.
6. Scott, Jeremy. 2009. *The Demotic Voice in Contemporary British Fiction* (Basingstoke and New York: Palgrave MacMlllan), p. 102. Scott devises this concept about Kelman, and applies it to Donovan's, Warner's and Niall Griffiths's works.
7. Burgess, Moira. 1998. *Imagine a City: Glasgow in Fiction* (Argyll: Argyll Publishing), p. 181.

8   Bissett (Schoene, 2007: 62) speaks of the 'levelling effects of an omnipresent popular culture', its democratising potential. Donovan, in *Buddha Da*, stresses Anne Marie's admiration for pop singer Madonna, a willing concession to global pop culture which, according to her father Jimmy, extends to the American turns of phrase that she uses.
9   Bissett, Alan. n.d. 'Alison Miller Interviewed', www.laurahird.com/newreview/alisonmillerinterview.html, [consulted April 2010].
10 Donovan says so to Adrian Searle, when she explains that her choice of the Glaswegian demotic was made because 'that is the way people speak'. Searle, Adrian. 2008. 'Anne Donovan Interview', February, glasgowwriters.wordpress.com/featured-writers/annedonovan/ [consulted March 2009].
11 This attachment is described in a manner which is far from conventionally romantic, as Clare and Julian's 'relationship' starts with a rape while in Florence.
12 For a more detailed definition of cosmopolitanism, see the introduction.
13 Galloway, Janice. [1989] 1991. *The Trick Is to Keep Breathing* (London: Minerva), p. 235.
14 Gray, Alasdair. [1981] (1991). *Lanark, A Life in Fours Books* (London: Picador), p. 243.
15 Johnson, Dorothy. 2001. 'Laura Hird – Born Free', in www.spikemagazine.com/1201laurahird.php [consulted December 2011].
16 See MacNeil, Kevin. 2005. '100 Best Scottish Books of all Time', *The List*, January, www.list.co.uk/article/2736-laura-hird-born-free-1999/ [consulted 12/13/2011].
17 Ibid.
18 McNeill, Kirsty. 1989. 'Interview with James Kelman', *Chapman* 57, Summer, p. 1.
19 Hird and Donovan, as well as Miller started their novels with the voice of their young female character, whom they describe as 'speaking' to them: Anne Donovan intended *Buddha Da* as a short story about Anne Marie's life, and Miller says that she 'heard' Clare's voice when she herself was on her way back from an anti-globalisation rally in Florence. As to Hird, she gives both Joni and Angela pride of place.
20 See Jill Adams Interview in *The Barcelona Review*.
21 Even if one takes into account the fact that this title is borrowed from a song written in 1966 by John Barry and Don Black for the film of the same name, the song being later recorded by both Andy Williams and Frank Sinatra, the relevance is external to the plot.
22 See Innes in Schoene (ed.), p. 305.
23 See Haywood, Ian. 1997. *Working-class Fiction: From Chartism to* Trainspotting (Plymouth: Northcote House), notably his description of McIlvanney's *Docherty* (1975): '[McIlvanney] looks back to the Edwardian period to illuminate the historical process of the formation of working-class respectability in an environment of economic hardship and emotional volatility'. p. 155.
24 On the Big Man, see Haywood p. 156.
25 Hird, Laura. 2006. *Hope and Other Urban Tales* (Edinburgh: Canongate), pp. 79–92.
26 Angela is much more of a stepmother figure to her own children than a mother. Not only does Hird call the mother a 'bitch', but she also points out that she is a 'monster', See the Jill Adams Interview.
27 Watson, Roderick. 2007. *The Literature of Scotland* II (London: Macmillan), p. 261.
28 Bissett, Alan (ed.). 2001. *Damage Land: New Scottish Gothic Fiction* (Edinburgh: Polygon), pp. 4–5.
29 Gifford and McMillan, p. 597. In this passage, they are describing women's contemporary writing.

30 Lehner, Stephanie. 2011. *Subaltern Ethics in Contemporary Scottish and Irish Literature: Tracing Counter-Histories* (Basingstoke: Palgrave McMillan), p. 3. Lehner is concerned with the impact of class division, gender inequalities, ethnic discrimination and poverty in a manner that compounds the class analysis with precisely other forms of discriminations.
31 Quite fittingly so, as their first song is destined to be sung for Hogmanay at a party that ushers in the new millennium.
32 Lehner is quoting Edward Said.
33 Strachan, Zoë. 2007. 'Is that a Scot or am Ah Wrang?', in Berthold Schoene (ed.), p. 55.
34 See March, Cristie L. 2002. *Rewriting Scotland: Welsh, McLean, Warner, Banks, Galloway and Kennedy* (Manchester and New York: Manchester U.P.), for her description of 'Janice Galloway's newly gendered vision', pp. 108–33.
35 'Zoë Strachan'. 2002. *Sunday Times*, quoted by Nick Turner, Contemporary Writers website, 10 February, literature.britishcouncil.org/zoe-strachan [consulted November 2009].
36 See also p. 306. In Hird's novel, in spite of the reversal of male-female stereotypes of agency, both Angie and Joni are depicted as being the 'victims of men' according to Dorothy Johnson (2001), which prompts the critic to actually attribute to the novel a 'reactionary outlook', explaining that the implication in *Born Free* is that 'However tough Joni will continue to be a victim'. (www.spikemagazine.com/1201laurahird.php)
37 See Innes in Schoene (ed.), pp. 305–06, in particular her description of the misandric violence that concludes *Spin Cycle* and her comments on the power of the word 'cunt' in the narrative.
38 See Lehner, chapter 5.
39 This scene's status is ambiguous too, seeming to mutate from that of a dream to the real world of Stella's apartment and the actuality of the intercourse taking place.
40 In his article 'Cosmopolitan Scot' (pp. 71–92), Berthold Schoene describes Stella's journey from Glasgow to Orkney to London as a journey towards self-recognition, and emphasises the importance of Orkney as a place of entry into her past and of ritualised identity finding and cultural belonging, which leads her to become what he calls a 'newly emancipated cosmopolitan woman'.
41 See also the first chapter in which the characters seem to co-exist within the cramped space of the launderette in an isolated, lonely fashion, an impression conveyed by the strict internal perspective, which does not afford any discursive means of interaction for the three characters.
42 Rawlinson, Zsuzsa. n.d. 'Zoë Strachan interview', www.britishcouncil.org/hungary-arts-literature-strachan.htm [consulted June 2011]
43 See for instance p. 34.
44 In a manner coincidental with Strachan's description of her novel as an exploration of circular patterns, the last insertion of Agnes's memories of Vina is one of the very first memories of their time together, therefore making the end (of the novel) fold back upon the beginning (of Vina's story).
45 Strachan speaks in the interview quoted above of her choice of Orkney for its evocative power of the history of humanity.
46 'Still standing' is the title of the last chapter.
47 This notion of what connects, or disconnects, individuals is taken up again in a different context in chapters 5 and 6 of this book.

48 Scott sees this as showing Donovan's concern with an authentic expression of the self rather than just a concern with a survival of the language.
49 Donovan in Searle interview.
50 Moses, David. Spring 2004. '*Buddha Da*. By Anne Donovan', in *Scottish Studies Review*, 5.1, p. 130.
51 . Searle. See also *The Barcelona Review*, interview at www.barcelonareview.com/37/e_ad_int.htm.
52 Searle interview.
53 The word 'pet' comes up as 'no such concept' on Irina's transference tool, a judgment which many a non-British reader will concur with.
54 Significantly, the email exchange is dated 2001, a date which connects the arguments with the political situation of Scotland.
55 Galloway, Janice. May 2009. *The Scottish Review of Books* 5.2., p. 6.
56 Searle interview.

2. Female Crime Fiction: The Space of Transgression

In the wake of Janice Galloway's or A. L. Kennedy's success came, alongside the mapping of a space of fiction by female writers such as Anne Donovan, Laura Hird, Alison Miller or, even more recently Jenni Fagan, another somewhat contiguous space which adds to the equation a generic dimension, as well as openly reflecting on the issue of gender – crime. Denise Mina and Louise Welsh in Glasgow, but also Scottish writer Val McDermid who lives and works in Manchester, carved out a space for themselves in a genre dominated in Scotland by the totemic figure of Ian Rankin, a space situated at the crossroads of gender and genre, in order for them to go beyond both gender and generic stereotype. This space is not a negative space in the sense of the kind of fictional territory delineated in Strachan's novels,[1] but rather a transitional space, conceived as a locus of revelation and of questioning of the assumptions made by readers of the genre. This chapter, therefore, focuses on crime novels written by women – leaving aside their many male counterparts, not only Ian Rankin or Alexander McCall Smith, but also, for example, Stuart McBride, Christopher Brookmyre or Paul Johnston – in order to comment on the doubly marginal space from which they hail.

To start with the question of generic and historical constraints, crime fiction is a tradition in British literature that can be said to have Scottish roots, as it dates back to Arthur Conan Doyle's famous short stories, which themselves have been said to have been inspired by Edgar Allan Poe's Auguste Dupin and Emile Gaboriau's Inspector Lecoq. Ian Campbell notes that Conan Doyle was also possibly influenced by popular nineteenth century Edinburgh crime writers James McLevy and James McGovan.[2] In the twentieth century, the genre earned its credentials with the American hard-boiled crime novels of Dashiell Hammett and Raymond Chandler, while in Britain crime fiction refers us back to the golden age of Agatha Christie and Dorothy L. Sayers. Over the years, it has segued into a variety of subgenres such as the thriller, psychological thriller, police procedural, PI or hardboiled detective novel to name but the best known, while critics have devised new labels to account for subgenres which cater for very specific markets, for example the fairly recent 'Chick Dick' novel which is a mixture of crime novel and lesbian novel, a cross-generic genre in itself, written, for instance, by Sarah Paretski, an author cited by Val McDermid as one of her inspirations.

In Scotland, ever since James Ellroy coined the term 'Tartan Noir' to refer to Ian Rankin's work, the genre has steadily developed, to the extent that Edmund O'Connor judges it the most noticeable publishing trend in the last fifteen years. This fact makes the critic wonder if the phenomenon is just a marketing success (the happy result of 'publishers' spin machine') or if there is 'something genuinely dark and disturbing scuttling the streets [of Scotland's cities]'.[3] One of the elements that can point to the suitability of crime fiction as a genre in a Scottish literary context is that it accommodates two of its fundamental tenets. The first of those is the *topos* of the divided self, the study of duplicity, of the monstrous hiding behind the mundane, a theme in Scottish fiction since the seventeenth century, on to James Hogg and later Robert Louis Stevenson.[4] The second is the influence of the monstrous and the gothic, with Scottish gothic detective writing a tradition well established from the mid-nineteenth century. Those two aspects provide some backup to Gill Plain's definition of crime fiction as being 'about confronting and taming the monstrous',[5] an endeavour both endorsed and challenged by Mina, Welsh and McDermid in their fiction. For McDermid, this dual influence has to do with the particular historical context that weighs upon Scottish fiction:

> We didn't find ourselves in the tradition of Agatha Christie and Dorothy Sayers, nor in the American one of Chandler and Hammett. Our tradition is much darker, with psychological mainsprings and black humour – it comes from writers like James Hogg and R. L. Stevenson, and what Hugh MacDiarmid called the Caledonian antisyzygy.[6]

Louise Welsh in particular shows an unflinching interest in gothic fiction which she intertextually integrates into many of her novels, particularly *The Cutting Room* (2002) but also, in a parodic manner, in *The Bullet Trick* (2006). She redefines it by playing with its codes, more particularly emphasising its eroticism, claiming that it is 'a very sexual genre'.[7] In a manner that is in keeping with this position, the 'King of Tartan Noir', Ian Rankin, stresses the connection between the novel and the gothic characteristic of our world itself, therefore setting up a space of transition between the fictional and the non-fictional:

> What crime fiction needs is a sense of the *incomplete*, of life's messy complexity. The reader should go to crime fiction to learn about the real world, not to retreat from it with comfortable reassurances and assumptions. Crime writers in Great Britain – my contemporaries – are beginning to realise this. Good does not always triumph in today's crime fiction; evil cannot always be rationalised.[8]

Rankin further delineates this transitional space, insisting on the nature of crime fiction's appeal for its readers, in the process characterising this space as a space of transgression of various borders, be they psychological, formal or ontological:

> People are interested in crime fiction because they are fascinated by the margins of the world, those places where society's rules break down. [...] They learn to deal with fear and the unknown.[9]

In this advocacy of the triumph of the gothic as a convenient, if fairly orthodox, expression of an evil which, in a diverging movement from the convention, can no longer be rationalised away – 'tamed' – in contemporary fiction, Rankin points to a trend since the 1980s which has been to suppress the safe dividing line between murderer, victim and investigator.[10] Plain (2001: 3), focusing on the mechanics of detective fiction, sees it as a process whereby the inexplicable, unspeakable and the excessive is fed into the 'machine of genre', worked on by specialists of logic, to give up certainty and closure, but she simultaneously underlines the erosion of the detective's centrality more recently, noting that, over the years, only the presence of crime has given the genre coherence. This uncertainty in the distribution of roles in a codified genre raises the stakes in the depiction of horror and fear, while also looking back on the centre and denying the reader the comfort of a safe, out-of-reach or removed position. As Lee Horsely indicates, '[b]y writing novels centring on the victim or the transgressor, writers offer kinds of awareness, accounts of society as seen from the margins, that act to expose the perspectives of those at the centre'.[11] The shift characterised by both Horsley and Rankin as a decentring of the genre results in crime fiction exhibiting an adaptable formula, capable of carrying a complex social and political agenda while still attracting a mass audience.

All of those aspects can be found in the novels by Mina, McDermid and Welsh who, between them, have been able to redefine the famous Tartan Noir label. With their differences and specificities, all three Scottish female writers strive to produce novels, be they detective novels or thrillers, which, in order to eliminate safety and closure,[12] move away from the traditional reliance on the figure of the detective in a manner consistent with the contemporary evolution of the genre, in particular with the necessity for women crime writers to imagine alternatives to masculine modes of investigation. They create a space of fiction which acts as a space of transition from, of interpretation of, the real; ultimately a space of transgression where the safety of borders is questioned.

The first reality which is integrated into the space of transgression is that of female agency. Plain (2001: 5) characterises the collapse of the detective's agency in crime as coterminous with what she calls the genre's concentration on 'the sexual politics of detection'. Welsh, Mina and McDermid focus on the feminine, opting for a female or an unconventional investigator. This choice confirms Lee Horsley's remark about literary noir, which she defines as an exploration of the condition of powerlessness in a world in which dominant males are the antithesis of Chandler's 'knight of the mean streets' (2005: 281). In women's noir, according to Horsley, female protagonists are impaired, lacking social power and effectivity. Community is as important, if not more important, than agency, and the subjectivity of the central female is made available to the reader in texts which reveal women who are suffering from 'the loss of recognition' (2005: 281). As Mina's choice of protagonists among a group of suffering women confirms, the Noir world is a world of loss and dispossession. It is also a world of contamination of the present by the past, a world in which the removal of safety and closure has to do with the opening up of the present time to the past. In that respect, women's noir problematises Martin Priestman's description of the detective thriller which 'divides our interest between solving a past mystery and following a present action in which the protagonist may confront a dangerous conspiracy alone, or step outside the law, or both'.[13] This issue is tackled by all three writers, especially by Louise Welsh whose novel *The Cutting Room* hinges on the sleuth's attempt to discover the reality of a murder seemingly committed almost half a century before and which reaches out to him in the shape of snuff photographs.

Another characteristic of Scottish crime fiction which is complicated, and on occasions decentred, by female writers is the concentration on the harsh realities of urban life already at work in McIlvanney's famous *Laidlaw* trilogy, and later in the novels of Christopher Brookmyre and Ian Rankin.[14] Plain, writing on Tartan Noir, links literature with the political and historical context by noting what she calls the 'symbiotic relationship between text and context' in Scottish fiction, which she describes as an expression of 'the inarticulable resentment of a stateless nation', as well as of its 'oppositional identity' (2007: 133). Noting that Mina's work in the 1990s, like Rankin's, conveys a bleakness at odds with the political optimism in the possibility for a new Scotland, Plain contrasts the dystopian impulse with the utopian political ideal of devolution to wonder about the possibility for post-devolution crime fiction to endure. Indeed, the continuance of crime fiction in Scotland is a factor of its position, not only in a political context, but also in a literary one. The marginal space that is occupied by crime fiction in general enables a projection of the most gloomy, the worst of the historical and contextual space. As Alex Thomson notes in his editorial to the 1999 *Edinburgh Review* issue on crime, '[c]rime [...] will always have been a question of borders. After all, what else is a crime if not the crossing of some boundary or other; a *trespass* against us [?]'.[15]

The mention of the outside world – the world of the reader – in this assessment of the function of crime fiction in Scotland ties in with an important element in the works of Mina, McDermid and Welsh, their insistence on the reader's position, and the idea of the porosity of the border between the world of fiction and the real world in works in which evil and oppression are shown to 'trespass', to contaminate the world of the reader, offering their novels as a space where this transgression can be played out.

'A missing splinter': death, violence and the woman's body

Louise Welsh is herself a border crosser as her first novel *The Cutting Room* is situated on the dividing line between literary fiction and crime fiction.

As such, she questions the validity of the division of literature into genre and subgenre while resisting the genre's strategy of containment by endeavouring to create a space of transition between fiction and reality, or rather a space of fiction that seeks to annex the real. *Tamburlaine Must Die* is a historical thriller focusing on the last days of playwright Christopher Marlow, while *Naming the Bones* provides the reader with a murderous plot which ultimately appears as an excuse for the main character and narrator to delve into the complexities of identity and narration. This prompts Val McDermid to point out that in this novel the main focus is storytelling, which 'take[s] us to another world'.[16] This other world, however, is a dubious territory, as it travels from fiction to the real world and back again. Val McDermid herself, still today hailed as one of the most popular proponents of female Tartan Noir, but also described by Ian Rankin (1999: 13) as a political writer, mixes police procedural with psychological terror in her novels in order, like Mina and Welsh, to adopt and foreground a decentred position from which to narrate. All three increasingly emphasise the ubiquity, diffuseness and fundamentally inexplicable character of violence and death, while also toying with some of the conventions of the genre as well as writing to an agenda they clearly define as a feminist one. Indeed, Welsh defines herself as a feminist writer, placing the focus on the trope of the female body in crime fiction in a more general context of exploitation:

> I guess I consider myself a feminist. I'm very concerned with the way women's bodies are sometimes used, especially in films. You'll see a movie and the woman's body will be there to just hold your interest as a prop, like this table – there's been a murder, and there's a naked female body on the floor. This idea of the dead supine female somehow being more arresting in a way – you see it a lot in advertising, this very passive naked female who might as well be dead, so when I came to write *The Cutting Room* I was worried about writing about what I don't like, in a sense. How do you write about sexual exploitation or its visual use without recreating it? In the end you come down to your own tightrope, and some people will think you've got it right, some people might think you haven't. That was part of the idea of using photographs as well, trying to make one removed from this body on the floor, and also try to

point up the way in which photography is very much a powerful medium that we can use in that way.[17]

Mina, whose fiction substitutes ordinary women for the figure of the professional investigator, makes a similar point on the way the female body, in crime and in society, comes across as a commodity. She also reflects on the nature of victimhood which she extends well beyond the codes of the genre, while also working on a model of agency which she blends with the archetypal victim trope. In a manner similar to Patricia Cornwell's Kay Scarpetta novels, Mina's fiction hinges on the insecure nature of the protagonist's identity, as the latter shifts from the status of victim to that of murderer or investigator, thereby breaking down the conventions of the genre, and placing the investigator, as well as her investigation, in a problematic position.[18] For Mina, this has to do not just with the status of women, but with society's representation and unquestioning acceptance of this status:

> Women are labelled mentally ill through the criminal justice system in different ways from men. When women are deemed 'mad' it takes all their agency away; it means she can never have meant to do anything, whereas a man might still have rationality. This all ties in with the idea of women being passive – which is a stereotype the courts preserve very strongly. I wanted to have a female detective who... had to be proactive and have agency and make moral decisions, though she has a history of mental illness.[19]

Mina clearly assesses crime fiction's power to displace the issues it tackles from the fictional to the real world, thereby reshaping the space of fiction as a space from which to reach the reality of the condition of women in the contemporary world, giving a much more definite, gender-conditioned shape to the pronoun 'us' to Thomson's assessment of crime as 'a trespass against us'.

Val McDermid, who is often described as a writer of socialist feminist fiction,[20] started her publishing career with a series of novels published by the Women's Press featuring a lesbian journalist turned detective (the Lindsay Gordon series), followed by a series recounting the adventures of Kate Brannigan, a Thai-kickboxing private investigator, before launching into her most successful series to date, the bestselling Tony Hill/Carol Jordan series inaugurated in 1995 by *The Mermaids Singing*.²¹ This series of psychological thrillers set in the North of England where McDermid lives and serialised by ITV to great success, banks on the contemporary reader's fascination with all the new professionals associated with crime solving, in particular the figure of the police profiler. Denise Mina is the acclaimed author of the Garnethill trilogy²² with its amateur investigator Maureen O'Donnell, and of the Paddy Meehan series, with its blundering and determined journalist heroine/detective. Both series are set in Scotland and depict social deprivation, the hopelessness, the ruthlessness of violence, especially violence to women, and the stigma which is attached to poverty.²³ Mina is indeed almost militant when she values the genre in which she is classified for its accessibility and therefore its publicity powers:

> I did [set out to be a crime writer]. [...] I think people read crime without any intimidation [...]. I think people should read literature with that sort of empowerment and that sense of valuing their own opinion. Really what I'm doing is writing feminist stories in a really accessible medium. That is what I'm really interested in, just getting those sort of feminist stories out there, because I don't see representations of women in a lot of literature that I recognise as the real experience of women.²⁴

And indeed, both her work and McDermid's strive not only to focus on the 'real experience of women', which includes Paddy's sister Caroline's beating at the hands of her abusive husband or Maureen's own sexual abuse by her father looming in the background of all three Garnethill novels, but also to shift the perspective by adopting that of the disempowered amateur female detective as in *Exile*:

> She stood up and looked through to the kitchen, out of the window, past the drizzling rain and the dark clouds to the grey shadow on Ruchill.²⁵ She wasn't coming back to this, whatever happened. She wouldn't come back to a house where she was afraid to look out of the widow. [...] she [...] cried again, curling small with misery and grief, longing to be anyone but herself. (*E*, 222–23)

The physicality of the threat represented here by the absent father, who regularly enters the narrative in Maureen's nightmares, is made more acute both by focalisation and the structuring of the narrative which makes the father's threatening presence a recurring reality. Maureen, at once the victim of impending crime and the investigator into the fate of other victims, is poised on the brink of violence and abuse, which she can see from different angles. Similarly, in *The Dead Hour*, the traditional description of the dead woman's body is replaced by a disturbing one of the victim shortly before her death, as glimpsed by Paddy in the reflection of a mirror:

> The pretty blonde was standing in the door that led to the living room, listening. She was slim necked and fine featured, the tips of her bob stained pink with blood. As she watched Paddy through the mirror her slender fingers cartwheeled the curtain of hair behind her ear, revealing a bloody jaw. A thin slash of scarlet ran from the side of her mouth to her chin, down her neck and over her collarbone, soaking into the wide Lady Di lace ruff on her white blouse.
>
> For a slither of a moment their eyes met and Paddy saw the vacant expression she'd seen many times at car crashes and fights, a look saturated with shock and pain. She raised her eyebrows at the blonde, asking if she wanted help, but the woman gave a half shake of the head and broke off eye contact, sliding backward in the doorway and out of the mirror. (*DH*, 8–9)

The apparition-like quality of the woman described, Paddy's missed opportunity to rescue her, the universalisation of her predicament, as well as the fact that her disappearance is indeed enacted even before her actual death, all add another dimension to the traditional inquiry into the murder of a woman, that of an attempt to make up for the gap, the unspeakable, almost unimaginable moment when the murder is committed. It is an enquiry into the process and trigger of violence to women but also into their being suppressed from the account of crime, an aspect taken up by the plot of the Garnethill trilogy, where the fragility of even women's status as battered wives or murder victims is also tackled. Indeed, the finding of the woman's corpse, itself the starting point of the plot in *Exile*, is described as merely accidental:

> London is a savage city and she didn't belong there. She might never have been found but for Daniel. She would have disappeared completely, a missing splinter from a shattered family, a half-remembered feature in a pub landscape. (*E*, 15)

This sustained theme of the disposability of women to the extent that they are sometimes not even granted a 'proper death' in the narrative is matched by Louise Welsh's use of the motif of snuff photographs in *The Cutting Room*, which hinges on the auctioneer-narrator's search, not so much for the victim, as for the actuality of a murder based on the photographs he has found at a house he is emptying.[26] The question which governs the novel is phrased by the narrator: 'Were they real? They felt authentic, but that meant nothing. [...] If there had been a murder, she'd been dead a long time' (*CR*, 36). In a manner very similar to Mina, Welsh, thanks to the hypotheticals and conditionals in this sentence, displaces the enquiry onto a more conceptual level, to show up a system which devalues women to the point of turning them into phantom victims, suspended between two states. So that, rather than containing, or 'making safe', the narratives in *The Cutting Room*, *Exile*, or *The Dead Hour* question the function of women in crime novels, and the illusory safety granted by traditional closure and a return to a society made safe by the disposal of the murderer. In that respect, they conform to Kathryn and Lee Horsley's concept of a-heroic noir, in which 'the protagonists do not act to "reconstitute order" [...] but are themselves victims or perpetrators', and in which 'the normal world is shown to be vulnerable and easily disrupted', making the genre an 'exploration of the conditions of powerlessness'.[27] Significantly, when at the end of *The Dead Hour* Paddy Meehan rescues the hunted down upper-middle-class drug addict Kate just before she is caught up at last and murdered by her pursuer, in effect saving her from a certain and brutal death, the sound that comes out of Kate's mouth is interpreted by Paddy as 'a death rattle, a gurgle at the back of [her] throat' (*DH*, 315), which makes the neat boundary between danger, death and safety a – momentarily at least – disturbed idea.

Val McDermid's novels integrate irony and vulnerability by adopting a position which emphasises violence and threat through both victim's and murderer's point of view. Taken to an extreme, this strategy enables the serial killer to turn the table on the detectives, as in *The Wire in the Blood*, where a final ironical twist has the murderer meditating and eventually almost actualising his release on the novel's last page:

> Vance sat upright, stretching out his arms like a hero accepting the adulation of the crowd. He'd worked it out. He was as good as a free man. Murder was indeed like magic. And one day soon, Tony Hill would find that out for himself. Vance could hardly wait. (*WB*, 496)

The whole novel therefore, considered with its closing words, is not about taming the monstrous, but showing how prone to escape it is, thus suggesting the profound mutation of a genre which cannot adequately stem the tide of violence anymore.

'A place to put our anger'

Faced with this unstoppable threat, women crime writers chose to expose it, as Val McDermid states quite unequivocally, when she explains: 'I think that's one of the reasons why a lot of women both write and read crime fiction – it's a place to put our anger.'[28] Her own psychological thrillers precisely emphasise anger, without restricting that insight into an examination of women's anger only. Psychological profiler Tony Hill's function is to make sense of the rage that spurs men and women killers into action, but also of the anger occasioned by the victimisation, mutilation and general abjection of the (often female) body. Sarah Dunant notes how 'terrorised, battered, sexually assaulted, mutilated, even dismembered, [female] bodies have become part of the grammar of the form',[29] an idea which is taken up by McDermid's epigraph to *The Mermaids Singing*, 'The soul of torture is male', and implemented in her novels, which usually feature graphic descriptions of mutilated corpses. In *The Wire in the Blood* the purpose of the gory description relies on the careful choosing of the victim, in this case police investigator Sharon Bowman:[30]

> The deformed freakish head that faced him bore so little resemblance to anything human.

> He could see dark holes where her startling eyes had last looked out at him. Gouged out, he guessed, judging by what looked like threads and strings trailing from the wounds. Blood had flowed and dried round the black orifices, making the hideous mask of her face even more grotesque. Her mouth looked like a mass of plastic in a dozen hues of purple and pink.
>
> There were no ears. Her hair stuck out in spikes above and behind where the ears should have been, held in place by the dried blood that had sprayed and flowed over them. (*WB*, 214)

This scene caused outrage among McDermid's readers, many of whom wrote to the Amazon website to complain about the ruthless killing of a character they saw as 'the heroine'. Ironically, this outburst comforted McDermid in the idea that she had achieved her goal of actually displacing the debate from within the narrative to the real world, setting up the novel as the place of transgression of the border between fiction and reality, and in a way forcing the readers to export their anger into the here and now, as the author herself indicates in an interview, saying that she 'wanted the readers to be shocked, for it to be a pale simulacrum of what happens in real life when people are murdered'.[31] In other words, like Mina, she claims to hitch up the conventional level of violence of crime fiction in order to turn the space of the novel, the space of fiction, into the space of reality as it is hitting the reader, therefore justifying Rankin's depiction of her as a political writer. McDermid's argument here – and her transfer from one plane to another – rests on Julia Kristeva's concept of the abject, with its emphasis on the corpse as a symbol of 'death infecting life':

> The corpse [...] is the utmost of abjection. It is death infecting life. Abject. It is something rejected from which one does not part, from which one does not protect oneself as from an object. Imaginary uncanniness and real threat, it beckons to us and ends up engulfing us.[32]

The description of DS Sharon Bowman's body emphasises the double bind of abjection: that of being a necessary condition of the subject, and of being what must be expelled or repressed. It therefore 'engulfs' the reader, contaminates him, displacing the possibility of closure and escape into our safer real world, and stressing instead our 'incrimination': just as Paddy in *The Dead Hour* is incriminated by her passive behaviour with the victim of a crime about to be committed,[33] Rilke in *The Cutting Room* is also involved by his finding the photographs, a fact which makes it impossible for him to give up the enquiry in spite of the various warnings and threats he receives that all induce him to let things be, and in spite of the requirements of verisimilitude for the novel which would prompt him to pass the photographs on to the police. The reader, himself a viewer of the photographs through their numerous and detailed descriptions, is also not only engulfed by death as it infects life, but equally incriminated by this voyeuristic complicity – a trespasser, in Thomson's words. Similarly, in Mina's *The Dead Hour*, the reader is implicated by the use of internal focalisation, which makes it impossible for him to stand at a safe distance from the murder.

The Mermaids Singing relies on another shock tactic, that of reversing our preconceptions about victim and murderer. The killer, who at first seems to be targeting gays, finally turns out to be a transsexual, a transvestite parody of femininity,[34] who turns the agency wheel on its head by placing each of her male victims in an entirely subjected, powerless position that she enjoys as a woman, in a masquerade of a more conservative pattern in thrillers. McDermid wants to exploit the full range of this reversal, again by focusing on her readers' reaction, declaring that, in this book, she was interested in finding out 'how it would affect peoples' [sic] perception of a crime if the victims were males rather than females'.[35]

Mina also focuses on anger, taking as her central symbol abused, damaged women, like Siobhan in *Garnethill* or Pauline Doyle – the arch-victim – in *Exile*. All of them, together with Maureen O'Donnell herself, stand for the 'most often subordinate and impaired' protagonists of a-heroic noir,[36] as is for example shown by this description of Pauline Doyle:

> Admitted to the hospital weighing five stone and aiming for three, Pauline could never bring herself to tell the police what her father and brother had been doing. If her mother found out it would kill her. She had been discharged for all of two weeks when a woman out walking her dog found her in the scraggy woods near her house. She was under a tree, curled up into a ball, her face covered by her

skirt. She had dried spunk on her back and the police thought she had been murdered until they found the letter in the house. (*E*, 48)

Sexually abused on repeated occasions, once post-mortem, Pauline symbolises the topos of death as a substitute for erotic stimulation in thriller, albeit with a crucial shift in point of view, and therefore in readerly sympathies. Louise Welsh takes this up in a humorous fashion in *The Bullet Trick*, with the grotesque pantomime that accompanies the conjuror's performance of his 'murdered woman' trick:

> I grabbed a scalpel from my top pocket, held it high so they could catch its quick sharp glint, eager as a shark's grin, then I stabbed her hard in the solar plexus.
> Fake blood from the gel packs concealed in the napkin's lining spurted red and unforgiving over my gown, face and hair. I spluttered against its bitter tang and laughed like a crazy man. An echoing ripple of laughter came from the audience. (*BT*, 162)

True to her metaphorical role as a conjurer, Welsh provides the reader with her own trick when Sylvie, the conjuror's young female assistant, looking to add a little sex appeal to finish off the trick's effect, moves the story from grotesque parody to frightful reality, and pantomime murder into (apparently) real killing. In *The Cutting Room*, whose plot actually hinges on the topos of murder for sexual titillation, death seems to avenge itself for the stereotypical use it is put to by invading the narrative, spilling out of the snuff photographs not only to the world of the characters, but seemingly onto the very pages of the book itself.[37] When Rilke, the protagonist and narrator, examines or handles the photographs, colours gradually become muted and silence descends upon the narrative: 'I showed him the scenes of death first. He studied them closely, silently, the crowd around us receding, uproar subsiding, as the images took on their dreadful focus' (*CR*, 79). In a silenced, colourless universe, Rilke realises that even he has been turned into a corpse ('My body seemed the repository of a dead man' (*CR*, 154)), that light is fleeing from his world ('I [...] walked from the darkness of the house into the dark of the night' (*CR*, 195)), and that the other characters of the book do not fare much better than him ('The man looked like death. He looked like me' (*CR*, 198)) until, in a quasi-metaleptic moment, he realises that 'death reached out from [the books'] pages' (*CR*, 228).[38] In an echo of the scene in which the presumed murderer's angry sister, Madeleine McKindless, draws crosses on a page until it has become colonised by death, prompting Rilke to describe it as a graveyard, the narrator watches as death revengefully and inexorably fills up the pages of his own narrative.

Subjects, not objects

As with Welsh and her anonymous female victim on the snuff photographs, for Mina, Pauline represents the all too present figure that she is writing to eradicate from her vision of the world; Pauline stands to be replaced by a different type of woman, the type symbolised by Maureen O'Donnell, who takes social and sexual justice into her own hands, or Paddy Meehan, the working-class journalist who gradually fights her way up to a position of power. In *The Dead Hour* the premise of a budding sisterhood of women of agency is, somewhat naively, underlined:

> 'I've always supported myself.'
> 'You've made your own way.'
> 'I have.'
> They smiled at each other, these two working women, both keeping jobs from needy men, betraying nature by escaping the kitchen sink, these two women who were out in the world, active not passive, subjects not objects. (*DH*, 159)

In order to challenge patriarchal order and allow their women to become 'subjects not objects', Mina, but also McDermid and Welsh, first of all changed the gender and sexual orientation of their sleuths (they chose a lesbian, a gay man, a sexually active bisexual, a female DCI, a down-at-heel magician, or a sexually abused woman). Another reinterpreted figure is that of the psychiatrist in noir thrillers, who conventionally represents 'the provision of an authoritative patriarchal judgement with the intention of explaining the crime'.[39] In Mina's *Garnethill* the psychologist is the abuser and murderer. In McDermid's Hill/Jordan series, Tony Hill both works towards an explanation and solving of the crime, and is presented as an anti-normative figure by being made sexually impotent, a choice McDermid justifies by saying that she wanted to get away from the macho image.[40] In *The Wire in the Blood* she even excludes him from the system by stripping him of his regulative and normative power at the hands of a brutal detective:

> 'You are making one hell of a mistake, McCormick,' he said, his voice rough with anger.
> The big detective gave a snort of laughter, 'I'll take that risk, son.' He gestured with his thumb towards the door. 'Away you go, now.'
> Realising he couldn't win on this battleground, Tony bit down hard on the flesh of his cheek. The flavour of humiliation was the coppery taste of fresh blood. (*WB*, 226–27)

Thus dismissed and divested both of his adult and masculine attributes, tasting blood like so many victims whose deaths he investigates, Tony Hill becomes an agent in the destabilising of the certainties of the genre. This fundamental characteristic of Tony Hill, his 'mutability', is exploited in the *Wire in the Blood* TV series which features frequent shots of him in his role as a profiler, adopting the murderer's or the victim's position as he tries to understand much more than the crime by very literally stepping into their shoes. While this choice illustrates one aspect of McDermid's complex representation of society's deviances and shortcomings, it also successfully reconfigures the tenets of the genre and its distribution of power and order. In a similar reversal of the status of the psychologist in crime fiction, in Mina's *Garnethill*, Maureen takes justice into her own hands and decides to lure the psychologist-cum-abuser into a trap, drugs him and burns him in the carefully staged arson of the flat she takes him to.[41] In this paroxystic gesture, Maureen turns justice into revenge, against not just the man or what he symbolises, but also against the complacency of the genre. The figure of the detective, or psychiatrist, therefore no longer serves as the upholder of normative order. It becomes the figure of dissent, of upset, of the refusal to let the genre conform to the status quo.

However, reversals in agency are realised in a non-didactic manner. Female DCI Carol Jordan of *The Mermaids Singing* experiences a sort of epiphany of powerlessness, in spite of the careful construction of her character as a figure of domination and official power manifested through her appropriation of masculine discourse:

FEMALE CRIME FICTION: THE SPACE OF TRANSGRESSION

'Fraser Duncan? Hello, this is Detective Inspector Carol Jordan of Bradfield police,' she said. Carol had never grown used to referring to herself by her full title. She felt as if, any moment, someone was going to jump out and shout, 'oh no, you're not! We found you out at last.' (*MS*, 324)

The method is non-Manichean, McDermid showing that a 'feminist' version of the crime novel, even if it works on a series of reversals, cannot be reduced to a mere reversal of the symbols of institutional power or a simple transfer of agency. Indeed the author herself points out that her feminism is attributable to her focus on justice rather than on solving a whodunit, as well as her concern with the way we deal with victims, male or female – another way to escape from the normative function of both gender and genre.[42]

'One foot in the grave, the other on a banana skin': renegotiating the boundaries of the genre

Going against the containment potential of the genre for Mina, Welsh or McDermid also means resorting to pastiche and parody. McDermid's Lindsay Gordon novels in particular present a parody of the illustrious but very conservative model provided by Agatha Christie's novels. *Report for Murder* (1987), with its plot involving the murder of a famous ex-pupil in an upper-middle-class private school for girls, the school headteacher's appeal to Lindsay Gordon and her friend Cordelia Oliver[43] to solve the mystery and offset the wrongful arrest of one of the mistresses at the school, the *huis clos* atmosphere of the enquiry, down to the tone, method of interrogation and of solving the crime and even a few playfully heavy-handed allusions, all gesture towards the illustrious model. The parodic dimension is made clear by integrating the pastiche into a lesbian novel as Lindsay and Cordelia become lovers in the course of a book very openly discussing issues connected with lesbianism and lesbian love. This parodic yoking together of seemingly incompatible worldviews can be encapsulated – in this otherwise conventional whodunit series – in the very short dialogue between Cordelia and Lindsay, when the latter tells her lover, 'If I was Hercule Poirot, you wouldn't fancy me, would you?' (*RM*, 123). In that sense, the Lindsay Gordon novels, because of their playful parodic undertones, at least in part conform to Plain's assessment of lesbian crime fiction:

> Lesbian crime fiction is characteristically multiple: its version of the crime story is parodic, didactic and erotic – and there can be no guarantee that these fictions are read in order to establish 'whodunit'. Lesbian crime fiction thus provides a basis for reading *away from* the ending, and suggests practices which destabilise our conception of the pleasure of the generic text. (2001: 197)[44]

Louise Welsh, in her own literary version of the crime novel, uses various strategies that playfully assess and reconsider the genre she is writing in, to the extent that her second novel, *Tamburlaine Must Die*, a pastiche of a historical novel combined with a thriller, has the journalist and writer Mark Lawson wonder in the *Guardian* if she can make the boundary between crime fiction and literary fiction disappear.[45] In this invented memoir of the last ten days in the life of playwright Christopher Marlowe, Welsh revisits her theme, broached in *The Cutting Room*, of death as a form of voyeuristic entertainment, and steeps her main character into a dark story of gothic inspiration, as he is looking for the author of a libel signed in the name of a character in his play, Tamburlaine, and attributed to him. The fictional Marlowe follows in the footsteps of his historical predecessor, while abruptly warning his readers that he '[cannot] imagine what future [they] inhabit' (*TMD*, 1). With that statement, the transitional – or transgressive – space, here the ontological border that is the object of the protagonist's (and the reader's) quest, is not that between the historical past and the present, but rather that of fiction, in that case fictionalisation or rather dramatic representation, and reality, an issue which is linked to the impending threat of death. Indeed, Marlowe's actor-friend Blaize, cast in the role of Tamburlaine, eventually crosses the boundary when he tells Marlowe, 'you cast me in the role of murderer and so I became one' (*TMD*, 135–36). When he kills Blaize, Marlowe suggests that the reason for this execution is that the latter '[was] never Tamburlaine, […] just a half-rate actor' (*TMD*, 138–39), therefore crossing the ontological barrier between life and drama once again, while simultaneously suggesting that death can be the punishment for failing to achieve the impossible postulate of precisely destroying the border between two separate ontologies. The process becomes self-reflexive when Marlowe is told that 'your enemy Tamburlaine is a man who wishes to be you and yet wishes to kill you ... and so invites his own death' (*TMD*, 118), and can be connected to Welsh's own relish for the gothic and for Poe.[46] But the problematisation of death that this genre supplies stretches beyond its usual scope, as the reader is invited to recognise the quasi-metaleptic irony in Marlowe's description of death:

> Death makes the world a brighter place. I've seen the shape danger gives to things, an edge so sharp that if you like your head atop your shoulders and your entrails tucked safe in your belly it's best not to stop to admire the view. Yet the prospect of death renders everything lovely. (*TMD*, 28)

At first deprived of the false reassurance of the last sentence (which comes quite late in the description), the reader has no choice but to go by the oxymoronic description provided by the early lines of this extract, belatedly aware as he is that he has stopped to watch the view (as a reader of thrillers) and that the safety of inhabiting a removed, unimaginable future time might no longer be a valid protection.

The Bullet Trick presents a pastiche of this situation by playing on a fairly commonplace figure metaphorically associated with the serial killer: the conjuror.[47] Just as the conjuror-protagonist presents his various tricks and their attendant difficulties, the narrator relentlessly equates the literal with the metaphorical, showing how he can conjure himself, and the other characters, into the book, either in a straightforward, basic-trick manner, as with Sylvie:

> 'Let's just say I come from here, now.'
> 'The here and now?'
> 'You better believe it.' (*BT*, 105–06)

Or by using the flat, deadpan tone of the comedian, as with the mother who seems to materialise out of nowhere at an awkward moment:

> I said, 'Who the fuck do you think you are?'

> He shook his head, and started to walk towards the waiting queue.
> I made to follow him, then a small figure caught my eyeline. I turned
> and said, 'Hi Mum'. (*BT*, 90)

But as is usual with a conjuror, all those are just distractors, meant for the reader to look elsewhere while the real trick is going on, the reversal of the basic plot structure of the crime novel. Indeed, the dual plot involves chapters on William Wilson in Glasgow, on the run after committing a crime he cannot bring himself to face, interspersed with chapters set in Berlin which painfully recount the events that led William to commit the murder. The overall structure, however, as in a movie played backwards, is a journey from death and murder to un-death, as the victim – ta da! – finally turns up, alive and well in the last chapter. The trick may be a little hackneyed and obvious (the reader guesses quite early on that Sylvie will 'magically' spring back to life), but it remains that the novel reflects upon the construction of the thriller story, while gesturing towards Louise Welsh's refusal to take the genre, and her own distortions of it seriously, as is indicated by one of her epigraphs – an obviously apocryphal one – to *The Cutting Room*: 'One foot in the grave, the other on a banana skin' (*CR*, 50).

The Imp of the Perverse

In spite of the occasional antics shown by the narrators of their novels, the exploration of darkness is a territory shared by all three writers, who all claim to want to displace this darkness from the fictional, the imaginary, to the real. Louise Welsh, for instance, claims that 'fiction is someplace we can face our fears', and, as she elaborates, insisting that 'we can go places in novels which would perhaps be dangerous or undesirable for us to physically tread', we can trace a link with her allusion in *The Cutting Room* to Poe's short story 'The Imp of the Perverse'. This story describes the dangerous, indeed lethal lure of murder:

> We stand upon the brink of a precipice. We peer into the abyss – we grow sick and dizzy. Our first impulse is to shrink from the danger. Unaccountably we remain. [...] If there be no friendly arm to check us, or if we fail in a sudden effort to prostrate ourselves backward from the abyss, we plunge, and are destroyed.[48]

Welsh's fiction, as well as McDermid's and Mina's all describe the lure from all possible angles, managing to monitor, destabilise or even create our reactions. From that point of view, they set up a new space for the crime novel to occupy, or rather shift the genre from its conventional marginal space to a space of transgression. This space enables them to endanger the stability of metaleptic borders, destroying the sense of containment that is provided by definition by its fictional status, and to trespass against the reader's comparatively safer world. In so doing, they provide us with the deeply unsettling thrill of that ultimate transgression: the infringement upon our own safety. As Poe's narrator confesses that 'I am one of the many uncounted victims of the Imp of the Perverse', it seems reasonable to argue that so are Welsh, McDermid and Mina, as well as their numerous readers.

Notes
1. See chapter 1.
2. See Campbell, Ian. 2007. 'Disorientation of Place, Time and "Scottishness": Conan Doyle, Linklater, Gunn, Mackay Brown and Elphinstone', in Brown (ed.), vol. 3, p. 107.
3. O'Connor, Edmund. 2007. 'Tartan Noir', in *Chapman* 108, pp. 58, 50.
4. This constant reference to Stevenson and Hogg is particularly present in crime fiction, a fact which prompts Plain to speak of the 'obligatory reference to Stevenson', which she identifies as a trope of national identity, Plain, Gill. 2007. 'Concepts of Corruption: Crime Fiction and the Scottish "State"', in Schoene (ed.), p. 133.
5. Plain, Gill. 2001. *Twentieth Century Crime Fiction: Gender, Sexuality and the Body* (Edinburgh: Edinburgh U.P.), p. 3. Plain notes a breakdown of the genre, with a focus on the inexplicable and monstrous.
6. Jakeman, Jane. 2003. 'Val McDermid: The dying game,' *The Independent*, Saturday, 24 May, www.independent.co.uk/arts-entertainment/books/features/val-mcdermid-the-dying-game-590995.html [consulted August 2007]. Incidentally, McDermid does recognise elsewhere her connections with the American tradition of hard-boiled fiction.
7. Louise Welsh, in a conversation with writer Patrick McGrath on the theme of Gothic Nightmares. The occasion for the conversation was the 2006 exhibition at the Tate Gallery: 'Gothic Nightmares Fuseli, Blake and the romantic imagination' (15 February – 1 May 2006), www.tate.org.uk/tateetc/issue6/gothicnightmares.htm [consulted May 2006]. James Hogg's *The Private Memoirs and Confessions of a Justified Sinner* (1824), which has been described as a proto-detective novel, is mentioned by most crime writers in Scotland as having influenced their work.
8. Rankin, Ian. 1999. 'Why Crime Fiction is good for you', *Edinburgh Review* 102, pp. 12–13.
9. Rankin, Ian. 2007. 'Foreword', in Forshaw, Barry, *The Rough Guide to Crime Fiction* (London: Rough Guides Ltd.), p. vii.
10. On the insecure nature of the protagonist's identity (as victim or as murderer's alter ego) see Horsley, Katharine and Lee. 1995. 'Body Language: Reading the Corpse in Forensic Crime Fiction', *Paradoxa* 20, pp. 17–18. See also Pittin-Hedon, Marie-Odile. 2009. 'Scottish

Contemporary Popular and Genre fiction', in Ian Brown and Alan Riach (eds), p. 195, on the importance in Rankin's own fiction of Rebus's villainous alter ego Big Ger Cafferty, and the symbiotic, ultimately quite literally vital connection between them.
11 Horsley, Lee. 2005. *Twentieth Century Crime Fiction* (Oxford, Oxford U.P.), p. 252.
12 According to Plain (2001: 3), crime fiction is 'a literature of containment, a narrative that "makes safe"'.
13 Priestman, Martin. 1998. *Crime Fiction: From Poe to the Present* (Plymouth: Northcote House), p. 2.
14 This is indeed recognised by the writers themselves, as they very often acknowledge the influence of Chandler and Hammett rather than that of Agatha Christie for example.
15 Thomson, Alex. 1999. 'Editorial', *Edinburgh Review* 102, p. 3.
16 Welsh, Louise. 2010. *Naming the Bones* (Edinburgh: Canongate), back cover.
17 Renton, Jennie. 2006. 'Death and Literature' *Textualities* (online magazine); textualities. net/writers/features-n-z/welshlo1.php [consulted March 2007].
18 On this issue, see Horsley, Katharine and Lee (1995).
19 Wright, Jude. 2000. 'A Glasgow kiss for legal lads', *The Independent*, 19 August, www.independent.co.uk/arts-entertainment/books/features/a-glasgow-kiss-for-legal-lads-697303.html [consulted June 2008].
20 See for example Munt, Sally. 1994. *Murder by the book? Feminism and the Crime Novel* (London: Routledge), p. 71. McDermid herself admits to having been spurred into writing by the two writers described as the – feminist – founding mothers of contemporary female hard-boiled private eye genre, Sarah Parestky and Sue Grafton.
21 In addition, McDermid has also written standalone thrillers, either psychological thrillers or serial-killer narratives.
22 The first volume of the series, *Garnethill* (1998) was awarded the John Creasey Dagger Award for best first crime novel.
23 The novels stretch back to the 1980s, the period when *The Dead Hour*, published in 2006, starts. The novel therefore alludes to the worst of the Thatcher era for the poor, in particular in mining communities.
24 Lewis, Georgie. n.d. 'Denise Mina Is a Wee Cheeky Cow!' www.powells.com/authors/mina.html [consulted March 2009].
25 The housing estate where her abusive father has taken a flat.
26 On the notions of objectification and depersonalisation, see Miller, Gavin. Winter 2006. 'Aesthetic Depersonalization in Louise Welsh's *The Cutting Room*', *Journal of Narrative Theory: JNT*, 36:1, 72–89.
27 Horsley, Katharine and Lee Horsley. 1999. '*Mères Fatales*: Maternal Guilt in the Noir Crime Novel', *Modern Fiction Studies*, 45/2, pp. 371, 376.
28 McDermid quoted in Hume, Samantha. 2003. '"Here's tae Us Wha's Like Us": Val McDermid's Lindsay Gordon Mysteries', in Dorothea Fisher-Hornung and Monika Mueller (eds), *Sleuthing Ethnicity: The Detective in Multiethnic Crime Fiction* (Cranbury: Associated University Presses), p. 237.
29 Sarah Dunant quoted in Munt, p. 51.
30 It is to be noted that Val McDermid does not specialise in the female murder victim. In fact, after a 2007 newspaper-mediated fallout with fellow crime writer Ian Rankin, who was quoted as saying that lesbian crime writers were relentless killers of men, she produced a body-count of all the characters she'd murdered, which came to twelve men,

twelve women, and one gay. (See McDermid. 2007. 'I start my day in a condition of rage', *The Guardian*, August 17)

31 Hadley, Mary. 2003. 'An Interview with Val McDermid', *Storytelling*, p. 35. *The Mermaids Singing*'s exploratory technique of focusing every alternate chapter on the mind of the killer by reproducing his diary also fictionally externalises the murder by forcing the reader into uncomfortable proximity with the first-person narrator of the various atrocities he commits.
32 Kristeva, Julia. 1982. *Powers of Horror: An Essay on Abjection* (New York: Columbia U.P.), p. 4.
33 In the scene quoted above, where Paddy gets a glimpse of the victim just before she is murdered (*DH*, pp. 8–9).
34 Technically a transgender, as Dr Hill points out in the ITV series.
35 Hadley, p. 35.
36 Horsley, Katharine and Lee, 'Mères Fatales', p. 376.
37 For a fuller analysis of this aspect, see Pittin-Hedon, Marie-Odile. 2009. 'Scottish Contemporary Popular and Genre Fiction', in Brown and Riach (eds), pp. 193–203.
38 The books mentioned in the narrative do not, however, include the actual book we are reading.
39 Horsley, Katharine and Lee, 'Mères Fatales', p. 389.
40 See Hadley, p. 31.
41 It is to be noted that, Terminator-like, he survives to haunt and almost destroy Maureen in the second instalment, a true if melodramatic embodiment of the monstrous.
42 See Hadley, p. 35.
43 The naming of those two characters after two famous critics can be seen as a sign that McDermid is nodding towards literary criticism in a facetious way. Lindsay Gordon was in the 1980s and 1990s Visual Arts Director of the Scottish Arts Council and is now director of Peacock Printmakers in Aberdeen, while Cordelia Oliver was long-time drama and visual arts critic in Scotland for *The Guardian*. Surely the fact that the real-life Lindsay Gordon is a man can also be considered as a bit of a private joke considering the sexual orientation of the protagonists in the novel. My thanks to Ian Brown for pointing all this out to me.
44 The second part of Plain's assessment of lesbian fiction, however, that 'these novels also present a profoundly disturbing reworking of the violence inherent in crime fiction' (2001: 197), would more easily apply to McDermid's other novels, both the standalones and the Hill/Jordan series in particular.
45 Lawson, Mark. 2006. 'And for her next trick …' *The Guardian*, July 22, books.guardian.co.uk/reviews/crime/0,,1826032,00.html [consulted August 2007].
46 She uses Poe's story 'The Imp of the Perverse' as a chapter title for *The Cutting Room*, and nods to the American writer once again when she names the murderer and his sister Roderick and Madeleine, or the protagonist of *The Bullet Trick*, William Wilson.
47 The serial killer in Val McDermid's *The Wire in the Blood* also deems himself a conjuror.
48 Poe, Edgar Allan. 1845. 'The Imp of the Perverse' (Electronic Text Center, University of Virginia Library, etext.virginia.edu.), p. 364.

3. James Robertson: The Contagion of History

As Scottish literature has regularly been described as "Constituting Scotland", "Rewriting Scotland" or "Questioning Scotland",[1] it has now become a critical commonplace that creative writing in Scotland has, since the 1980s, been part of the political process that led to the devolution. *And The Land Lay Still*, a novel which engages with the political and social history of twentieth-century Scotland, and which has been acclaimed as a great state-of-the-nation novel, seems to conform to the pattern. The six-part novel, whose title is borrowed from 'The Summons', an Edwin Morgan poem from the *Sonnets from Scotland* collection, starts and ends on a retrospective on the work of photographer Angus Pendreich set up by his son Mike Pendreich, also a photographer and one of the main protagonists. The subtitle for the retrospective, 'Fifty Years of Scottish Life 1947–1997', indicates the scope also covered by the novel, which follows the trajectories of various characters from all classes of society as their destinies are woven together with British and Scottish history in what Robert Alan Jamieson calls a 'sprawling matrix of subtle connectivity'.[2] It portrays working-class socialist Don Lennie with his wife Liz and their sons Billy and Charlie who, in the fourth and fifth sections, are shown to take diametrically opposed routes; Ellen Imlach, whose childhood with parents Jock and Mary is depicted in section one and who reappears in the fifth section as a writer, raped and abused by thuggish Charlie Lennie; conservative David Eddelstane whose political and personal destiny is offered to the reader in the shape of a scathingly funny portrayal of the rise and fall of a Tory MP; Mike's partner Adam; Jack Gordon, his English wife and their daughter Barbara; Angus's former lover Jean Barbour, a political icon who can be seen as the novel's pivotal character in that she has links with the history of Scotland, its politics, and the process of telling a story. These characters all brush shoulders with the wider historical context, which includes the decommissioning of the Dounreay power plant, the setting up of the Scottish parliament, numerous by-elections and general elections, the introduction of the poll tax in Scotland or, south of the border, the Profumo scandal or the 1980s miners' strike, as well as various events on the international scene, among which are the Vietnam and Korean wars. All those events are mediated to the reader through the discourse of an authoritative extra-diegetic voice who sometimes comes across as offering historiographic lectures. As Mike is drawn to the nationalist cause, or at least shows an interest in understanding its tenets and attends various meetings hosted by Jean Barbour, Peter Bond, who believes his birth-name *James* Bond to show that his parents were 'oblivious to the bigger picture' (*ALLS*, 247), also makes his entry into the novel first as an MI5 agent under the supervision of his English superior Croick, subsequently to be summarily dispatched to Edinburgh as a freelance spy to keep an eye on the nationalists only to increasingly lose substance and stay on in the narrative as a ghostly presence. All six sections are introduced or concluded by a short lyrical italicised passage written in the second person. The reader gradually comes to realise that those passages convey the voice of Jack Gordon, who disappears from the narrative in the first part,to roam the land, picking up stones as he goes to give to people he encounters, among whom are Mike and Ellen, and only reappearing at the very end of the novel at the opening of the exhibition as a blurred figure in one of Angus Pendreich's picture taken at Dounreay.[3]

In this big, sprawling work, James Robertson, hitherto typecast as a writer of historical fiction, slightly displaces his focus, first by concentrating on a very recent period, the second half of the twentieth century, but also, and more importantly, by engaging in a reflection not just on the importance of history and the bearing of the past on the present, but on the influence of the present on the past and the connection between the concepts of history and story. Colin Milton, writing on modern historical fiction, states that the advantage of fiction over history is that it can 'focus on the part played by "'ordinary'" people in shaping events through their membership of groups representing historically significant causes, interests or principles', stressing fiction's capacity to literally *embody* historical events and thereby to enhance their significance and emphasise their multiple points of origin.[4] Milton also suggests (2007: 115) that in Scotland, recent historical fiction's interest in groups that so far had not been part of the political nation, in works such as Robertson's *Joseph Knight* (2003), which 'links a number of such "hidden" histories – of gender, class and colour', has led to a more inclusive re-examination of the nation's history and identity. In *And The Land Lay Still*, Robertson takes the reflection further by focusing on the relation between the narrative of the facts of the past and fiction, or more generally between historicity and creativity. This move involves a shift in both the generic and the intertextual make-up of the novel. Indeed, in this epic recreation of the Scottish nation, which encompasses representations of the notions of class and national identity, the emphasis is ultimately laid on formal and generic issues far removed from the typical state-of-the-nation narrative, with incursions into the ghostly, a reappropriation of the mythical and an emphasis on storytelling, on the construction/reconstruction of the narrative of the past. The novel indeed challenges the static division between the historically accurate, the documented evidence of the past's existence, and the fictional and mythical, in a geographical and cultural context in which the past is precisely a function of a mythic narrative. Robertson's enterprise is one of demythologising the mythical, by re-injecting its discourse with a new dynamism, while fictionally examining the most important development of contemporary Scottish history: the run up to devolution. It is therefore based on the dialectic of imagination and politics, while concentrating on the circulation between the two. It is, in other words, a creative, fictional counterpart to, and an update on, Craig's 1999 analysis of the interaction between the political and imaginative representation of the nation in *The Modern Scottish Novel*.[5]

An epic recreation of the nation or an imaginative one?

Willy Maley, in a 2008 booklet on new Scottish writing subtitled 'border-crossing', continues almost ten years after Cairns Craig to underscore the necessary connection between nation and imagination:

> Imagination stands in for the reality of a nation, storytelling substitutes for sovereignty. So, for Scottish writers, working across forms and genres is second nature. They're border-crossers by design: challenging, experimental, provocative. For Nations, like notions, exist only in the mind till they're put down on paper.[6]

Symmetrically to this programmatic assessment, James Robertson speaks of Scotland – past and present – as 'an amazing repository of ideas and images for a novelist',[7] while some reviewers hark back to the dilemma raised for fiction in Scotland, and to Robertson's novel in particular, pointing to the country's specific political status:

> *And The Land Lay Still* is very long, in places very fine, and afflicted too often by the need to lay out the facts and headlines of recent history. Implicit in its creation, nevertheless, is a teasing question: can Scotland hope for one of those state-of-the-nation epics when the nation of Scotland remains a submerged and stateless entity?[8]

Donny O'Rourke, former director of the Ullapool book festival before being succeeded in 2010 by James Robertson himself, answers this very question in the affirmative in his review for the *Scottish Left Review*, while elaborating that this 'political primer' can be seen as a 'search for the renascent nation's soul'.[9] The novel therefore cannot just be seen, as Robertson himself put it, as 'a story of Scotland', not even more inclusively, as Irvine Welsh has it, as 'looking at the world through a Scottish lens',[10] but also as one of those works of fiction which succeed in putting the nation down on paper, in other words in contributing to the fictional representation of national identity. This, as reviewer Bella Bathurst reminds us, places Robertson in a long line of Scottish writers, stretching from Robert Burns to Alasdair Gray and Irvine Welsh.[11] Robertson's particular achievement, however, lies in his use of historical fiction and its connections with the concept of national identity, defined by Mariadele Boccardi as 'the result of the various interactions between the cultural, political, economic, legal and religious institutions of a country, on the one hand, and the people's sense of the nation's common purpose and trajectory, on the other'.[12]

Boccardi's argument is that the collective sense of purpose, the connections established between individuals and institutions, is 'crucially fostered by the nation's production of credible imaginative accounts of its historical trajectory' (2007: 97). This notion of the credibility of imaginative accounts has been at the heart of historians' and critics' preoccupations since Tom Nairn and Benedict Anderson, the latter pointing to a commodification of national identity in *The Spectre of Comparisons* (1998), while the former famously argues in *The Break-up of Britain* (1977) that Scottish nationalism has often been perpetuated through forms of romanticism. Cairns Craig's concept of 'national imagination', which he defines (1999: 10) as 'the means by which individuals relate the personal shape of their lives, both retrospective and prospective, to the larger trajectory of the life of the community from which they draw their significance', avoids the romantic pit by declining to use the word 'myth', but nonetheless poses the question of the relationship of individuals with their 'nation's common purpose'. In that context, Nairn's cynical remark that the assertion of the 'thistle patch' by political and cultural nationalists 'proved very useful'[13] in the absence of a political status for Scotland leads Eleanor Bell in *Questioning Scotland* to examine (2004: 59) the dangers of nationalism when it fictionalises nationhood and invents fictitious pasts, leading people to accept such myths as truthful. Bell (2004: 49) uses the term 'overdetermination' to describe questionable generalisations on Scotland's 'character'. To her, overdetermination occurs 'when the nation is reduced in convenient, seemingly unproblematic ways, thereby assuming a level of "national truth"', when the nation is perceived as being limited to those formulations, without any critical awareness of their potential contradictions. James Robertson, by focusing on contemporary history, dwells on the nation's contradictions, and tackles the risk of overdetermination first by using a multiplicity of focalisers, with their own vision of the nation and of their participation in it – the socialist vision of Don Lennie, or the perceptions of nationalist Jack, feminist Sarah, and unionist conservative David Eddelstane. Those diverging, sometimes conflicting visions are rendered in free indirect discourse which, together with the central photographical metaphor of the book emphasised by the exhibition title, The Angus Angle, reminds the reader of the intrinsic but key notion of perspective that is inherent in any reconstruction of national identity in Boccardi's or Craig's sense of making the link between people's individual sense of the meaning of the nation and its political and cultural institutions. Those varied voices and perspectives are contrasted with a much more wooden voice and account, the 'historical' account provided by an external narrator who is resolutely set apart from the characters and their points of view, first by providing the long updates on historical events, at home and abroad, in the process surrounding the private lives of the characters in a decidedly heterogeneous voice, and second by adopting a style and tone that also demarcate it from the rest of the book by often switching into pamphlet mode, as in the example below:

> Here is a situation: a country that is not fully a country, a nation that does not quite believe itself to be a nation, exists within, and as a small and distant part of, a greater state. The greater state was once a very great state, with its own empire. It is no longer great, but its leaders and many of its people like to believe it is. For the people of the less-than country, the not-quite nation, there are competing, conflicting loyalties. They are confused. (*ALLS*, 534)

The pared-down and voluntarily simplistic style and tone of this address, its argumentativeness may call to mind Alasdair Gray's pamphlets on independence *Why Scots Should Rule Scotland* and *Why We Should Rule Ourselves*, but they also, in places, provide a stylistic and thematic pastiche of the state-of-the-nation narrative, particularly of the most famous Victorian state-of-the-nation novel, Benjamin Disraeli's *Sybil, or the Two Nations*. This dimension is made clear when the book volunteers a presentation of Scotland in the 1950s in terms of economic hope and hardships in a highly anaphoric style which takes on Victorian undertones:

> This was Scotland in 1950: coast to coast Jock Tamson's bairns stood or sat, lugs cocked to the wireless for news of home and abroad [...]. This was Scotland in 1950: land of 250 pits and 80,000 colliers, 100,000 farmworkers. [...] This was the land recovering from war, the land of nationalisation and council-house building [...] this was the land that had change coming to it, like it or not, the closure of factories and the shedding of skills. (*ALLS*, 199–200)

The emphatic tone, the melodramatic anaphoras, the seemingly ineluctable economic outcome clearly echo this famous passage from *Sybil*:

> 'Yes,' resumed the younger stranger after a moment's interval. 'Two nations; between whom there is no intercourse and no sympathy; who are as ignorant of each other's habits, thoughts, and feelings, as if they were dwellers in different zones, or inhabitants of different planets; who are formed by a different breeding, are fed by a different food, are ordered by different manners, and are not governed by the same laws.'

'You speak of—' said Egremont, hesitatingly.
'THE RICH AND THE POOR.'[14]

The narrator's voice in *And The Land Lay Still*, by its capacity to emulate Disraeli's style, not only places the subgenre of the state-of-the-nation novel at the centre of the narrative, but also sets itself apart by means of the temporal gap it intertextually creates. By introducing a very sharply individualised, 'intertextualised' narrative voice, Robertson integrates the notion of over-determination to his fiction, and by sometimes making this voice invade the characters' narrative, he indicates the contagious nature of predetermined discourses of the past or indeed of the present. The contagion of history in that case is to be seen as the contagion by monolithic, univalent discourses of the nation, in the sense of pre-writtenness that the pastiche of former works implies – be they romantic or not. The main criticism that has been levied against *And The Land Lay Still*, that the historical elements are totally divorced from the fictional ones and that, to quote but one reviewer, the book reads like 'a history textbook that has swallowed a novel',[15] may well fail to address the very coexistence *and* discreteness, whether deliberate or not, of precisely two possible representations of the nation, one dynamic and innovative, the other entrenched, didactic and fossilised.

In that context, the implicit but very often overlooked contradiction inherent in the representation of national identity, which prompts Eleanor Bell to advocate what she terms (2004: 51) a postmodern approach to notions of nationhood in order to challenge essentialist nationalism, that is to say, to adopt a more open-ended framework that would question the limiting restrictive framework of the argument that posits nationhood as inherent or factual, is fictionalised in the novel by the use of the enigmatic character James/Peter Bond. This character's dual moniker, as well as his schizophrenic relation to the world, indicates the necessity to evade a totalising posture while simultaneously underlining the dangers of such departure. His very position as a Scottish spy with the London-based secret services, his being cut loose from this position to become a freelance agent within the complex nature of the historical and political developments in Scotland in the run up to devolution, mark him out as the locus of all seemingly irreconcilable contradictions. This is exemplified in his ambivalent relationship to one of the historical emblems of Scottish nationalism in the 1920s and 1930s – and an important historical realeme in the book – Hugh MacDiarmid. Acting as a secret agent, Peter Bond dismisses MacDiarmid and his followers, judging that '[T]hey're powerless [...] and penniless. The more Scottish Nationalism is associated in the minds of the people with Grieve and others like him, the less likely it is that it'll ever have any kind of mass appeal' (*ALLS*, 269).

At the same time – and somewhat paradoxically if one overlooks the allusion to the power of creativity to succeed where mere political rhetoric has failed – Bond privately acknowledges the deep resonance of MacDiarmid's words to him:

> [H]e could see [the lyrics MacDiarmid had made up] as mere sterile arrangements of dead words. But they were more than that. He felt, reading them, that they put him in touch with some kind of throbbing undercurrent of life, something simultaneously ancient and modern, tiny and huge, parochial yet soaring into space. (*ALLS*, 269)

With this contradiction, which governs the whole novel because of the epic project behind it, and also because of the specific pact of reading of the novel as a genre, which as Craig indicates, precisely establishes a continuity between past and future,[16] *And The Land Lay Still* strives to achieve what is necessary to escape the dilemma faced by its character Peter Bond: a creative narrative of history. The contagion of history in that context would take the shape of a two-way contamination, of story by history, and history by story, emphasising the crucial fluidity between the two notions.

'There is fluidity in time': the fluidity of history

'I'm interested in how the past continues to influence the present,'[17] Robertson explains of his novel, while adding another comment which gives a more accurate account of his treatment both of time and history:

> For me, the really interesting thing about past, present and future is the fact that they interact, that there is fluidity in time. The past acts upon the present, but equally – as I tried to show in *The Fanatic* – the present acts upon the past, it reshapes how we see the past and therefore what it says to us. [...] History is very important to me

but only if I can see some kind of connection with now and with tomorrow. Otherwise it's dead and dry and has no interest for me.[18]

In the novel, the element that conveys the fluidity of time and the necessary interaction between past, present and future which defines Robertson's conception of history is to be found not in the historical and realistic plot, but in several episodes precisely removed from the constraints of temporality and realism, as for example the story within the story of the mouth in the box. The young student sent into a metaleptic level inferior to his own in order to find the end of one of Jean's stories significantly encounters narrators who get older and older, and finally receives from the oldest of them all, 'the mouth', reduced to her function as narrator of the future, a lesson on the inseparable nature of past, present and future, of individual and collective time. The antiquated and metonymic narrator first asks him about yet earlier and earlier personal memories, before giving him her verdict:

> [A]nd the mouth says, 'And what happened before *that*? 'I don't know,' he says, 'I don't know.' 'And *I* don't know how the story *ends*!' The mouth shrieks, and it starts to cackle, and the eye never blinks. (*ALLS*, 62)

In this logical puzzle, it seems that one's own personal past cannot be separated from the future of a story external to oneself, the future of what Craig (1999: 10) would call 'the larger trajectory of the life of the community', and therefore that the anonymous young man is being asked to perform exactly what the critic describes as the necessary condition for the creation of a national imagination, with Robertson, by the display of this array of narrators of the past, emphasising the diachronic dimension.

Robertson makes use of figures of the artist to embody the difficult concept of a narrative of history, by choosing to represent Jean Barbour and Angus Pendreich respectively as a voice, and a photographer, therefore as the bearers of the creative impulse, of the 'throbbing undercurrent of life'. Jean is first introduced as '[t]hat voice [...] A voice thick with years of storytelling, hoarse from the speaking and the smoking but not harsh; knowing and kind, mostly, though the cutting remark and the quick putdown are not absent from her repertoire' (*ALLS*, 31). The teller of stories, the impersonator with her 'repertoire', who famously ventures into tales that can best be described as fantastic parables, symbolises the departure from the here and now of her living room, which is also the locus of the staging of her narratives.

This leads the reader to the dual generic make-up of the novel, which has given rise to such neologisms as 'faction' or 'infotainment',[19] and to the experimental intent behind it. Robertson says that he wanted to build his book around the question: 'what is it that happens when you force diverse events into a story?', therefore underlining the naturally heterogeneous nature of facts and story. The duality embodied by Jean Barbour is staged by the encounter of two views on photography, Mike's and his father's, as they diverge on Angus's status as a photographer. Whereas Mike sees his father as an artist, Angus himself, who clearly separates creativity from the recording of facts, insists that what tells him apart from artists is their capacity to *make* things whereas he 'just record[s] what already exists' (*ALLS*, 42), a disagreement which once again problematises the imagining of the nation. So while the father would see a retrospective of his photographs as merely a jigsaw puzzle composed of disparate pieces, the son can discern the photographs' capacity to tell a story out of facts, a story that, in true compliance with the 'Angus Angle', is made up of individual stories that run parallel to, or look in the opposite direction from, the grand history of the nation's monuments, thereby steering away from what Benedict Anderson calls the commodification of national identity[20], which requires the identification by all of the objects of official history. When Angus turns to 'something in the shadow' of the obvious subject, 'the ridiculous next to the sublime, the commonplace made special by association' (*ALLS*, 48), he blurs the limit of history itself, and makes possible a new reading of it, which depends on the artist's capacity to turn it into his own narration. This achievement, which goes beyond mere paraleptic continuation,[21] exploits an opening up of the narrative of history which is made in the drier, more factual part of the plot. In this part, the external narrator voices a programme for the narrative of history, in true concurrence with Jean's actions, which consist not in forcing events into stories, but stories into events:

> What if, what if, what if? If only, if only, if only. Those phrases sit like crows on the passage of the years. They settle on politics, they

settle on love, they settle on life. You clap your hands but not all the crows fly away. What if Mike has not ended up with Adam that night at Jean's. If only he had been sure of his sexuality at thirteen, or sixteen. [...] What if Jim Callaghan had called a General Election in the autumn of 1978, before the so-called Winter of Discontent? (*ALLS*, 118)

The hypotheticals, the wishful tone, applied to both fictional and historical events, show this programme for the narrative to be a necessary opening of the present to the past and to the imaginative, re-creative process, in spite of their heterogeneous nature. This movement is symbolised by Jean's forceful insertion of herself into history by being associated with the Stone of Destiny.[22] Another of Jean's functions in the narrative is precisely to point to this difficult relation of history to story, to the contagion of one by the other in terms of narrative structure, when compared with the structure of life:

'Chronological order,' she says. 'Interesting phrase. Arranging things by time. It seems to be the natural way of releasing a narrative, but maybe it isn't. It's not how we remember our own lives, our own stories, after all. Bits of them come at us in any old order. Mixed-up memories. [...]'
'Most of us can only take so much chaos,' he says.
'I'll tell you something I've always wanted to do, Mike. I've always wanted to tell a story with no beginning, no middle and no end.'
'How would that work?'
'I'm not sure. That's the point. There's a tyranny about beginnings and endings and the routes between them but we seem to like being tyrannised.' (*ALLS*, 40)

To give flesh to this hypothesis, Jean, the voice of the story, uses the classic metaphor of the story as a journey and discards the notions of continuity and order, of the sacrosanct chronology in order to provide her own (hi)story, in a manner very similar to Angus's project of taking isolated pictures without trying to order them into any particular narrative, which, at the receiving end, leads Mike to have to choose one route. The voice/storyteller, as well as the photographer, therefore shows that a national imagination, and by extension the elusive concept of national identity, will not be a monolithic or fixed whole, but rather a multiplicity of possible journeys through a dense historical *and* creative landscape, as is asserted in Maley's statement. Mike, creating his narrative of Scotland through his father's photographs, chooses to describe time in spatial, cartographic terms:

> So in doing what I've done, making the selection I have, have I laid a false trail? Or am I simply able, from where I am now, from where *we* are now; to see the route we came, to look back and see the trail clearly marked? If my father were alive we would have an argument about that too. I'd say I can see the lines on the map, and he'd say the map is covered with many lines, you only see the ones you want to see. And we'd both be right. (*ALLS*, 643)

So just like Angus takes pictures which capture the past without thinking of them in terms of an underlying narrative, needing Michael to make the connection between the events of the past, therefore to construct a story, his own story, out of his father's pictures, so does Robertson provide a narrative of the past which is fragmented, with a variety of narrators, some of them actually represented inside the narrative as narrators of their own past, with variety in typography to reflect the variety of the stories and discourses. Robertson also integrates a character to serve as Michael's counterpart in the book, a character who will create a story out of the historical/fictional snippets he is given. With the help of that guideline, the reader, like Mike, Jean or Jack the endlessly wandering 'spectre of nationalism',[23] can therefore choose to find his own way in the panoramic landscape provided by the historical overview which makes up half of the narrative.[24] In fact, just like Angus's pictures, which can be seen as vehicles for an epic portrayal of the nation, or Jean's stories, which point to the necessity *and* difficulty of relating history to one's own stories, the historical facts provide the novel not just with its scaffolding, as has been noted, but also and more importantly with the sort of historical map that keeps all the lines in view for the reader.

The novel therefore presents the reader with a narrative of history which, because it has captured a voice and a series of pictures, can break free from the romantic narratives of the past condemned by Tom Nairn, from a romantic or essentialist approach to nation and identity. This liberation is represented in the novel by Ellen Imlach's encounter with the stalely mythical, thistle-patch history lessons of her childhood, where the girl, in the part suitably entitled 'scenes from the olden days', with the *passé* connotation of the choice of the archaic form of the adjective, is introduced to such symbols as the lion rampant ('the proper word for the way the lion was standing' (*ALLS*, 396), 'a *royal* emblem' which 'belonged to the Queen' and which 'you could only fly [...] if you had permission from a very important person called the Lord Lyon, who was spelled with a Y not an I' (*ALLS*, 397)), the Saltire, Saint Andrew, as well as the thistle. All those emblems of the mythical Scottish past, complete with tartan, today sold to tourists on Edinburgh's Royal Mile, are dutifully transferred onto her notebook whose title, 'Ellen Imlach, Ace Reporter', is redolent of the naivety of children's books (particularly of the children's books of the 1950s) and their disconnection from real life. After thus summarily disposing of those cliché symbols of the past by consigning them to a child's notebook, the novel opens up the future for a new sort of narrative of history, which a grown-up Ellen will in turn write by going back to the Scotland of her own past, her own lifetime in a way that is far from romantic. In so doing, she takes the historical narrative into her own hands, as do the multiple narrators of *And The Land Lay Still*. As Adam, Mike's partner, indicates in a comment that is meant to be self-deprecating, but which can take on a positive and dynamic overtone, 'We're frae the olden days just the same as Robert the Bruce and Bonnie Prince fucking Charlie' (*ALLS*, 619). In this statement, which curbs the effects of the mythification of the past with the tmesis in 'Bonnie Prince Charlie' and by putting the present time of experience on a par with myth, the contagion of history in this case means that history may well determine story, but that stories will project history, both for the past and for the future. Characters can look at a history which spans their own generation.

This opening up of the scope both of history and story finds its counterpart in the generic diversity of the novel, as is noted by Donny O'Rourke:

> For this is historical *fiction* and the story in the history is told through, between and across genres. *And The Land Lay Still* is a family saga, an oedipal psychodrama, a story of artistic formation and a coming of age narrative, a *bildungsroman* in the fullest sense, a testament to

coming out, a 'buddy' or 'bromance' narrative, pit disaster ballad in prose, a love story, a national foundation myth, a spy story and a mystery novel.[25]

This sustained generic multiplicity which also encompasses a capacity to keep both the ghostly and uncanny in view is what marks the novel off from other British state-of-the-nation novels of the period. It certainly separates it from Sebastian Faulks' *A Week in December*, a book published in the same year as *And The Land Lay Still* and which portrays a very contemporary Britain 'atomised by the unrealities of reality TV, online-networking sites, broken families, bad schools, drug and alcohol abuse, psychosis and religious delusion'.[26] This novel, also hailed as great state-of-the-nation novel, is emphatically presented as 'the era's definitive, panoramic novel',[27] while Faulks himself, interestingly also a writer of historical novels, insists on his intention of writing a realistic – though philosophical – story when he claims that '[w]e don't have a serious, deep, modern philosophical novelist who writes realistic books. It doesn't happen. It can't happen. Apparently'.[28]

This singular generic attribution contrasts with the generic multiplicity which Michael Gardiner sees as a defining feature of Scottish writing, past and future:

> [T]he undoing the flexibility and the radical rethinking of [genre] as a means of organising texts[,] [a]nd this will to keep typologies open is what will really separate Scottish literature from Eng. Lit. in coming decades.[29]

In a manner similar to Robertson's novel capacity to drive a wedge between history as myth and fiction as separate from reality, generic multiplicity allows him to draw lines on a map for his reader to choose from. It has to do with the vital necessity for Scottish fiction to present the reader with a diachronic as well as a synchronic approach to contemporary history – a three-dimensional map, in other words.[30] And indeed, the other important difference with Faulks' novel is that the latter, although panoramic, rather concentrates on the variety that composes British society at present, covering a period of one week. The historical dimension omnipresent in Robertson's novel is absent from Faulks' project, making his work a social *summa* rather than a reflection on the state of national identity. The reason for that fact can be found in *And The Land Lay Still*, in the words of Duncan Roxburgh, art dealer and gallery owner, who is very proud of the fact that the name of his gallery does not include the word 'Scottish'. He explains this to Mike with an argument that leads us straight back to the notions of national identity and statelessness, when he complains that '"I'm sick of the word [Scottish] [...]. Why do we always have to be qualifying ourselves like that? The English don't do it. They just *assume*"' (*ALLS*, 37). Roxburgh, who by coincidence bears a name which phonetically means 'city of rocks' and who can therefore be connected with the Jack plot and the apocryphal legend of the giant who, by gathering stones he has amassed in his sack, creates the Hebrides, seems to be the character who, liberated by such historical narratives as the novel of which he is part, can start to 'assume' by letting go of the most obvious identity marker.

Land and myth

Robertson introduces a key figure to embody the active, dynamic part each individual is to play to connect his own story to a history whose fluidity makes the composition possible: Jack the wanderer, a character capable of moving both in space and time, his italicised, second-person narration seeming not to be tied to the chronology of historical time, nor to respect the chronology of the narration. The stones he picks up to give the children he encounters are linked in the plot to the Stone of Destiny,[31] while they also construct a story of their own, which blends with a form of elemental history to recreate a mythical narration of origins where nation is brought back to its primeval element, land:

> You kept a pocket full of stones. The stones had no purpose, they were just a story. You kept the story going. That was what you had to do. You picked the stones up where you found them and you took them on, and every so often you laid them down again. You were making a pattern but you didn't know what the pattern was. You didn't know where you were in the pattern or where or how or if it would end. Sometimes you took a pebble from a beach, sea-washed and smooth as a pearl, and left it under a tree miles up a glen; sometimes you took

> *a rough, ragged stone from an inland field and weeks later you threw it into the sea. And sometimes you handed the stones on, to small, unknowing hands, and let the pattern take care of itself.* (ALLS, 145)

In Jack's atemporal and rambling narrative, which moves through an elemental rather than purely geographical landscape,[32] the character seems to be putting into practice Mike's dilemma of finding his own path on the map traced by his father's photographs. The extract further emphasises how history is *itself* haphazard, a 'pattern' that entails permutations, chance occurrences, and therefore gives Mike's eventual realisation that 'the past is not dead, it's not even past' a literal meaning. Jack's narrative short-circuits the chronology and distinctiveness of historical time by borrowing from the time of the story and projecting it towards the future. The 'pattern' can endlessly be altered because the story is multiple and because the 'small, unknowing hands' are yet to contribute their share to it. It is therefore a 'geologic', or 'geophilic' process as Randall Stevenson puts it, insisting on the essential concatenation of space and time in Jack's narrative:

> Throughout, the 'fierce grace' of Jack's encounter with Scotland's stones, skies and seas contribute a background less historical than geologic or geophilic: a sense – once again like Grassic Gibbon's – of an immutable foundation subtending phases of people and their politics. (2011: 99)

This 'geophilic' characteristic also occurs in *The Fanatic* when the narrative stresses the connectedness between the 'land' and Carlin, the character:

> The shape of the city renewed itself to him instantly, clear and precise. But now he took in its hills and hollows and saw it not as a city but as land with the city draped and poured over it. The buildings and streets were at once solid and ephemeral. [...] Edinburgh was there, but it was no barrier. He skited and stauchered back down the steep side of the hill and every step connected him with the land. When he reached the road he could still feel the beat of it pumping up through the soles of his feet. (*F*, 114)

THE SPACE OF FICTION

What is alluded to here, and conveyed in *And The Land Lay Still*, is a 'sense of the land itself, its mythic variety'[33] which, because of the realistic part of the narrative and its treatment of the myths of Scottishness, reinvents a narrative for Scotland that could be described with the oxymoron 'mythical realism', a blend of demythologising the stereotypical myths and of flaunting the shortcuts of history to reinvent myth, by giving it an elemental and mineral quality, but also by connecting it with the human.

The fluidity of time, of history, leads Robertson back to the basic components of any mythic narrative: man and the elements. The novel in the Jack narrative destroys the idea of time and chronology in order to make room for the remythologising process that is necessary if one is to avoid the divorce between history and human life, history and the here and now, as Robertson puts it. All the narratives and many of the characters are connected precisely by the handing over of pebbles. Robertson's enterprise is, therefore, one that transcends the realistic-mythical divide and the divisions between the various stories and their centres of consciousness, an enterprise which ultimately connects the human with the elemental. In a final, highly symbolical scene at the end of Jack's narrative, the character/narrator slowly swallows his last remaining pebbles, finally managing to be at one with the stones, and lays down at the end of a long beach, at the very north of Scotland, therefore at the edge of the land, to die, echoing the novel's title and replacing the human within the land, the land within the human. As a consequence, the whole novel, and with it, the whole account of twentieth-century Scotland, can move back to its mythical *and* human roots. In a dizzying historical backward sweep that reduces time to an inessential factor, because of the power of the story to shorten, expand, suspend or rewind it, the narrative leads the reader back to those basic components of myth *and* history – man and land:

> *Once we were all strangers. Before these folk there were Pakistani pedlars speaking Gaelic to their island customers. Before them were Poles and Italians, before them Irish, before them Jews, before them English, French, Danes, Scots. [...] Once were Irish and Picts and Egyptians and Britons and slaves and cave-dwellers and hunters of mammoths and gatherers of clams and berries and once they were not here and once they will not be here again. Only the land will remain.*

[…] 'It is we who must reconcile ourselves to the stones, not the stones to us.' You picked up the stones and carried them for a while, then you released them. You yourself were released. You were a skeleton walking out of the jungle, you were a man, you were alive, you were dead, you were bones crumbling into the earth. You were a shadow on the land, someone else's glimpse, their fading memory, then nothing. (ALLS, 521–22)

As people's memories are the only way of connecting man and land, as the return into the past leads to a suspended time (or space) of nothingness, which is neither past nor future, but which annihilates this distance, Jack's last, suspended words, which read like an epitaph, connect 'you' and the elements for eternity:

You knew the meaning of dogs barking.
You knew the meaning of rain, of wind.
You knew the meaning of stones.
You knew.
You knew.
You knew. (ALLS, 524)

In this ultimate return to the roots, to the stones, the wanderer-historian passes on the sign of the earth that will remain and lay still for the world to move on.

The fluidity of form

In order to achieve this goal, at once very open and very vague, and to open up the possibility for fiction to mix with 'the passage of the years' rather than just watching them go by, or 'just record[ing] what already exists', Robertson uses the character who can cross ontological boundaries, a fact which is made even more blatant as it is paralleled with a crossing of other borders. Peter Bond travels geographically from England to Scotland, politically from the conservative government to the Scottish nationalists, intertextually from the popular novels of Ian Fleming to the Theatre of the Absurd, and narratively from facts to story and back again. In addition to encountering fictional characters from various parts of the plot, he comes into contact with historical figures such as Hugh MacDiarmid and Major Boothby. This device, a common feature of postmodern fiction in a book which cannot be described as postmodern, is one of the most economical ways of creating an ontological disturbance in a fictional world, by creating what Benjamin Hrushovski calls a 'double-decker structure', and what Brian McHale describes as a transhistorical party.[34] In *And The Land Lay Still*, it creates a circulation between two ontologies that challenges the historical pedigree of the facts being narrated and therefore throws a new light on the whole of the factual and historical part of the book. Bond, who is free-floating, is aptly presented from his very first appearance into the plot as a ghost, a 'spook', the narrator punning on the double meaning of this word. This ghostly characteristic, which he shares with Jack the wanderer, enables him to underline for the reader precisely the points of contact between the story and history, by crisscrossing their ontological frontier, in a manner fairly similar to Jack's crossing and re-crossing of the land. As Bond tells his supervisor Croick of his uneasiness at making up stories about people he watches in order to incriminate them, an activity which he describes as 'this mixing of [...] fact and fiction' (*ALLS*, 309), Croick, himself another ghostly figure whose reality status in Bond's world is ultimately open to question, reckons that '[f]eeling uneasy is what this is all about' (*ALLS*, 309), with possible dramatic irony in the fact that neither he nor Bond realise that their position is indeed uncomfortable, because their function as characters is precisely to link two ontologies, to straddle a gap that is made wider by the fact that the very novel of which they are part emphasises the distance between what critics have called 'historical chunks' and fiction.

In *The Fanatic*, where historical events and characters set in the seventeenth century and the present-day fictional universe are made discontinuous by a clear-cut division into separate and alternate chapters, James Robertson stages an encounter that suggests in a humorous mode the possibilities offered by such ontological disturbances. Andrew Carlin, an impersonator of Major Weir for an Edinburgh tourist tour, encounters other historical figures from disparate historical periods:

> He was still in the Weir gear: it was strange, you could wander around this part of town in this rig-out and people hardly paid you any attention. A couple of times he'd met another ghost on the street,

going to or from his work. Deacon Brodie, or a monk or something. 'Aye,' the monk nodded as he passed. 'Aye,' said Major Weir. They were from different centuries but they never even blinked. (*F*, 131)

In *And The Land Lay Still* Robertson has enlisted a whole crew of characters (Bond, Croick, Canterbury, Jack but also the enigmatic and polymorphous Edgar, who belongs to a world of fantasy) to turn this kind of ontological flicker into a regular pattern: one interpretation of the novel may be that Bond – among other characteristics such as that of being lifted from a work of popular fiction, although he claims to be 'the original Mr Bond' and then turns into an anti-Bond by losing all the glamour and sleek manners, the effective spying of his namesake – a reversal best conveyed by the nickname Jean's circle has devised for him, 'Duffelcoat Dick'– is a psychologically challenged loser of a character, whose paranoia and schizophrenia stem from the job he may or may not have held with the MI5. But another interpretation is that like Jack, crisscrossing both Angus's maps and Mike's history, he is the carrier of that crucial possibility for Scotland, which goes beyond the historical watershed that devolution represents: the possibility to connect the present with the past and the future, the imaginary and the real, the fictional and the historical. Bond, but also Croick, Canterbury and Edgar, inhabit a zone which is properly speaking borderline. Those characters who have been living in the shadow of history – 'So if he's a ghost. How would that have happened? Ex-spook becomes ghost. One thing he knows from his life in the shadow is how people fade in and out. They matter, they don't matter' (*ALLS*, 236) – end up being lost in the shadows of the story, getting a glimpse of the ultimately impassable border between the real and the fictional:

> Lots of people are definitely still alive but you can't speak to lots of other people. You're a ghost. You made yourself a ghost some time ago. You're on the other side of an invisible something. People see you but they don't speak to you, and you can't speak to them. (*ALLS*, 231)

The narrative makes it clear why those 'people' can't be reached – it has to do with their ontological status. As characters who travel in stories and disappear, Bond, Croick or Edgar '[are] here, then they're not. Stories without endings. Like a book you can't be bothered finishing' (*ALLS*, 237). And predictably, Bond, travelling as he does in a world that increasingly appears to be the world of the story, encounters its basic components, words, '[t]housands, tens of thousands of words [...] battering through the inner walls of [his] skull' (*ALLS*, 231). This realisation links him once again to his uncle Jack, who is the one who hands out the component-elements of history, pebbles, each one of which is 'just a story' (*ALLS*, 145). Because of the fluidity with which Bond can shift from the realistic narrative to the world of magic where words, and even stories can make a flimsy appearance, the narrative seems to start metamorphosing around him, in a way that draws attention not just to the fluidity of the story, but also to its plasticity, its capacity to always accommodate, or engulf or turn into another form. The Bond episodes cross a formal divide by shifting from showing and narrating to direct telling, as well as borrowing the formal conventions of the theatre, by shifting from free indirect speech to direct speech presentation, a dramatisation reinforced by the presence of what appears to be theatrical cues. It also turns the narrative into an intertextual voyage which is less obvious than the ones conducted in *The Testament of Gideon Mack*, which revisits James Hogg's *Confessions of a Justified Sinner*, less directly allusive than the sustained reference in *And The Land Lay Still* to Grassic Gibbon's minerality. Indeed, the bare indications that read like stage directions, such as 'Croick's dead and Canterbury's God knows where. In some care home for the politically deranged maybe' (*ALLS*, 231), seem to plunge the characters into a Beckettian universe where, ironically, there is no 'persistence of memory',[35] where time and history have been evacuated of meaning, and where all that the characters are left with are indeed words.

La fabbrica de la narration

In the staging of the story that ensues, Edgar, the 'buttlefish [...] posing as a butler' (*ALLS*, 275) or the magic character who has the ability to turn into any of the other characters from any of the ontological levels visited by the narrative, including the real world, shows the presence of yet another actor of the narrative, who acts in many disguises. This actor first euphemistically describes himself as the distributor of snippets of facts or stories in the shape of pebbles, or also as another character who has the ability to transgress boundaries and enter another world than his own, though without being able to interact directly with those he encounters. He is also presented as an eminently malleable entity who can enter all fictional levels and impersonate all the characters at once, from Jean Barbour to MacDiarmid, and whose task consists in a synthesis of Angus's and Mike's approaches of the depiction of the world. This authorial-historian figure, this figure of the artist who seems to be able to enter the narrative in various costumes, just like the Major Weirs, Deacon Brodies and such like who quite literally haunt the streets of the Edinburgh's old town in *The Fanatic*, is a crucial actor of the book, as he is there to manage the synthesis that the text can but imperfectly manage, a position at the centre of what Jean-François Lyotard, precisely defining the role of the historian, calls 'la fabricca de la narration':

> This position of the problem of the story is the position of a theatric: outside, the fact, external to theatrical space; onstage, the narrative unfolding its drama; hidden backstage, under the stage, in the theatre, the director, the narrator, with all the machinery he has at his disposal, which makes up the narration's *fabbrica*. The historian is supposed to strip away the machinery, the machination and, having brought down the theatre's wall, to restore what was excluded.
>
> But of course, the historian is but another director, his narrative is but another product, his work another narration, even if all this is compounded by the *meta-* prefix: meta-diegesis, meta-narration, meta-narrative. History is certainly about story, but a story boasting that it can reach out and refer to the thing itself, to the facts, that it can establish and retrieve them, is no less crazy, in fact crazier, than this powerful deployment of force and freedom that is the story, which is borne by the thousand discourses from which for example *The Odyssey*, that huge legend, was born.[36]

James Robertson, by bringing together history and story, by combining a theatrical space that actually flaunts the theatre's walls, and by introducing various characters who can be seen as the mechanics of the theatrical apparatus, manages to reconstitute, to bare the mythology that goes into any historical as well as any fictional construction. The reader of *And The*

Land Lay Still is therefore left with the storyteller's words, as Jean Barbour indicates that one should always '[t]rust the story' (*ALLS*, 128), while simultaneously arguing that '[a]ll stories are lies' (*ALLS*, 539). She, like Jack Gordon who gives out pebbles that can be arranged into a multitudes of possible combinations for the creation of myths, histories and stories, like Mike who wonders if his choice of photographs for his father's exhibitions might not end up telling the wrong story/history, like Edgar, who can rearrange a fictional character's individual story in order for it to be able to meet with the larger picture, or even like Bond, who navigates a world simultaneously made up of history and story, annihilates for the space of the novel the sacrosanct distance, making the narrative of Scotland not just a historical, but also a fictional possibility.

Notes

1. Respectively Craig, Cairns. 2001. 'Constituting Scotland', *Irish Review* 28, pp. 1-27, March, Cristie L. 2002. *Rewriting Scotland: Welsh, McLean, Warner, Banks, Galloway and Kennedy*, Manchester and New York: Manchester University Press, and Bell, Eleanor. 2004. *Questioning Scotland: Literature, Nationalism, Postmodernism*, Basingstoke and New York: Palgrave Macmillan.
2. Jamieson, Robert Alan. 2010. *The Bottle Imp* 8, www.thebottleimp.org.uk, p. 1. Jamieson also speaks of the book as presenting a 'symphonic structure, with five main movements and a shorter coda – themes and motifs introduced in the opening section are subsequently developed and explored, as characters come and go accordingly', p. 1.
3. He is also the body that is found at the end of the beach, this discovery being made towards the end of the novel as well.
4. Milton, Colin. 2007. 'Past and Present: Modern Scottish Historical Fiction' in Brown (ed.) vol. 3, p. 115.
5. According to Craig (1999: 9), 'in the work of the historical novelists of the nineteenth century what was being created was a national imagination: an imagining of the nation as both the fundamental context of individual life and as the real subject of history'.
6. Maley, Willy. 2008. *Literature and Diversity: Border-crossing: New Scottish Writing*, Scottish Book Trust, online publication, www.scottishbooktrust.com/files/Border-crossing%20-%20New%20Scottish%20Writing%20by%20Willy%20Maley.pdf [consulted Sept 2009].
7. Interview with James Robertson. 2006. www.scotgeog.com/interview.php [consulted June 2011].
8. Turton-Smith, Ian. 2010. 'Is this a Novel I See Before Me? James Robertson's *And The Land Lay Still*', *Scottish Review of Books*, Volume 6, Issue 3, www.scottishreviewofbooks. org/index.php?option=com_content&view=article&id=348:is-this-a-novel-i-see-before-me-james-robertsons-and-the-land-lay-still-ian-bell&catid=36:volume-6-issue-3-2010&Itemid=85 [consulted July 2011].

9   For O'Rourke, 'it is *a* book of which the stateless nation has long been in need', O'Rourke, Donny. 2011. '*And The Land Lay Still* – James Robertson', *Scottish Left Review*, March–April, Reviews 63, p. 26, www.scottishleftreview.org/li/images/stories/pdf/i63.pdf [consulted July 2011].
10 Welsh, Irvine. 2010. '*And The Land Lay Still* by James Robertson: Irvine Welsh enjoys a sweeping look through a Scottish lens at a turbulent era', *The Guardian*, July 24, www.guardian.co.uk/books/2010/jul/24/land-lay-still-james-robertson [consulted May 2011].
11 Bathurst, Bella. 2010. '*And The Land Lay Still* by James Robertson: An epic portrait of postindustrial Scotland is almost too painful in its accuracy', *The Observer*, Sunday 15 August, www.guardian.co.uk/books/2010/aug/15/and-land-lay-still-robertson [consulted May 2011].
12 Boccardi, Mariadele. 2007. 'Pedlars of the nation's past: Douglas Galbraith, James Robertson and the New Historical Novel', in Schoene (ed.), p. 97.
13 Nairn, Tom. 1977. *The Break-up of Britain*, quoted in Bell, Eleanor. 2004. *Questioning Scotland: Literature, Nationalism, Postmodernism* (Basingstoke and New York: Palgrave Macmillan), p. 60.
14 Disraeli, Benjamin. [1845] 1956. *Sybil, or the Two Nations* (Oxford: Oxford U.P.), Book 2, chapter 5, p. 67.
15 Waters, Colin. August 2010. 'Scotland is the subject of a state-of-the-nation novel with a Dickensian scope', *The Herald*, www.heraldscotland.com/arts-ents/fiction-reviews/james-robertson-and-the-land-lay-still-hamish-hamilton-18-99-1.1045894?50883 [consulted 04/07/2011].
16 Craig (1999: 11) stresses that the novel is 'a medium by which a common past and a common stock of cultural memories can be defined, and by which a possible route towards the future can be chartered without loss of continuity with a founding past'.
17 Campbell, James. 2010. 'A life in writing: James Robertson', *The Guardian*, 14 August, www.guardian.co.uk/books/2010/aug/14/james-robertson-land-still-profile [consulted 04/11/2011].
18 Interview with James Robertson. 2006. www.scotgeog.com/interview.php
19 O'Rourke, p. 27.
20 See Benedict Anderson (1998), *The Spectre of Comparisons: Nationalism, Southeast Asia and the World*, London: Verso, Part I, chapter 3, 'Long-Distance Nationalism'.
21 A term coined by Genette in *Palimpsestes* to refer to the narration's use of historical facts in a story by filling in the blanks left by history, by adding details, like encounters with some fictitious characters, which cannot be disclaimed, because they take part in a private part of the historical figure's life which has not been documented by historians. For instance, in *And The Land Lay Still*, Bond encounters Hugh MacDiarmid and Major Boothby.
22 She tells Mike the story of how, with his father Angus, she stole the Stone of Destiny from Scone.
23 Welsh, '*And The Land Lay Still* by James Robertson'.
24 For more detail on the question of the map as narrative metaphor in contemporary Scottish fiction, see Pittin-Hedon, Marie-Odile. 2008. '"Learn Your Own Way to Read the Map": rôle et place du roman écossais dans le processus de dévolution', *Babel*, 17, pp. 195–210.

25 O'Rourke, p. 27.
26 Galvin, Cathy. 2009. 'Sebastian Faulks on the state of the nation', *The Sunday Times*, August 23, entertainment.timesonline.co.uk/tol/arts_and_entertainment/books/fiction/article6803845.ece?token=null&offset=0&page=1 [consulted July 2011].
27 'It aspires to be a state-of-the-nation book, a satirical comedy of metropolitan literary life, a sweeping, Dickensian look at contemporary London, a serious examination of Islam and the reasons for radicalism among young Muslims, a thriller, a satire on the Notting Hill Cameroonians and a detailed look at the sharp financial practices that led to the collapse'. Cartwright, Justin.2009. 'A Week in December by Sebastian Faulks', *The Observer*, Sunday 23 August, www.guardian.co.uk/books/2009/aug/23/week-in-december-faulks [consulted July 2011].
28 Ibid.
29 Gardiner, Michael. 2006. *From Trocchi to Trainspotting: Scottish Critical Theory since 1960* (Edinburgh: Edinburgh U.P.), p. 2.
30 See the next chapter for a fuller analysis of this recurring concept of the three dimensional map in a different context.
31 See Randall Stevenson who states in his review of the novel that 'the pebbles [...] come to seem miniature stones of destiny'. Stevenson, Randall. 2011. '*And The Land Lay Still*', *Edinburgh Review* 131, p. 99.
32 See chapter one, for another example of the symbolical importance of the mineral Scottish landscape to the persistence of a Scottish immutable originary identity.
33 Turton-Smith.
34 McHale, Brian. [1987] 1991. *Postmodernist Fiction* (London and New York: Routledge), p. 17.
35 'The Persistence of Memory' is the title to the second section.
36 'Cette position du problème de l'histoire est position d'une théâtrique : en extériorité, le fait, au-dehors de l'espace théâtral ; sur la scène, le récit déroulant sa dramatique : caché dans les coulisses, dans la herse, sous la scène, dans la salle, le metteur en scène, le narrateur, avec toute sa machinerie, la fabbrica de la narration. L'historien est censé défaire toute la machinerie et machination, et restituer l'exclu, ayant abattu les murs du théâtre. / Or évidemment, l'historien n'est lui-même qu'un autre metteur en scène, son récit encore un produit, son travail encore une narration, même si tout cela est affecté de l'indice *méta-* : méta-diégèse, méta-narration, méta-récit. Histoire où il est question de l'histoire, assurément, mais dont la prétention à atteindre la référence à la chose même, le fait, à l'établir et à le restituer, n'est pas moins folle, plutôt plus folle à tout prendre, que la puissance de la fiction librement déployée dans tous les mille discours d'où naît l'immense légende qu'est, par exemple, l'Odyssée'. Lyotard, Jean-François. 1973. *Des Dispositifs Pulsionnels* (Paris : UGE), p. 180–81. My translation.

4. Suhayl Saadi: The Third Space of Fiction

Writing from yet another perspective than Strachan, Donovan, McDermid or Robertson, Suhayl Saadi published *Psychoraag* in 2004, a novel considered as one of the first novels of Scottish-Asian identity and which, as such, was compared with both Salman Rushdie's and Irvine Welsh's works. Saadi's work brings an added dimension to Habermas's concept of the 'postnational constellation' in which, according to Jürgen Neubauer (1999: 12), 'interaction[s] are both more local and more global than the nations'.[1] This definition is indeed particularly fitting for a writer who sketches the contours of a national identity that takes into account how the British-Asian component segues into a *Scottish*-Asian sense of identity. As can be seen from Zaf's assertion in *Psychoraag* that 'we were all Glaswegians' (*P*, 360), the space of fiction that is mapped out by Saadi's works redefines the national, the postnational, but also the ideas of multiculturalism and post-ethnicity in that they examine identity 'from perspectives broader than race'.[2] It is indeed a third avenue, that will be called a third space of fiction in connection with Homi Bhabha's concept of the third space, which Saadi's ambitious fiction sets out to delineate, by giving the 'mongrel nation' a distinctly, militantly Scottish-Asian flavour.

Psychoraag indeed presents itself as a multilingual, Scots-Asian stream of consciousness narrative, which incorporates Persian, Urdu and Arabic words, but also 'Weedgie patter',[3] and which follows the thoughts of a DJ through his last show on Radio Chaandni – moonlight – before the station is closed down. The *Junnune Show* – the show of madness – is a six-hour rant during Zaf's stint on the graveyard shift of the radio programme (midnight to six). The narrative, divided into six sections to cover the six-hour programme, takes the listener and the reader on a musical and ruminative trip in Zaf's consciousness, in which memories and stories are kick-started by the various songs he plays, a hotchpotch of influences which range from psychedelic songs by sixties bands like the Beatles, the Byrds or Kaleidoscope, to Celtic rock, Pakistani bands, jazz material like the music of John Coltrane, Bombay films songs from 1902 to the 1990s, and various contemporary bands, not least of which is contemporary British-Asian music by the likes of Susheela Raman, Sheila Shandra and Cornershop. For

Sarah Upstone (2010: 201), this eclectic musical selection serves to evidence the 'identity remix' achieved by Saadi's fiction, as well as bolstering its post-ethnic credentials.[4]

Joseph's Box, published in 2009, is an epic narrative of a different kind, as the protagonists, Zuleikha and Alex, embark on a geographical and spiritual journey which takes them from Glasgow to England, then to Italy and Pakistan, as well as into the mysteries of identity as represented by the initiation trip guided by the seven chambers and six boxes contained in the large box they fish out of the Clyde. Saadi, who was born in Yorkshire and has lived most of his life in Scotland, but who is of Pakistani origin – a 'ScotPak', like his protagonists Zaf and Zuleikha – describes himself as a dissident writer, pointing out that he does not belong to 'the Hyper-Hip Multicoloured Multicultural Metropolitan London-Oxbridge "Liberal" Literary Mafia'.[5] In his own definition of the categories of writers to have emerged in Scotland in recent years, he is one of those writers who are 'moving in', 'writers who hail from other cultures bringing something of their own ancestors' experiences with them, those experiences exerting themselves, either consciously or otherwise, in fresh contexts in their writing'.[6] He insists that those writers produce novels which move away from 'safe multiculturalism', that is the 'fashionable tracts where normative absolutes are almost never thrown into question'[7] or, to borrow Asif Farrukhi's words, the 'pre-packaged "multicultural" stuff which so many people are dabbling in to [sic] these days'.[8] *Psychoraag* – and to a lesser extent *Joseph's Box* – can therefore be seen as one of those novels written against what Edward Said describes as disempowering Orientalism or, more recently, Stanley Fish's updated description of a peculiar contemporary form of Orientalism, 'boutique multiculturalism':

> Boutique multiculturalism is the multiculturalism of ethnic restaurants, weekend festivals, and high profile flirtations with the other in the manner satirised by Tom Wolfe under the rubric of 'radical chic'. Boutique multiculturalism is characterised by its superficial or cosmetic relationship to the objects of its affection.[9]

Saadi, for whom 'every novel embodies a unique political act', writes uncompromising novels at odds with the propositions of boutique multiculturalism. He indeed sees this kind of fashionable multiculturalism as a renewed form of imperialism:

> The systems of imperialism have merely adapted – their iron grip, on our consciousness, our labour and our purse, remains as tight as ever. At times, the system seems irredeemable. This is very dangerous for society.[10]

His novels show an attempt to achieve transculturation, namely a capacity to transverse both Western and Eastern culture and to translate (a term which is at the core of Homi Bhabha's theory of postcolonialism), negotiate and recreate affinity and difference within a dynamic of exchange and inclusion.[11] The term 'transculturation', when it was coined in 1940 by the Cuban anthropologist Fernando Ortiz, meant that this dynamic of exchange lead to the creation of a new, original cultural product, therefore assuming a counter-hegemonic function. In order to mediate this process of creative inclusion, Saadi uses the power of music, integrated into both *Psychoraag* and *Joseph's Box* as a theme, but also as a narrative voice and a structural device, a 'unifying force'[12] which can take various guises, as is indicated by the literal translation of the word 'Pyschoraag', 'symphony of madness' or 'symphony of the mind',[13] while the lute, the instrument played by Alex in *Joseph's Box* and elevated to the rank of protagonist in the novel, is described by Saadi as a voice, a means to express melancholy.[14] In the glossary to *Psychoraag*, Saadi provides a useful explanation of the term 'raag':

> Raag: a pattern of notes in Indian music used as the basis for melodies and improvisations [...] Personalised descriptions of a raag enable a musician to meditate on its characteristics and to unite his or her personality with a particular mood and, thereby, instil the same mood in the audience. (P, 428)

This description, with its insistence on improvisation and on a highly personal approach to composition, can be seen as a delineation of the method of composition, and of the pact of reading the novel is built on, to the extent that Katherine Ashley sees the novel as a whole as 'Saadi's raag'.[15] *Psychoraag*, and to some extent *Joseph's Box*, are indeed improvisations on the idea of an epic journey into the self, and into the concept of identity, individual, social and national. This journey compresses history into the space of a few hours in a manner reminiscent of Joyce's *Ulysses*, or later of Angela Carter's *Wise Children*, as Zaf's ruminations are sporadically interrupted by analeptic accounts of his father's story of leaving Pakistan with his wife Rashida and their settling down in Scotland, only to occupy a sublevel of history, as Jamil spends most of his life working in the city's sewers. It is therefore a journey into history as well as into the self, but from a different standpoint from that adopted by Robertson in *And The Land Lay Still*, with an undercurrent of the narrative in both *Psychoraag* and *Joseph's Box* providing a historicised perspective on Pakistan, the 1971 Partition as well as on emigration. In both novels, this perspective, while not constituting the mainstay of the narrative, is made up of outbursts from narrators-focalisers (mostly Zaf and Zuleikha respectively) keen to keep up the connection between the interior quest and the external historical events irrevocably mingled in that quest.[16] In Saadi's words, '*Psychoraag* is not an exotic theme park of "The Asian-Scots experience"; rather, it traverses the rivers of history and memory and the courses these rivers take through our lives'.[17]

In *Joseph's Box*, the eponymous Giuseppe (also featuring as Yusuf), significantly defined as a bridge, a point of passage rather than separation, a 'great bridge between heaven and earth, protector of innocence, he who breathed life into the forms of the dead' (*JB*, 426), tells Zuleihka that 'history is not blind' (*JB*, 426). The narrative strives to enforce that principle, which rings like a declaration of intent, by creating in this novel as well as in *Psychoraag* a historicised vision of Glasgow and Pakistan, a need recognised by Zaf who claims that 'he knew nuthin about [...] Pakistan-before-it-wis-Pakistan, before the land had become suddenly pure' (*P*, 198), just as he 'knew nuthin of the Scotland before. It wis a complete mystery to him and would remain so always' (*P*, 199). In Zaf's on-air outbursts, the emphasis is generally laid on the dislocation of the individual, because, as Peppe also tells Zuleikha in the other novel, 'where you're from is not necessarily where your family is from. The world has changed' (*JB*, 345). This comment raises a point that Sarah Upstone (2010: 199) terms the post-ethnic dimension of Saadi's writing, by which she means a definition of identity relying on location rather than ethnicity, therefore advocating a brand of nationalism which she describes as civic. Indeed, for Upstone (2010: 203), 'nationalism speaks to the importance of geographical affiliation, even as it denies race as a basis of this'. This dislocation in the geographical conundrum of identity is particularly obvious in the description of Zuleikha's mother, and it comes to include time, in the shape of history, as well as space, geography:

> And Zuleikha thought of her own mother; of how, through the bluster, the domineering attitude, Zuleikha had known – or at any rate, had sensed – that above all else Nasrin Zeinab had felt fear. Perhaps it had been the deep scar of having been brought up in a country which had an ambivalent attitude towards immigration from what, in those days and for some time afterwards, had been termed the New Commonwealth – but which really had been the old empire. Or perhaps it had been simply the existential dislocation of a woman living in a post-industrial society who had never worked outside the home. (JB, 371)

As Catherine Woodward acknowledges, the historicised approach to identity is a condition of the geopolitical and religious definition of the present:

> The replacement of sacred art with the manufactured self righteousness of God appears to Saadi as what initially choked Pakistan. The horror of the now is so horrible because it is juxtaposed with the immediacy of what went on before and the present becomes a gross and shameful pantomime in the face of the past it tried to kill. Here I really admire Saadi for his active rehistoricising where it is so very important, not just for Westerners but for anyone who has forgotten the past and what has been rubbed out with it.[18]

Woodward, pointing as she does to the necessity for all narratives to take the recognition of the past's impact on the present as containing a geographical component, acknowledges Saadi's wish to widen the scope of the re-historicising process he is attempting and to speak to the here and now. Incidentally, as Ali Smith notices in her review of *Psychoraag*, it is highly ironic that a book driven by the overarching theme of whether anybody is listening received no critical attention from English reviewers, in spite of being named by *The List* as one of the 100 best Scottish Books of all times.[19] It still remains that *Psychoraag*, and *Joseph's Box* after it, attempts the complex process of historicising the characters' lives, a reality which appears as unstable. *Psychoraag* is indeed an exploration that stretches into the past of Zaf's origins, the social makeup of Glasgow, and his own problematic definition of identity, mirrored in the various characters, Zilla, Zafar the Kinning Park gangster, and Zafar the boy in the photograph, who, together, compose a summation of Zaf's own identity. His quest is made up of a reflection of broken images, of fragments combining to depict a complex, self-contradictory psyche and identity which finally needs hallucinations and projections of the future onto the present to be completed, as Zaf in the last chapter embarks on a journey in the streets of Glasgow at the same time DJing for the Junnune show. Similarly, in *Joseph's Box*, Alex, Zuleikha and the characters they encounter hover between reality and hallucinations. The novel, which Saadi describes as a return to the primitive style of the epic,[20] with a central motif referring to the Islamic story of Yusuf and Zuleikha, is a quest narrative which he describes as 'a search for unity through the attainment of spiritual beauty'.[21] This journey, which is both geographical and spiritual, can be described as a three-dimensional journey, the protagonists progressing through time, geography and constantly shifting versions of an underworld, a journey which crosses and re-crosses the borders of life and death in a way that brings to mind Zaf's comment to his listeners at the beginning of his own nightly crossing – in the first chapter of *Psychoraag* – with the words 'Ahhh, thur's nuhin better, in the deeps ae the nicht, than a wee bit ae clean terror' (*P*, 60).

For Zaf, as for Zuleikha and Alex in the next novel, the epic journey into the night, into the wee bit of clean terror, is a trip that is both internal, exploratory and external, outward, expanding, a voyage towards the root of all identity, a voyage 'in the cosmic karmic darkness ae space 'n' time 'n' Glasgae' (*P*, 88), or, as Alan Taylor explains, taking up the famous postulate of the mongrel nation, an attempt to make sense of the elusive, slippery nature of all boundaries:

> It is as if he is desperately trying to define the indefinable, to find a label where none is adequate. What does it mean to be Scottish?

Who among us is truly Scottish? All of us are made up of many components. We're all mongrels noo.[22]

Crossing boundaries

For Saadi, Glasgow is a good place for crossing over, and Scottishness 'a metaphor through which [he] perceive[s] things',[23] a place from which to observe what he sees as the metamorphosing system of imperialism, a system that challenges the idea of mongrelisation. The need for Saadi to cross borders, for which he invents a unique language, a 'Babel of tongues' or 'midnight choir'[24] made up of Glaswegian Scots mixed with Urdu, Arabic, Gaelic and Punjabi, as well as with songs lyrics, registers the consequences of the system of imperialism on the Asian Scot, but also, in a way that adapts Bhabha's programme for the writer in *The Location of Culture*, strives to explore a particular confluence of cultures and identities.[25] For Bhabha:

> What is theoretically innovative, and politically crucial, is the need to think beyond narratives of originary and initial subjectivities and to focus on those moments or processes that are produced in the articulation of cultural differences.[26]

The task that Zaf assigns himself is quite similar to Bhabha's prerequisite:

> Of course, it wis all rubbish, this stuff, this ascribin of characteristics to a whole group of people based on their tribe or their religion or the *mulk* from which they had journeyed. Aye, it wis impossible to get it out of your system. [...] Nonetheless, Zaf would try. (*P*, 23)

In order to achieve this articulation of differences, this depiction of confluence, Saadi chooses the 'cosmic karmic darkness' (*P*, 88) of Zaf's journey into the hyphenated, the Asian Scot, both in touch with the cultures of the world, and connected with his own sense of whether he is truly Scottish and/or Asian. Like Saleem in *The Satanic Verses*, Zaf can be described as a figure in '*Hamlet* haunted by bad dreams and self-doubts, melancholiacs thoughtfully liable to bouts of self-reproach',[27] a figure roaming his own memory and consciousness in an attempt to articulate, to daily create a sense of Asian-ness that can only be complete if the connections can be made to a certain sense of Glaswegian-ness:

> [A]fter all, it is an Asian station, he thought. All the bits, past and future, that daily jostled and sang the state of Asianness into being, that reconstructed somethin that wasn't real from somethin that wis. A dancer's shadow hoverin over the hot red soil of South Asia. Old India wis shaped like a crucified Jesus. An, like some white-walled cavern chapel, Radio Chaandni bellowed out its hymns into the unlistenin darkness of Glasgow. (*P*, 22)

Zaf's voice, which goes on air to address an audience who may or may not be listening, is a voice that is anchored in Scottishness as much as in Asianness, as is indicated by its critical, ironical eulogy of multiculturalism:

> [T]his is the *Junnuuuune Show* oan ninety-nine-point-nine meters FM an we're broadcastin oan that wondrous an exciting an pioneerin multicultural, multi-ethnic, polyglottal stop ae a radio station, Radio Chaandni. Aye! (*P*, 188)

The phonetic rendering of the Glasgow voice as well as the pun on the 'polyglottal stop' not only offer, as Upstone asserts (2010: 198), 'the most effective alternative to birth as an assertion of Scottish identity',[28] therefore insisting on an identity which is defined not by ethnic origin but by location, but they also amount to an ironical vision of the superficial multiculturalism introduced by the words 'Junune' and 'Chaadni'.[29] As such, they express Saadi's distrust of safe multiculturalism for an author who wonders, as quoted above, how many more Zadie Simthereens we can stomach, and who insists in interviews on the necessity to avoid what he calls 'ethnic reading':

> It is important to be wary of 'ethnic' readings of all output produced by an artist who happens to belong to a group which is in the minority in a particular locus [...]. One must avoid the ghetto-ising of talent, or the exoticism of that which was always intrinsic.[30]

Instead he suggests a narrative identity that includes a variety of points of origin, which are allowed to combine in a voice which he describes as 'existential heteroglossia':

> Like most people, [Saadi] said, his consciousness comprised a swirling mass of inchoate energy, with elements of Asian-ness, European-ness, British-ness, Scottish-ness, Muslim-ness, Pakistan-ness, Afghan-ness, Indian-ness, middle-class-ness, left-wing-ness, artist-ness, physician-ness, twenty-first-century-ness, and male-ness. For many people, he thought, this state – he called it 'existential heteroglossia' – was closer to the truth than wrapping a particular flag around one's midriff as though it were a shroud.[31]

And indeed, to Zaf, who 'had never known where his own reality lay' (*P*, 279), the journey is a journey through Scotland, across to Scotland and back again, a zig-zagging itinerary the description of which is contained in the meaning of the word 'Scotland' in Urdu according to the novel – 'a wee man in a coracle, croassin the ocean' (*P*, 189) – itself a description which is in no way unproblematic, or, as Zaf himself puts it, 'a dangerous philosophy' (*P*, 189). The journey, or crossing, implies the destruction of a series of constructed ideas of identity; it implies moving away from the language of memory, of the 'community', which can only lead back to formulas of the past, to 'the sons and grandsons ae the *kisaan* who had powered the buses, the underground trains, the machines of the sweatshop underwear-manufacturers' (*P*, 242). It is a transcultural enterprise that needs to go beyond the slick description which can verge on cliché, as when Zaf, on air, claims that 'this is today music – it knows nae boundaries an we know nae boundaries' (*P*, 30), or as shown by several social or racial clichés which are introduced into the narrative as if they were incontrovertible facts, going back to the casual racism of the period when Jamil first emigrated, or to that when Pakistani bus drivers first made their appearance in Scotland.[32] The necessity for Zaf is therefore first to confront the clichés, including his own version of them, in order to avoid the danger of confining himself to one identity, one language, as the name of another radio station, radio Pardesi – foreigner – indicates. For Zaf, who symbolically at the beginning of the novel has a long night ahead of him, a night when he is not going to interact with his listeners as he usually does by taking requests, but only with himself, the stakes are high. They involve broadcasting from a place that is not Pardesi, while avoiding to resort to commonplaces about identity that fail to come to grips with reality. They involve confronting first the boundaries of identity provided by his origins, rather than just willing for an escape from them:

> Zaf hated those kinds of boundaries – hated bein defined by his status of bein other – felt trapped by that whole thing. Mibbee that wis why he'd dumped Zilla – because he'd not wanted to be cast in his own skin. [...] Zaf wanted to be like a lizard and to be able to slip from one skin to another, whenever it suited him – to go from pub to club to mosque to whore and not even to sweat in between. To be like a white man. Well, that wis the fantasy, anyhow. (*P*, 45)

This fantasy, this temptation, to escape into whiteness, represented in the novel by Zaf's white girlfriend Babs, is an impulse that, the texts tells us, leads to erasure, to disappearance:

> Zaf had felt like escapin with his new white girlfriend, runnin away from the eternally judgemental, hung-up families of East Pollokshields and Kinnin Park – far away to some vast, empty place where they would be able to lose themselves, where they would be able to become just two tiny figures, specks of dust in a classical European vista. (*P*, 77)

In order to escape the fate of disappearing, of dissolving into a culture – or into a 'classical European vista', an expression which Saadi borrowed from Robert Alan Jamieson – Zaf embarks on a journey, first into personal and then into social history, with the interpolated story of his father and mother's emigration from Pakistan mostly focalised by the father. This first generation of immigrants whose trip ended up in an underworld symbolised by the city sewers in which Jamil worked for most of his life, encounters a world made up of two words, 'izzatt' and 'sharam' (*P*, 206), 'honour' and 'shame'. Those twin concepts epitomise the fate of immigrants and their children, the second one harking back to Salman Rushdie's 1983 novel *Shame*. In it, the narrator expands on the meaning of that notion:

> *Sharam*, that's the word. For which this paltry 'shame' is a wholly inadequate translation [...] A short word, but one containing encyclopaedias of nuance [...] embarrassment, discomfiture, modesty, shyness, the sense of having an ordained place in the world, and other dialects of emotion for which the English has no counterparts [...] What's the opposite of shame? What's left when *sharam* is subtracted? That's obvious: shamelessness.[33]

Saadi's novel suggests a different trajectory from Rushdie's, by opposing shame not with shamelessness, but with honour. But the basis for the trajectory is the same, as Zilla, Zaf's alter ego, his black girlfriend whom he wishes had been white, occupies the narrative as a traumatic memory visited by Zaf throughout the long spell of his journey through his own mind and his own Asianness; she is a figure 'broadcasting', or rather, not being able to broadcast, from a place which is recurrently associated with silence, with the absence of music.[34] This silencing of Zilla's voice, of the character insistently presented as the 'black girl' refers the reader back to the silencing of Pakistanis in general through the sharing of both theme and metaphor:

> People were always seen as immigrants and never as emigrants or expatriates. They were pictured as nameless, liquid hordes that would pour in. [...] And lastly, in this great, pyramidal misapprehension of a whole people, Pakistanis had remained completely inaudible. They had no music, no voice, no breath. (*P*, 73–74)

When voice is life ('breath'), the silencing of the people is an act of violence that triggers violence in return. As a figure of the suppressed, inaudible voice, Zilla takes up a place in the background of the narrative only to finally break into the foreground in the fourth part in the shape of a monstrous figure reminiscent of Rushdie's Sufiya's magical transformation into an inhuman force, 'shame's avatar' (1983: 219) gathering itself to wreak havoc upon the world. In this climactic scene in both senses of the term, as Zaf and Zilla engage in hallucinatory sex, Zaf's nemesis, the 'human beast' (*P*, 301), the 'tiger' (*P*, 302) but also a 'fucking archangel' (*P*, 306), an 'avenging angel' (*P*, 308) who makes love like 'a mad duchess ridin a pig' (*P*, 302), appears to Zaf in a dramatic fashion that threatens to annihilate him:

> The sunes in the room wur disordered, frantic, as though time wis runnin oot. That wis it. Behind the darkness, time wis escapin like sand through a glass. The figure wis grouwin larger. She wis comin ower tae him. He hunched back against the waw, tried tae occupy the space between the waw and the flaer. Nae space at aw. 'Ye always wur a coward.' The voice. The hair. Nightmare. Zilla. (*P*, 286–87)

The intercourse which ensues, is indeed a hallucinatory scene, a coupling of the insect-like, insignificant Zaf with a looming, threatening predatory and ultimately destructive version of himself (as Zaf first identifies Zilla as a 'fuckin alter ego' (*P*, 47) finally to repeat that 'part ae him hud always been Zilla' (*P*, 305)). The love-making, a fight to death, or a near death experience, provokes an explosion of language, which scatters words on the page as so much shrapnel, tattered fragments of a language that needs to accommodate various realities.[35] This failing of language which reveals its own dark side, which seems to stem from chaos, can be seen as a representation of what Jean-Jacques Lecercle, writing about the violence of language, calls the remainder:

> There is another side to language, one that escapes the linguist's attention, not because of his temporary failure or failings, but for necessary reasons. This dark side emerges in nonsensical and poetic texts, in the illuminations of mystics and the delirium of logophiliacs or mental patients. [...] I have called it 'the remainder.'[36]

Faced with this surfacing of the remainder, this incapacitation of language, the text resorts to rhythm, and turns the passage into some repetitive, obsessive chant which revolves around the words 'Migra Polis', themselves words which are at once connected and separated from a socio-historical interpretation because of the context and manner of their utterance and introduction into the narrative. They trigger a hallucinogenic, trance-like experience both for the narrator and the reader, before finally leading the latter back to the comparative safety of the reality of Zaf's cubicle, a metaphor for Zaf's consciousness in this passage and in the novel at large. Indeed, the magic that is performed in the passage has to do with a slipping of meaning, from the literal to the metaphorical. The reader loses his bearings when, suddenly deprived of the safeguard of a realistic narration, he witnesses a shift whereby the setting and situation assume a metaphorical meaning. With this shift in the metaphorical signification of the cubicle, which throughout the novel can superficially be seen as a metaphor of Zaf's entrapment into an identity which both is and is not his own, an identity of opposites,[37] the other elements of the setting take on a new meaning. Deck A and Deck B, the two players that are part and parcel of the standard studio equipment, assume a new, 'magic' meaning in the junuune of the encounter with Zilla. They become metaphors of Zaf's split consciousness, as he plays tunes that are culturally widely different (but by no means restricted to the dual opposition Indian versus European music) and that overlap. When the two decks play the same tune out of synch (*P*, 331–32), they also seem to portray the two poles of Zaf's mind, sanity contrasted with madness, and the gap between them, before the narrative forces the two selves into synchronicity again (*P*, 345). With this shift in the metaphorical value of the setting for the book (which, in keeping with the magic of that singular night, will go on shifting as our understanding of the text follows the sinuous route traced by the narrator), the reader is led to review his own position within or rather without the novel. Being as invisible, as immaterial to Zaf as his listeners, the reader needs to reconsider the rant, the moments when Zaf is on air, signalled by the narrative in the shift from justified text to unjustified sections. When, at the end of the explosion of words, Zaf plays the song entitled 'The Grace', warning his listeners that the pun, if there was one, 'wisnae intentional' (*P*, 312), this becomes a metafictional comment which goes over the listeners' head, to reach the only addressee who has access not only to Zaf's on-air rant, but also to his thoughts – the reader. John Stonesbury senses this metafictional strand to the narrative when, in his description of what he calls 'the politics of language', he interprets the mixing of linguistic codes as a valid way of reaching out to the reader, of involving him in the definition of identity. For Stonesbury, '[m]ixing linguistic codes, deploying dialect and alien tongue strategically in a narrative, can work powerfully to challenge the literary preconceptions of any reader willing to participate in the cultural dialogue'.[38] Yet the metafictional intent goes further than that. In *Psychoraag* crossing boundaries implies self-destruction, but it is also an encounter as well as an act of regeneration, a moment of grace, a self-creative act in the shape of a gathering of the words deposed on the page in the explosive connection with the self. Alan Bissett comments on the importance of the DJing metaphor in the novel, stressing that Saadi applies the technique of 'sampling' to his writing:

> For Saadi the trope of 'sampling' serves at once as a technical device and a major theme in his writing, demonstrating the matrix of deconstructed identities which emerge from a mixed backdrop of postcolonial, globalised and consumerist relations. As such, sampling constitutes a form of politicised (re)production, in which 'true' identities becomes inextricable from commercial or assimilated ones. (2007: 63)

For Saadi, however, DJing (a word the spelling of which evokes the magic of the Djinn) implies in Zaf's case a 'sampling' which not only mixes and re-combines, but which also finds it necessary to bring down language to its component parts, words, in order to construct a new fictional self again, an enterprise which the author describes as 'an attempt to explore the nature of meaning and being through words'.[39]

I need more words

In Saadi's fiction, the postulate expressed by Bella Baxter in Alasdair Gray's *Poor Things* that the story is made up of 'words words [...] that try to make much of little but cannot. I need more past'[40] can be reversed to 'the past that tries to make much of little but cannot, I need more words', a fact itself acknowledged in *Pychoraag* when Zaf 'cover[s] himself in words' (*P*, 403). This addresses the question of the profusion of words in Saadi's fiction, of his conception of the language of fiction and poetry, and of the synthesis of the two that he tries to create, being inspired by Urdu poetry, more precisely by the influence of the Urdu language on the poetic quality of the verse, as well as by the method of composition of the Ghazal.[41] In that respect, the language of *Psychoraag* and, to an even larger extent, that of *Joseph's Box*, can be seen as an experimental language which strives to incorporate excess and mélange.[42] It is a language conceived to achieve '[m]usic. Psychedelia. Transfiguration'.[43] While the critical reception of *Psychoraag* can be seen as mostly positive, notwithstanding the length of the novel and the occasional foray of the language into a hallucinatory, rhythmic chanting type of style that strives to cross the divide between poetry and prose at the expense of intelligibility, Saadi's second novel, which he describes as an even more ambitious project than the first one, a project that includes his reflections on language, was much less favourably received by reviewers. Their criticism mostly centred on the excessive verbosity – 'expansive verbiage'[44] – and the abstruseness of the language as well as on its overly and somewhat gratuitously poetic character, dismissed for instance by Simon Kövesi as 'hazy insipidly poetic' language.[45] Saadi stresses that his project consists precisely in underlining the musicality of the language that he created for *Joseph's Box*, a musicality partly inspired by Arabic, Persian and Urdu, in particular for their peculiar poetics whereby 'an idea is repeated at the end of every line but with a slightly different variation each time'.[46] Words, for Saadi, are used in this novel as instruments to 're-direct the flow' of the narrative, more generally in his search for what he terms 'the music', as an 'energy centre' which he equates with the third protagonist at the core of the novel, the lute.[47] What he attempts in *Joseph's Box* therefore, is to create a language that can 'sing with an "open" voice',[48] an enterprise which has as much to do with musical composition as with prose, as can be seen, or maybe felt, in this extract:

> The priest's eyes stared out at Zuleikha, boring a hole in her skull and pouring his consciousness, like wine, in through the orifice. And the wine made her begin to chant and sing like a poet or a sufi in search of the power of the Doric reed, and mathnawis, qasidas and ghazals flew from the opened mouth of her skull, the cantastorii of Khanqahs that sprang in the middle of the desert and the songs of sacred goats who could change form, die and be resurrected at will, who could empty their souls from their bodies and then, through devotion, have their skins filled with the spirits of Sufi Masters seeking truth, the muwashshahat of mountain trees which were older than the gods themselves, the songs of jugglers, whores and slaves and of the memory, life, obedience and beauty which they all sought to possess, the chants of soldiers who, through sacrifice, became sages

and who climbed to the tops of hills to light naphtha fires, the irregular rhythms of Kufic texts that wrote themselves in a thousand tongues in a single night and the murmurings of headless corpses who sang the neck verse and stepped along the points of the spider-dance, the Moorish dance, and who turned slowly black beneath the gaze of stone Madonnas. (*JB*, 321)

This music, which Saadi is looking for, and which he situates at the crossroads of Eastern and Western semiotic forms, is an encounter, maybe even a clash between the two.[49] The linguistic hybridity and convoluted syntax in this passage, the patterns of repetitions, the long sentences which strive for the hypnotic but also seek to imprint a musical, oriental quality to it by evoking the Ghazal, the shifting referents and diversity of personal pronouns, the cultural contrast emphasised by the proximity of the words 'Moorish dance' and 'Madonnas', all those features aim to create a new language, a sort of poetic prose which is the narrative form closest to music.

While this attempt to 'shift the gravitational possibilities of the English language [...] in terms of thought processes'[50] may sound rather grandiloquent, it resonates with Bhabha's concept of articulation, developed in his essay 'Articulating the Archaic'. As Bhabha explains, this articulation has to do with setting the language into motion in a new way that cannot simply result from an encounter of languages and words:

> I was attempting to describe the way in which the articulation of cultural differences has to deal with what can't be translated; what may be incommensurable in the moment of cultural difference emerges in language as an evacuation of the very signifying and symbolic register that is required, in another moment, for its representation. It is a kind of enunciative disturbance that throws the process of interpretation or identification into flux.[51]

In *Joseph's Box*, the protagonist's highly charged name, Zuleikha MacBeth,[52] represents the disturbance that is at the basis of the concept of articulation, and prepares the reader for a much wider perturbation of interpretation played out at the level of the narrative itself. Zaf in *Psychoraag* formulates this concept of articulation by resorting to the field of music, by refusing the association of Asian-ness and the Asian language with a monolithic tradition, that of the Bhangra, or religious song. For him, articulation can take place only when one has taken into account the rejection of separate stereotyped means of artistic expression, which cannot cover the intricacy of integrated rather than hyphenated identity:

> We're no jist spinnin, grinning dancers – we're no jist clowns in glitterin dresses. We're mair than that. Deeper. We've been here, there an ivirywhur, fur thousands ae years, an we can draw on onyhin we like. (*P*, 93)

Zuleikha and Zaf, both hailing from 'here, there and ivirywhur', are placed at the centre of narratives which are governed by an overarching metaphor of flux. *Joseph's Box* is actually predicated on this metaphor – as the author indicates that '*Joseph's Box* is like the Ganges; it moves slowly'[53] – and it takes its source by the side of the river Clyde, a river to which the narrative returns after a long course that takes it literally across the globe. As such, it articulates a series of events experienced by the reader along with the protagonists themselves as a current which carries them like so much flotsam, a narrative which tumbles the protagonists along in the same way that the Clyde carries the box. As the characters come to be seen not as epic heroes but rather as material for the narrative to carry along in its unstoppable course towards a river which is both its source and its end, the epic travellers increasingly appear to be the words themselves. In that context, the peculiar narrative technique which is used in *Psychoraag*, a stream of consciousness separated from its usual acolyte – the first person – becomes a strategy in Saadi's politics of writing, articulating the desire to find a voice that, rather than being guided by the controlling first-person instance, places an emphasis on the free play of words let loose to interact in a manner that ultimately leads them back to themselves. This freeing process, which comes at a price, notably that of the intelligibility of some of the passages from the books as well as of the overall design, particularly with *Joseph's Box*, leads both narratives to experiment with not only the verbal, but more importantly with the structural core of the work of fiction as well as the very definition of what constitutes a novel.[54]

In order to achieve that goal of liberating the narrative by setting its words loose without falling back on the old deconstructionist premise of the postmodernists,[55] Saadi provokes a relapse of the rules of strict narrator's control, by allowing, or indeed by forcing his narratives to ramble in a way that again conforms to the image of the flux. In *Psychoraag* the narrative sometimes moves seamlessly back and forth between incompatible events which happen in two different ontologies, between the 'dreams' and the reality of Zaf's cubicle,[56] or it places Zaf simultaneously on the streets of Glasgow or in a disused underground station and in his cubicle. In *Joseph's Box* a short passage of less than a page shifts both point of view (from Zuleikha's to Margaret's) and timeframe (from the 1940s to 2010) while strictly controlling the narrative by the use of the pronoun 'she' which applies to both focalisers. This effectively splits the narrative into two separate strands which only coalesce again with the image of the two women jumping across the water (*JB*, 260). In this episode, the two narratives are kept in sight of each other, in the same way that Margaret sees Zuleikha jumping across. The novel therefore manages to both estrange and naturalise the origins of the act of representation. For Saadi, representation cannot be separated from interpretation, and this dialectics acknowledges the power of words: Zuleikha realises in a moment, both magic and metafictional, that her body is made up of words; it is broken down into words which in turn can be separated from a specific worldview:

> Through this journey it was as though her sight had been restored. It was as though, having seen words merely as squiggles on a page, now finally she had learned to read. It was as though she had passed through a house of seven doors, as though her body had been flayed to the bare letters of a text, as though she, Zuleikha Chashm Framareza MacBeth, had been burned into stone. (*JB*, 657)

In order for the narrative to free itself from the constraints of the worldview they carry, words in Saadi's fiction are transformed into metaphors in a way that makes them more diffuse, more likely to flow.[57] They are turned into the all-encompassing idea of the 'voice' (with its various metaphorical possibilities), the existential heteroglossia, but also the voice of music, both of which enable the transformation of the language of words into one that is more conceptual as well as resorting to all the senses. For Zuleikha, who states that her identity is the result of 'troubled macro-history' (*JB*, 516), travelling to Baltistan is an experience which forces her to acknowledge her split nature as she starts 'thinking like a typical Farangi, [...] a memsahb, an Anglo-Indian' (*JB*, 559). As for Zaf, he proclaims the ultimate truth and reality of his and other voices that reach beyond the moment, even beyond history, when he claims that '[o]nly their voices, spirallin out towards the far end of the solar system, would still be real' (*P*, 78).

Reversing the usual preconceptions about the nature of reality, Zaf sees it as becoming conceptual.[58] On air, with the vehicle that alone can carry the flux of identity, the flux of his own very personal version of 'reality', his voice, he can reiterate every night what he sees as the ultimate human truth:

> On the radio, everythin he did felt real. It wis the only place where he felt human – when he wis alone with just his voice. Every night, he wis goin back to the beginnin. To Altaqween. (*P*, 200)

Going back to the beginning imposes a new definition of the narrative that borrows from Saadi's own conception of music, which stretches to include song lyrics, poetry, the language of Sufism and the Ghazal, a narrative that escapes Zaf's lips like a breath, as 'even the *saans* he breathed as it reddened turned miraculously into music' (*P*, 192). In *Joseph's Box* this flux is represented by the music of the lute, which assumes a life of its own, quite independent of the musician; it manages by itself to represent the transition, the translation from musician to listener:[59]

> Music always brought into being a certain telepathy between listeners and musicians. It was not so much an entertainment as a communing [...]. And every time this happened a new language would be forged, a language that was hot as Mongibello's many caldere, a tongue through which might be brought into being new thoughts, new ways of constructing reality. (*JB*, 422)

The music which, as Zuleikha senses, 'must flow towards light' (*JB*, 173) like water, is a representation of Saadi's conception of music (and storytelling) as 'a two-way communal transfiguration'.[60] In *Joseph's Box*, it carries the voice of the people deprived both of voice and life. It is a revolutionary force that can destroy and recreate our sense of the world:

> It was the music of the people who, one way or another, had been lied to, and whose wealth had been stolen from their calloused hands by pretenders bearing sulphur, salt, asbestos, oil and religion. It was the song of the people who had been turned into servants, serfs, slaves, saints. Etna. Kaf. When the music of the people exploded, the earth would shift its orbit. (*JB*, 423–24)

In the long night of revolution that is represented in *Psychoraag* by the last night of broadcasting, a night which stretches across several months in *Joseph's Box*, all music coalesces, as 'behind the Scottish music was the Italian, and behind that the Sicilian, the Arabic, the Persian' (*JB*, 547–48), and the magic transformation that is carried out logically ends up turning *characters* into music, in Alex's case 'a mess of music' (*JB*, 547), in Zilla's case 'a shadow music' (*P*, 35), and in Archie's case a music of repetition and circularity, a music of identity that crosses borders as is indicated by the fact that Archie, the Scot whose middle name sometimes changes to Idris, undergoes an impossible transformation, a disembodiment to become a Saadian voice:

> And Archibald Idris McPherson knew that all through this long night, which bore no relation to the chronological night of summer, he would be a ghazal, a plaintive song of terrible longing that would be sung over and over again until sunrise. (*JB*, 590)

The third space of fiction

The discourse of voice as music – or music as voice – thus created both in *Psychoraag* and *Joseph's Box* can be seen as a sort of third discourse that comes to supersede, incorporate or cover the other discourses of the text. This third discourse or, in Zaf's terms, a 'third tune', cannot be summed up as the mere juxtaposition of words and sounds. The novels therefore travel from a dialectical approach to language and identity to a transcending of that dialectics.[61] Zaf initially describes himself as a sample:

He liked samples, felt comfortable with them. He was a sample of
Pakistan, thrown at random into Scotland, into its myths. And, in
Lahore, he had felt like a sample of Glasgow in the ancient City of
the Conquerors. Yeah, the journey from the Clyde to the Ravi wis a
voyage through time, space and spirit. It required a leap of faith, a
sword dance but with scimitars instead of claymores. (*P*, 227)

The novel, however, thanks to the voice of music that creates its third, subterranean discourse, focuses on the description not of the sample itself but of the *method* of sampling, as is noted by Alan Bissett, who identifies this method of composition as a trope in the novel. The important shift here has to do with the idea of process, of translation from sample to sampling, from passive component element to active transformation of this element. As Bhabha indicates in his discussion of the 'third space', the notion of translation rests precisely on the necessity to eschew the customarily dialectical approach to the construction of identity:

> The intervention of the Third Space of enunciation, which makes the structure of meaning and reference an ambivalent process, destroys this mirror of representation in which cultural knowledge is customarily revealed as an integrated, open, expanding code. Such an intervention quite properly challenges our sense of the historical identity of culture as a homogenising, unifying force, authenticated by the originary Past, kept alive in the national tradition of the People. (1994: 37)

The necessity to abandon the dialectical (and linear) approach is thematised in *Psychoraag* by the recurrence of the two decks Zaf plays his music from. As Zaf goes over the many nights he has spent using the two decks of his mind, he becomes aware of the process that has led him to create the third tune, a voice which has achieved transculturation:

> Durin the ninety nights of his sojourn with Radio Chaandni, deep in the aureate darkness, through the walls and the floor, at times Zaf would hear two completely different pieces of music, just muted

enough not to be able to make out the melodies or words. In places, the notes would merge and, from somewhere, there would arise a third tune, one that nobody had ever written but which sounded better than either of its component parts. Here it goes, here it comes (P, 239).

The third tune, which cannot be frozen into a pattern, which 'comes' and 'goes', can be seen as the musical equivalent, or the metaphorisation of Bhabha's cultural third space, which the critic identifies as being manifest in the 'negotiation of incommensurable difference':

The non-synchronous temporality of global and national cultures opens up a cultural space – a third space – where the negotiation of incommensurable differences creates a tension peculiar to borderline existences. [...] Hybrid hyphenations emphasise the incommensurable elements [...] as the basis of cultural identifications. (1994: 218–19)

As Saadi points out, when claiming that in a context of isolation and dislocation, he 'had to breath[e] [his] own music',[62] this negotiation is a vital enterprise. Bhabha draws on Walter Benjamin's concept of the 'continuation of transformation' explaining:

His work has led me to speculate on differential temporal movements within the process of dialectical thinking and the supplementary or interstitial 'conditionality' that opens up alongside the transcendent tendency of dialectical contradiction – I have called this a 'third space', or a 'time lag'.[63]

The narrative in *Psychoraag*, relying on the metaphor of the two decks, constructs a fictionalisation of the third space, by presenting two narratives: Zaf's own rambling memories, which include events from his childhood as well as the present multicultural, multiethnic and multisocial world which relies on separation, and his father Jamil's narrative of emigration. The two narratives are governed by two controlling points of view, Zaf's and Jamil's, only to be brought together at the end of the novel as Zaf's vision finally is able to sample the two voices. As the narrative ultimately goes back to Jamil's night on the Afghan border, when he goes mad and leaves the car to climb the mountain in the moonlight, seemingly hauled up by the force of an unidentified music (*P*, 217–18), the correspondences with Zaf's own experience – the madness (Junnune), the moonlight (chaandni), and above all the music from which Jamil 'was unable to make out any melody – not even on the level of assonance' (*P*, 218) – not only samples from two narratives, but also describes a place which is a desert, an elemental place from which the narrative will finally flow:

> He wondered whether perhaps this deserted place was his natural home. Perhaps this was what he had been searching for all his life. Maybe they should stop here. Perhaps Rashida and he could eke out some kind of living from the rocks of this undefined land. (*P*, 218–19)

The place of transition represented by this desert spot is a blank, a nowhere space, which very much resembles Zaf's cubicle, the description of which insists on its isolation from the rest of the world. On the third floor of a disused building, soundproofed and empty but for a formica table and the console from which Zaf broadcasts his show by himself, the cubicle can therefore be seen as a space of narration and negotiation very similar to that 'undefined' desert, that empty space where the narration of Jamil and Rashida's story started. The cubicle is the place from which a voice is broadcast in the shape of a narrative made up of words and music, reminding us that, as indicated in Jamil's narrative of displacement, what travels in *Psychoraag* is a series of words with the playlist serving as a map:[64]

> He scribbled a title across the dog-eared piece of paper that wis lookin more and more like an ancient parchment map with a set of bizarre blue symbols for coordinates, sweepin curves for mountain ranges and no shore in sight. (*P*, 130)

But, as in *Joseph's Box*, the journey is not an easy one, as the coordinates, the topography and the very structure of the map seem to be elusive and dynamic elements: the playlist appears and disappears from the cubicle; between appearances, the names scribbled on it seem to change of their own accord, or even become graphic, adopting a code that is non-verbal in a way that the novel itself emulates with its illustrations, notably that of a map juxtaposed with the quotation above. As titles come and go, leaving traces and lines on the playlist, the journey appears as a difficult, tentative enterprise. But its goal, as Zaf indicates in one of his diatribes on air, is far from tentative. The show hinges on the necessity to redraw the map of its own narrative and, in a universalising process, on the need for all maps to be updated:

> Aye, that's whit we'll do. We'll redraw aw the maps an, whun we come oot ae here in the mornin, we willnae recognise the waruld, we willnae know oorsels. No one said this show would be safe, *samaaen*. If it's safety an caution ye're lookin fur, then mibbee ye'd be better tunin elsewhere. Radio Clyde mibbee. An these few tunes huv brought us oan this rockin boat as sune that we like tae caw Scoatlan, tae the hairt ae darkness, the quietest time ae the night, the period whun thur's only braith an thought an daith. (*P*, 208)

Redrawing the map is an enterprise that needs to hail from Scotland (even though it cannot issue from the safety of Radio Clyde) and not from the foreign roots of the past, because, according to Bhabha, those imprison the narrative into a dialectical position that cannot make room for a third space. In a manner that reinforces the novel's insistence on the pole of reception of the message, in order to add to the constant assumption that Zaf is talking to an audience the novel provides the reader, at an ontological level superior to Zaf's, with his own, perfectly organised and readable playlist, placed at the end of the book as an addendum, offering another version of the map necessary to navigate the narrative. This playlist/reader's map can be seen as a statement on the author's part that the redrawing of the map has been completed, in other words as a concluding message once again sent over the characters' heads that the narrative has successfully mapped out the new territory that it started out to delineate.

Joseph's Box, also dominated by a variety of maps and scrolls, introduces an element which makes for a complication of the usual metaphorical meaning of the map. As the woman in green met by Zuleikha at the end of the novel says, using the metaphorical association that Saadi applies to all his works of fiction, the stories have a music of their own, which the characters as well as the readers have to be able to understand in order to solve the mystery set by the boxes:[65]

> The music of stories has gone on since the beginning of time, but one will only hear the sounds, thoughts, actions which bind us if one is willing to become a reader, a listener and a watcher. (JB, 641)

The woman, who serves as a polymorphous guide to the protagonists (each of them being faced with a different version of her), insists on the importance of stories and, as she introduces the three protagonists associated with their reception, makes it clear by including a 'listener' that the flat, two dimensional concept of the reading of the map needs to be rethought if one is to get the 'music' of *Joseph's Box*. This is based on the postulate that there are different ways of interpreting stories by relying on different senses, and on the three-dimensionality of the story which requires three different and connected modes of apprehension on the part of the receiver – hence the 'reader, listener and watcher'. This somewhat abstruse injunction is nevertheless linked to the main map which appears in the novel in the shape of the rock found in the last of the six boxes. The rock, contrary to the maps and scrolls which so far have guided Zuleikha and Alex's progression, is a three-dimensional map[66] that enables them to use their sight as well as their reading skills, as it actually reproduces the mountains of Baltistan which their quest finally takes them to: 'the pattern formed within the rock was a chart, a facsimile of some mountainous valley. Yet it assumed this aspect only when held at a particular angle in a certain light' (JB, 542).

As with Zaf's playlist, the map is elusive and provisional, a feature quite at odds with the purpose of maps, which is to 'circumscribe geography, by enclosing, defining, coding, orienting [and] structuring [...] space',[67] and yet it traces the outlines of a third space which rests on the notion of the addition of a third dimension to the usual two. Saadi has commented on his desire to alter the 'gravitational possibilities of language'; this enterprise is to be extended to an altering of the gravitational possibilities of the narrative itself. The overarching symbol of this abstract concept is the ever-present lute, in its capacity in the novel to play outside of the musician's will and its physical mutability which enables it to turn into different instruments as the narrative goes on.⁶⁸ This transformation of the narrative is carried out in *Psychoraag* in metaphorical terms, with a reversal in the description of the territories conjured up by the narrative, from the Land of the Pure – or Pakistan – to the 'pure land of Zaf's imaginings' (*P*, 358), not only literally, as Zaf's imaginings invoke a Pakistan that would be the reverse of what it is now, but also symbolically, as the elusive but vitally important third space created by the narrative. In this shifting movement that uses reversals, metaphorisation, and stichomythia, what both *Psychoraag* and *Joseph's Box* are aiming for is a renegotiation of the borders of literature.

The borders of literature

The parallels that can be established between Saadi's work and some of Salman Rushdie's writing prompt us to examine the notion of Saadi's treatment of literary genre, in particular of magic realism. The magic that is very much present in both *Psychoraag* and *Joseph's Box* does not vouch for their generic description as magic realist. By calling his novels 'both magic and realist', Saadi is looking at the borders of the representational act itself. Commenting upon *Joseph's Box*, Saadi indicates that 'I didn't want to write a typical magical realist text where the characters don't question the magical things happening around them. […] I wanted to have that strong realist tradition, but inject it with this drugged, magical story'.⁶⁹ This desire to escape the magic realist generic pact stems from a necessity for Saadi to both connect to and disengage with the world which he sees as a rejection of all previously defined literary genres:

> Part of writing entails connecting with the world, part entails escape from it and that about defines my interaction with reality; the creativity that emerges from the need to seek meaning, issues from the fissures between the two.⁷⁰

In order for the fissure to emerge, Saadi has created complex works, in particular *Joseph's Box*, which he describes as 'a conceit of opposites',⁷¹ although reviewers have assessed it in less flattering terms.⁷² The fact is that, in order to produces the 'fissure' or third space of fiction, he has had to rely on strategies that upset our expectations of the novel.⁷³ Not least of these strategies is that of suggesting a third dimension to the narratives he creates.

This third dimension can also be envisaged very literally, as a particular emphasis on the notion of verticality in both novels, a dimension which is thematically foregrounded by the sheer number of tunnels and underground places present in them. Verticality grants the novels depth, therefore suggesting a third dimension. This verticality, however, does appear as problematic, as is for instance indicated by Zaf in the last chapter simultaneously walking through Glasgow down a disused underground tunnel and broadcasting his show from the top of the radio Chaandni building.[74] It is an impossible enterprise because it is a trip through the margins, the limits of literature.

Verticality, a new orientation for the narrative in Saadi's fictions, takes several guises. In *Joseph's Box* it adds to the thematic element an intertextual dimension, in a narrative being ostentatiously guided by the Koranic story of Joseph and Zuleikha,[75] and which at a symbolic level relies on the Greek myth of Pandora's box, while this circulation into various intertextual backgrounds is described in terms that are themselves intertextual: when Alex exclaims, 'I'm the white rabbit', the obvious reference to Lewis Carroll can be transferred onto the whole of the narrative as it whisks down tunnels and crosses borders.[76] In *Psychoraag* verticality is more than a dimension; it suggests a hypothesis for reading the text itself. As the two words 'izzatt' and 'sharam' (*P*, 206) appear in the text vertically rather than horizontally, they fleetingly suggest a reversal of the reading direction (an interesting suggestion in a book which, among other languages, quotes Arabic, a language read from right to left). Together with the narrative's capacity in *Psychoraag* to move downwards, a movement equally suggested at the end of *Joseph's Box* when the three protagonists are taken down separate narrative paths by the same polymorphous hermit,[77] therefore tracing different superimposed narrative routes, verticality suggests that the novel is playing with the form of the acrostic, with the various stories providing diverging illustrations of the points of entry provided by the letters composing the words 'izzatt' and 'sharam'. The six boxes, with the multiple, sometimes chaotic stories they contain, also make for an upsetting (even if only in theory) of the linearity of reading. It creates a third dimension of reading for a third space of fiction which puts a premium not only on non-linear, but also on non-horizontal reading, and underlines the capacity of the text to shift shapes, in a djinn-like fashion, that turns *Joseph's Box* in particular into a sort of metamorphotext. This metamorphotext, like the rock of the sixth box, is an elusive object that strives to present the reader, viewer and listener with a different aspect according to the angle in which he views it. It is a text that erases chronology, that plays with the directionality of personal pronouns[78] and keeps expanding and contracting, like Zuleikha's own vision of the box, which she describes as the repository of multiple stories compressed into one:

> She wondered whether perhaps the layers of boxes sealed by lids might form part of a simple structure. [...] What was this? Baboushka dolls? Scientific laws kept expanding while, like the universe, the box kept contracting. Perhaps it would go on forever. Like that book by some weird Ecuadorean, a story of mushrooms and Eros, which ended up being the story of just one letter that kept repeating, backwards and forwards across the text, from the first page to the last. Once you began to read the book, you would never be able to finish it. It was both infinite and infinitesimal. (*JB*, 121)

In that context, *Joseph's Box* appears as a novel that reflects not history, but the structure of the mind, as Saadi himself indicates in an interview, commenting on the embedding process that is at the heart of *Joseph's Box*:

> 'Worlds within worlds' mirrors the structure of our minds; the mind is thought to work like a series of overlapping fields, one part flowing through another to produce the unified and yet almost infinitely diverse phenomenon known as thought. The mind functions as an almost infinite series of mirrors; in this context, the search for self-definition, the need to read oneself, is the ultimate thought. Indeed, it is beyond thought. Writing is a crucial part of this quest.[79]

This embedding, enacted in both novels at the level of characterisation, with various characters finally appearing as different versions of the protagonists,[80] is represented by the image of the broken mirror, present in both narratives: it is only mentioned in *Joseph's Box* in the description of Petrus's house (*JB*, 519), while in *Psychoraag* it gives the reader a clue to interpret the narrative as a whole as a portrayal of the human mind:

Perhaps, like Z-A-F, Z-I-L-L-A, J-A-M-I-L and R-A-S-H-I-D-A, the singers, too, led quantum existences, lives split and burned through invisible mirrors. Show and illusion. Radio dreams. (*P*, 360–1)

The breaking up of the characters' names into their constitutive letters as well as their suggested immateriality turns them into abstract entities, physical realities broken down into fragments that can imprint themselves on the human brain, information that can travel – flow – through the nervous system. This ultimately leads the reader to a physiological dimension, which can be related to Saadi's own description of the workings of memory, which avers that '[m]emory is held in the nerves and muscles – maybe even ancestral memories. It's beyond the rational, beyond even thought'.[81]

In keeping with this physiological approach to narrative, Saadi, who is also a practising GP, resorts to biology in order to express the articulation process that is at work in his own novelistic language. *Joseph's Box* puts this theoretical approach to metaphorical use under the cover of magic and hallucination. In a moment of hallucinogenic epiphany, Zuleikha, who has previously described herself as being flayed to the level of letters (*JB*, 657), and who relates to her dying patient Archie in a way that foregrounds mingling,[82] finally sees herself as coursing inside Archie's brain:

> The last few months had been a pantechnicon of strangeness, and Zuleikha had felt as though, like a refugee, she was clinging desperately to its undercarriage, the river of the road flowing beneath her. She was swimming even deeper into the nucleic acid of Archie McPherson's consciousness, into the vestiges of his life. (*JB*, 207)

But the extreme experience goes both ways, as Archie also is described as 'entering' another character, in his case Laila's body:

> And Archie began to seep like liquid through her skin and into her flesh, so that the lake inside him began to heave and roar as it had done when he had gone to war or else to the whore, the woman whom he had almost killed with his own hands. (*JB*, 504)

In this final step of metaphorisation of the course of words in the novel as an organic process involving lymph and blood, *Joseph's Box* keeps Zaf's promise of a cosmic experience to his listeners in the other novel by conjuring up a fictional universe both contracting and expanding like the contents of the box or the dimensions of the lute. In the same way that Alex realises that 'time and space [are] rubber bands' (*JB*, 275), the reader is confronted with a novelistic universe which pulses in an organic fashion, a universe governed by the principle of morphing, where the metamorphotext thus created can alone conjure up for a brief moment the third space of fiction.[83]

At the end of politics lies language

Joseph's Box, as well as *Psychoraag*, is an openly ambitious novel which strives to tackle the age-old notions of identity, language and representation in terms of what Marc Augé terms 'a synthesis of the cultures of the world', by locating the 'synthesis', the coexistence of overlapping and contradictory drives within the same individual. Augé insists that the only possible way for multiculturalism to succeed is to achieve that somewhat paradoxical individualised synthesis, that process of transculturation:

> Any education should, in order to be worthwhile, take 'transculturalism', the crossing of borders and cultures, as its goal and ideal, rather than remaining entrenched in one single tradition; the notion of cultural diversity only acquires meaning when felt by each individual: the ideal of a global education revolution will be perceived on the scale of human history only when it becomes conceivable to define each individual as a unique and original synthesis of the cultures of the world.[84]

For Saadi, however, the creation of the individual is no simple act of will, and creating a third dimension in literature to attempt a representation of Bhabha's third space is, in the last analysis, not just a theoretical question, but also an intensely political one. He indicates in 'Songs from the Village Idiot' that '[a]t the end of politics, at the end of the subway line lies language. And so, it makes political sense, countering oppression, whether consciously or unconsciously, to begin with literature'.[85] Ultimately, therefore, his attempt to evolve the third space of fiction can indeed be read as a reversal of this last postulate, as his reader realises that at the end of language lies politics. For all the linguistic challenge they sometimes present, both *Psychoraag* and *Joseph's Box* can be described as strong political statements or, to borrow Saadi's own terms, as acts of faith in the transforming possibilities of art, 'in its narrow meaning of drawing and sculpting, or in the broader sense of creating, re-creating and transfiguring the world' (*JB*, 315).

Notes

1   See the introduction for more details on the notion of the postnational constellation.
2   Upstone, Sarah. 2010. *British Asian Fiction: Twenty-First Century Voices* (Manchester: Manchester U.P.), p. 202.
3   Calder, Angus. 2004. 'Saadi's all the rag' *The Sunday Herald*, April 25, sarmed.netfirms.com/suhayl/NEW/books/psycho/calder_review.htm [consulted March 2005].
4   On the part played by music in post-ethnic fiction in general, in particular in the works of Hanif Kureishi and Saadi, see Upstone pp. 203–04.
5   Saadi, Suhayl. 2006. '*Psychoraag*: The Gods of the Door', *Spike Magazine*, www.spikemagazine.com/0206-suhayl-saadi-censorship-in-the-uk.php [consulted March 2007].
6   Saadi, Suhayl. 2000. 'Infinite Diversity in New Scottish Writing', asls.arts.gla.ac.uk/SSaadi.html [consulted February 2011]
7   Saadi, Suhayl. 2006. 'Songs of the Village Idiot: Ethnicity, Writing and Identity', in McGonigal, James and Kirsten Stirling (eds), *Ethically speaking: voice and values in modern Scottish writing* (Amsterdam and New York: Rodopi), p. 134.
8   Farrukhi, Asif. n.d. 'Suhayl Saadi – Life of creative tension', sarmed.netfirms.com/suhayl/NEW/books/psycho/dawn_review.htm [consulted 11 February 2009].
9   Fish, Stanley. 1997. 'Boutique Multiculturalism or Why Liberals Are Incapable of Thinking about Hate Speech', *Critical Enquiry* 23/2, p. 378.
10 Saadi, '*Psychoraag*: the Gods of the Door'.
11 See Taylor, Diana. 1991. 'Transculturating Transculturation', in Bonnie Marranca and Gautam Dasgupta (eds), *Interculturalism and Performance* (New York: PAJ Publications), pp. 60–74, especially pp. 60–61 for her description of the way this social phenomenon was imported into culture. See in particular how Taylor links cultural aspects to social ones, by stating that 'Transculturation affects the entire culture; it involves the shifting of socio-political, not just aesthetic, borders; it modifies collective and individual identity; it changes discourse, both verbal and symbolic' (1991: 61).
12 Saadi, '*Psychoraag*: the Gods of the Door'.
13 See Saadi, Suhayl. 2007. 'In Tom Paine's Kitchen', in Schoene (ed.), p. 29.
14 See Saadi, '*Psychoraag*: the Gods of the Door'. Saadi quotes the words of lutenist Roman Turovsky.
15 Ashley, Katherine. 2011. '"Ae Thoosand Tongues": Language and Identity in *Psychoraag*', *IRSS* 36, p. 143.
16 Saadi himself, who describes his need to 'redefine myth and history', therefore to engage in a re-historicising process, explains the crucial importance of this focus: 'I try to elicit deeper, longer views, to tap into both human and inanimate geopoetics, as Kenneth

White calls it. But in my essays and articles, I do critique contemporary geopolitics. You'll see that in "Joseph's Box", there are references to industrial disease, the death of manufacturing industry in the UK, the Mafia economy in Sicily/Italy (part of the novel is set there), Islamism in Pakistan, the Indo-Pak confrontation over Kashmir, racism ... all these things are there, but they are not foregrounded. They are part of a much broader rubric'. 'Suhayl Saadi Uncensored' 2009. *Kitaab*, kitaabonline.wordpress.com/2009/10/01/suhayl-saadi-uncensored/ [consulted January 2010].

17 Saadi, 'In Tom Paine's Kitchen', p. 30.
18 Woodward, Catherine. 2008–9. '*Joseph's Box* by Suhayl Saadi', *The Glasgow Review*, www.glasgowreview.co.uk/ [consulted March 2011].
19 See Smith, Ali. 2004. 'Life Beyond the M25: Ali Smith enjoys new fiction from Scotland and Wales', *The Guardian*, Saturday 18 December, www.guardian.co.uk/books/2004/dec/18/fiction.alismith [consulted November 2009].
20 Erskine, Sophie. 2009. 'A New Literary Form Is Born: An Interview with Suhayl Saadi', www.3ammagazine.com/3am/a-new-literary-form-is-born-an-interview-with-suhayl-saadi/ [consulted April 2010]. Saadi adds that he chose the form of the epic, though in a democratised narrative form, thanks to the use of the third person which allows the narrator to 'turn away from the self-obsessed "I"'.
21 'Suhayl Saadi Uncensored', *Kitaab*.
22 Taylor, Alan. 2004. 'Fable bodied: Born in England to Pakistani parents, and now working', *The Sunday Herald*, April 4, findarticles.com/p/articles/mi_qn4156/is_20040404/ai_n12587975/ [consulted August 2009].
23 Ibid.
24 Ibid. See also Maggie Scott in *The Bottle Imp*, who speaks of 'a new, multi-faceted form of aureate Scottish prose', 'a new take on the traditional practice of "decorating" language by peppering it with prestigious terms borrowed from other cultures'. Scott, Maggie. 2008. 'Voices from Modern Literary Glasgow: *Buddha Da* and *Psychoraag*', *The Bottle Imp*, Issue 3, May, asls.arts.gla.ac.uk/SWE/TBI/TBIIssue3/Voices.pdf, p. 1. I would argue, however, that Saadi's use of language goes well beyond the decorative intent, being rather used as a tool for the transculturating process at work in his novels.
25 This is not to say that Saadi is the only writer to mix languages to an exceptional degree in a work of fiction, but rather to point to the unique quality of the language that results from such idiosyncratic composition. In fact, many African writers or writers of African origin practise this particular type of polyphony, as for example the Nigerian writer Ken Saro-Wiwa does in *Sozaboy* (1994). This novel, subtitled 'A Novel in Rotten English', mixes Nigerian Pidgin English, broken English, some idiomatic English and Khana (the language of the Ogoni).
26 Bhabha, Homi K. [1994] 1997. *The Location of Culture* (London and NY: Routledge), p. 1. The word 'confluence' is used by Saadi himself in an interview with Doug Johnstone. Saadi adds that 'civilisation [...] is not hermetically sealed boxes'. Johnstone, Doug. 2009. 'Suhayl Saadi', *The List*, Issue 636, edinburghfestival.list.co.uk/article/19858-suhayl-saadi/ [consulted September 2009].
27 Rushdie, Salman. 1992. *The Satanic Verses* (Dover, Delaware: The Consortium), p. 228.
28 Ashley (2011: 131) also notes Zaf's attempt to locate and connect with the Glaswegian community through language.
29 See Upstone, (2010: 197–203) for an analysis of the 'diaspora in reverse' and the part played by language in the constitution of his protagonist's sense of identity.

SUHAYL SAADI: THE THIRD SPACE OF FICTION

30 Saadi, 'Songs of the Village Idiot'. The rejection of the exotic is also a feature Saadi shares with Rushdie. See for instance David Brooks' 1984 interview with Rushdie, where the latter declares 'I *hate* the word exotic', Reder, Michael (ed.). 2000). *Conversations with Salman Rushdie* (Jackson: University Press of Mississippi), p. 59.
31 Sardar, Ziauddin. 2008. *Balti Britain: A Journey through the British Asian Experience* (London: Granta), pp. 77–78.
32 Some are integrated with the distance that is conveyed by the comic, as for instance in the episode of Jamil's decision to move north of the border in the 1950s, which fleetingly alludes to casual racism against the Scots, when Jamil is strongly advised against moving to Scotland on the grounds that it is populated by savages (*P*, 206).
33 Rushdie, Salman. [1983] 1984. *Shame* (London: Picador), pp. 38–39.
34 See for instance the description of Garngad street, where Zilla's flat is: 'There wis no rhythm to the street' (*P*, 178), a fact repeated in the phrase 'the waws ae the street-winae-music' (*P*, 183).
35 After the encounter, disconnected words – 'Sweat', 'Blood', 'Daith', 'Love' (*P*, 309), 'Red', 'black love', 'daith' (*P*, 312) – appear to have been thrown onto the page.
36 Lercercle, Jean-Jacques. [1990] 1999. *The Violence of Language* (London: Routledge), p. 6.
37 This is captured in Zaf's description of his parents as 'holdin apart the edges of the world' (*P*, 191).
38 Stotesbury, John A. 2010. 'Language and identity in the narration of Suhayl Saadi's Glasgow fiction', in Georgieva, Maria and Allan James (eds), *Globalization in English Studies* (Newcastle: Cambridge Scholars), p. 97.
39 'Suhayl Saadi Uncensored', *Kitaab*. See also chapter 3, on Robertson's fiction, which also tackles the way the narrative resorts to dwindling down to its basic words, to a slightly different effect.
40 Gray, Alasdair. 1992. *Poor Things* (London: Bloomsbury), p. 61.
41 Katherine Ashley (2011: 130) links Zaf to the multilingual Scottish tradition and describes him as 'a human tower of Babel'.
42 Sardar acknowledges this multilingual poetic quality in Saadi's prose, noting (2008: 70) that *Psychoraag* has 'the feel of the multi-levelled poeticism of Arabic, Farsi and Urdu texts, where a single word can imply twelve different meanings and suggest links with a host of ideas elsewhere in the text'.
43 'Suhayl Saadi, Interviewed for the Asian Writer February 2010', in Shaikh, Farhana (ed). 2010. *Happy Birthday to Me: A Collection of Contemporary Asian Writing* (Leicester: Dahlia Publishing), p. 151.
44 Hughes, Peggy. 2009. 'Book review: *Joseph's Box*', *The Scotsman*, 19 July, living.scotsman.com/bookreviews/Book-review-Joseph39s-Box.5472937.jp [consulted September 2009].
45 Kövesi, Simon. 2009. '*Joseph's Box*, by Suhayl Saadi', *The Independent*, Friday, 11 September, www.independent.co.uk/arts-entertainment/books/reviews/josephs-box-by-suhayl-saadi-1784898.html [consulted November 2009].
46 Erskine.
47 Ibid.
48 Ibid. See also *Psychoraag*, where Zaf says of the very old concubine songs he plays that the song stretches 'beyond the lyric' (*P*, 267), meaning that it is more expressive than words, that it exceeds words. This comment can be seen as a statement of purpose for the enterprise that is *Joseph's Box*.

49 See Erskine. See also, *Kitaab*, 'Suhayl Saadi Uncensored', in which Saadi states 'I wanted to shape the text from old English semiotic forms, to acquire that sense of long-history which one can feel very powerfully in certain places in Albion'.
50 Saadi in Erskine.
51 Mitchell, W. J. T. 1995. 'Translator translated: interview with cultural theorist Homi Bhabha', *Artforum* v.33, n.7 (March 1995), pp. 80–84, prelectur.stanford.edu/lecturers/bhabha/interview.html [consulted April 2012].
52 This is stated in a blunt way by Archie, who notes the yoking together of disparate cultures by expostulating, 'Zulie MacBeth –and how the fuck did she get a name like that' (*JB*, 24–5).
53 Saadi, in Erskine.
54 Indeed Saadi pursued the logic of *Joseph's Box*, by supplementing the book with a hypertextual continuation, Joseph Box's website (www.josephsbox.co.uk/) (no longer available), which provides tangential stories that can come into contact with the book, the latter being described by Saadi as no more than the hardcopy of the story. Those stories, which can be found on the 'storybox' page, attempt to break up even the physical boundaries of the book, by significantly hurling more words at it, in an elaborate *mise en scène* that enables the reader to have access to stories tangential to the main narrative, such as 'the tale of the Soldier', 'The tale of the Sufi', of the servant, the poet, the juggler or the whore, among others. A note from the author also explains how he got the idea for the book from a mysterious package containing manuscripts sent to him from Lahore.
    Interestingly, this 2009 project finds an echo with Ewan Morrison's own e-book project, *Tales from the Mall* which came in advance of the publication of the book with the same title. The agenda is different, the idea stems from different premises, but the questioning of the nature of fiction remains the same.
55 In the *Kitaab* interview, Saadi expresses his wish to 'undermine and eschew the tropes of modernity and postmodernity, alike'.
56 See, for instance, pp. 138–40.
57 This freeing is consistent with Saadi's conception of language: 'Language is of this planet, it consists of a set of symbols [...] Yet [...] these symbols are able to signify regions beyond themselves, regions that stretch towards the cold, blue light of infinity' in Saadi, 'Songs of the Village Idiot', p. 121.
58 Alex makes a similar statement in *Joseph's Box*, when he claims that 'only the dreams are real, and the five senses discordant liars' (*JB*, 74).
59 This is all the more significant in the parallel system of communication established by music in both novels as Saadi sees, in fact 'hears', the reader as a musician: 'I hear the reader as a musician, not a musician in the Western classical tradition, but a jazz musician who "breaks and enters" the text at will and who, through the act of reading, redefines old moralities'. 'Songs from the Village Idiot', p. 132.
60 Ibid., p. 122.
61 See the various references to Zaf or Zuleikha's identity in terms of a cultural dialectics.
62 *Kitaab*, 'Suhayl Saadi Uncensored'.
63 Mitchell.
64 As Ruth Maxey indicates, the map is a favoured device across British Asian imagery, mapping being a 'polysemic metaphor'. Maxey, Ruth. 2012. *South Asian Atlantic Literature: 1970-2010* (Edinburgh: Edinburgh U.P.), p. 46.

65 It follows that the mystery is about the stories, the inquiry into the music of the stories, and that the obvious mystery set by the boxes in the plot appears as a pretext for this more fundamental inquiry taking place. The quest, the chase, is therefore about the capacity of the story to figuratively draw up a third dimension for itself that would turn the interstitial, in-between space of Zuleikha's voyage into a third space of fiction, literally. Hence the comparative neglect of the plotline concerned with solving a puzzle.

66 In addition to being described as such on p. 555, the rock appears to contain many scripts from various areas.

67 Phillips, Richard. 1997. *Mapping Men and Empire: A Geography of Adventure* (London: Routledge), p. 14.

68 Zuleikha notes on several occasions that the instrument's shape has shifted, it becomes bigger or smaller, has a more or less plaintive or disembodied sound, until finally it turns into a different instrument altogether.

69 Saadi, in the Doug Johnstone interview.

70 Saadi, in *Kitaab*.

71 Erskine.

72 The reviews of *Joseph's Box* were on the whole fairly critical of the novel. See for instance Tom Adair in *The Scotsman* who wonders in his title 'Who killed the editor' (Adair, Tom. 2009. 'Book review: *Joseph's Box*, by Suhayl Saadi', *The Scotsman*, 15 August 2009, living.scotsman.com/bookreviews/Book-review-Joseph39S-Box-by.5556095.jp [consulted September 2009]), or Simon Kövesi's summary dismissal of the novel's intricacy in his *Independent* article.

73 A fact which itself explains the rejection of magic realism, as the genre, since Garcia Marquez, and Rushdie in Britain, comes to the reader with its own set of rules and preconceptions.

74 Zaf actually underlines the impossibility of the voyage for his listeners: 'OK, so here Ah am … here in the cubicle ae *The Junnune Show*, ae Radio Chaandni, broadcastin fur only forty-five meenuts mair oan ninenty-nine-point-nine meters FM. And, yet, at the same time, Ah'm roamin aroon the streets ae this magnificent city. How d'ye figure that wan?' (*P*, 377–78).

75 Saadi explains this reliance on the Koranic story by stating in the Erskine interview that 'Both Pandora and the Qu'ranic Zuleikha […] are representations of human flaws (we're talking patriarchal civilisations here) who yet contain a glimmer of hope within their souls and it is this glimmer which may come at last to define them'. In the novel itself Yusuf is characterised as 'Yusuf, the soul, the one who needed no key and whose love had had a unique effect on each of them' (*JB*, 659). See also the structural importance of the Bible/Qu'ran and of the use of Sufism for structural purposes in *Joseph's Box*, in Saadi's interview with Shaik Farhana (2010: 151), where the author explains that '[t]he book draws on Jewish, Greek and Buddhist legends and like the Biblical/Quranic Joseph, the main characters progress through the seven Sufi stations of sacrifice, truth, power, obedience, life, memory and beauty'.

76 Significantly, the narrative takes up the same intertext again when describing Zuleikha's descent inside the chimney/tower inside the Sicilian palazzu, in which she appears as an Alice figure, falling off the rung ladder into the dark and pushing a small trapdoor at the bottom (*JB*, 390–93), another sign that she is travelling across ontological boundaries.

77 See *Joseph's Box*, pp. 613–18, and the subparts covering the stories of the three protagonists, '*Zulfikar's Tale*' (JB, 628), '*The Story of Alexander*' (JB, 647) and '*The Story of Zuleikha*' (JB, 651).
78 See for instance pp. 578–79, where Zuleikha focalises the narrative which therefore uses the pronoun 'she', and where the pronouns shifts to 'he' referring, as the reader understands later, to her father.
79 Saadi, 'Infinite Diversity in New Scottish Writing'. This aspect is also present in the narrative when the map is finally compared with the inside of a skull: 'but then, as he gazed at the white paper; the coordinates seemed to shift and he was no longer certain whether what he was inspecting was a map of the land, or an anatomical drawing of the inside of a particular skull – a skull which, while bearing aspects common to all human crania, would nevertheless remain without mimic in the whole of history' (JB, 267).
80 In *Psychoraag* Zaf is Zafar the gangster, Zafar the boy on the picture, and also Zilla. In *Joseph's Box* the text fleetingly brings up the possibility that Laila might be a version of Zuleikha.
81 Saadi, 'Infinite Diversity in New Scottish Writing'.
82 See the end of part/box 3, chapter 12, in which Zuleikha and Archie have sex in a suspended portion of time and space that is later implicitly rationalised and dismissed as a hallucination.
83 This intensely conceptual approach to narration, informed among other things by Saadi's background as a scientist, deterred critics. Yet the text sometimes deflates that by resorting to humorous comments that could be metafictional, such as for instance Zuleikha's very lucid (if one is to take the metafictional postulate) realisation that the narrative is sometimes trying too hard: 'We should all go on psychotropic medication, she thought. Hearing voices, music, telepathic messages from the dead and the dying … This was the stuff of madness. Or else hilarity' (JB, 284).
84 'Toute éducation digne de ce nom devrait avoir pour but et pour idéal la traversée des frontières et des cultures, le "transculturalisme", non l'enferment dans une seule tradition; c'est dans chaque individu que la notion de diversité culturelle prend un sens: l'idéal de la révolution éducative mondiale ne sera perceptible à l'horizon de l'histoire humaine qu'à partir du jour où il sera concevable de pouvoir définir chaque individu comme une synthèse originale et unique des cultures du monde'. Augé, Marc. 2010. *La Communauté Illusoire* (Paris : Payot), pp. 50–51. My translation.
85 Saadi, Suhayl. 2006. 'Songs of the Village Idiot: Ethnicity, Writing and Identity', in McGonigal, James and Kirsten Stirling (eds), *Ethically speaking: voice and values in modern Scottish writing* (Amsterdam and New York: Rodopi), p. 137.

5. Ewan Morrison: The Non-Place of Fiction

At the other end of the spectrum from James Robertson's emphasis on history's problematic but fertile connection with the present, and presenting yet another facet to the definition of the postnational constellation, an angle which takes into account the increased globalisation of our sense of the local itself, is the work of Ewan Morrison. Morrison came to fame as a writer with the publication of his 2005 collection of short stories *The Last Book You Read* which, as evidence of its popularity, is now available as an e-book. The collection was praised by Berthold Schoene (2007: 14) as 'embracing globalisation as the new human condition' in a vision that provided 'a strong sense of planetary commonality'. Indeed the stories, as well as Morrison's three subsequent novels, *Swung* (2007), *Distance* (2008) and *Ménage* (2009), and the generically hybrid *Tales from the Mall* (2012), show the author's overwhelming, constant concern with the place of the human in a globalised world. Morrison defines the globalised world as a world taken over by American-style consumerism, and its attendant rampant commodification of everything including the human, a state of 'inauthenticity' which he parallels with what he sees as the false construction of a (Scottish) sense of identity:

> The construction of an authentic Scottishness is totally phony: the reality of daily life anywhere in the western world is that it is saturated with 'inauthentic' globalised media-generated images and experiences.[1]

The globalised world described by Morrison is the world which sociologist Zygmunt Bauman characterises as the world of 'liquid modernity', a world which, like fluids, 'neither fix[es] space nor bind[s] time' and in which modernity has filtered down from the 'macro' level of society as an organised system to the 'micro' level of social cohabitation, resulting in an increased burden for individuals to make sense of themselves in an unstable and unstoppable – an 'underdetermined' – environment.[2] For Bauman (2000: 7–8), '[o]urs is, as a result, an individualised, privatised version of modernity, with the burden of pattern-weaving and the responsibility for failure falling primarily on the individual's shoulders'. In the world of liquid modernity, Bauman continues, it is only solids which 'are cast once and for all' (2000: 8). The result for Morrison is a fiction which, according to Garan Holcombe, takes the shape of 'compelling narrative essays on fear and emptiness' with characters 'desperate for identifiable meaning',[3] while Schoene somewhat more optimistically describes the collection of short stories as showing the 'indispensable necessity of personal relationships' (2007: 14). In Morrison's own words, human relationships are the last retreat in a world that invests heavily in signs to be consumed, the author claiming that 'in the absence of all other values, relating to another person is perhaps all there is to go on'.[4] And indeed, what his three novels have in common is the sense of a problematised intimacy, an exploration of sex, of 'orgasm as the most intimate physical expression of love [that] has become part of a transaction that might drain rather than fulfil the self'.[5] Like many objects and symbols of consumption, the human in Morrison's fiction is placed at the centre of a nexus of separate, sometimes contradictory drives, which raises issues not only related to the creative process, or the process of writing fiction, but also to anthropology and sociology. It is therefore a reflection on space in many senses which is conducted in the three novels this chapter focuses on, on the meaning and values of space and place, the space of the human, as well as the space of fiction. In order to tackle these issues, this chapter will be based on the critical and theoretical thinking of Zygmunt Bauman, Marc Augé, Jean Baudrillard and Guy Debord.

Virtual space, non-place, no-place

Distance, as its title indicates, is very much about space, as well as about the intricate connections that can be woven between space and time. The two lovers, with a continent between them, try to make sense of an impossible spatial equation, while the organisation of the novel as a countdown to their eagerly-awaited reunion translates the spatial dimension into a temporal one. Tom and Meg live very much in time, and the space that they create to bridge the physical gap between them is made up of transcribed phone conversations, text messages and occasionally a few emails, all of which gradually build up an electronically based virtual world, ultimately a world that is made mostly of words. The part of the narrative devoted to Meg consists in various journal entries and a series of computer files all related to her love story with Tom, and created with a view to making sense of and ordering the narrative of their lives into a coherent pattern. In this transcript world, there is no place for secondary characters, who are all turned into types, and who play very little part in the narrative – Josh the American agent, McGregor the caricature entrepreneur, Morna the silent girlfriend, the predictably antagonistic ex-wife. The only character truly to have an impact on the narrative, to be given more than a walk-in part, is Sean, Tom's ten-year-old son. Significantly, Sean is afflicted with a severe stutter which prevents him from communicating with his father in the real world, a handicap for which he compensates by existing on the online computer game Second Life, in practice transferring his relationships into cyberspace – the new space of modernity, according to Paul Virilio – in a way that parallels his father's need for a virtual space of existence. For Sean, virtual space is also a world of words, although in a different way. It is a place where he, a child without an adequate voice, can exist by doing the only thing that is not available to him in the real world: using words. But this cyberworld is volatile, intermittent: as characters log on and off, they exist only in snatches of time, pointing to the fundamental shortcoming of this new space of modernity – that it can make people disappear.

Tom and Meg's story, which mostly takes place in their own private virtual space of words, is a place of transit, a fact mirrored by the way Sean and then Tom himself walk their avatars on the near-empty screen of Second Life. Additionally, the affair starts in a New York hotel, and the narrative first introduces the couple as they are waiting for a flight at Newark Airport, therefore placing the relationship firmly in the only space that they can pragmatically inhabit – two places which anthropologist Marc Augé describes as non-places. Augé chose this term in opposition to the notion of 'place', or 'ethnological place', associated by the ethnological tradition with the idea of a culture localised in time and space. For Augé:

> If a place can be defined as relational, historical and concerned with identity, then a space which cannot be defined as relational, or historical, or concerned with identity will be a non-place. The hypothesis advanced here is that supermodernity produces non-places, meaning spaces which are not themselves anthropological places

and which [...] do not integrate the earlier places: instead they are listed, classified, promoted to the status of 'places of memory', and assigned to a circumscribed and specific position. A world where people are born in the clinic and die in hospital, where transit points and temporary abodes are proliferating under luxurious or inhuman conditions (hotel chains and squats, holiday clubs and refugee camps [...]); where a dense network of means of transport which are also inhabited spaces is developing; where the habitué of supermarkets, slot machines and credit cards communicates wordlessly, through gestures, with an abstract, unmediated commerce; a world thus surrendered to solitary individuality, to the fleeting, the temporary and ephemeral, offers the anthropologist (and others) a new object.[6]

As Tom at the beginning of the novel wishes '[t]o live with Meg, forever in departures' (*D*, 19), he prophetically glimpses, even yearns for, the only space available for this relationship to endure in, which is an impossible combination: technically a non-place, but literally either a no-place, in the usual sense of a utopian space – '[w]hen they kissed they were nowhere' (*D*, 19) – or a place disconnected from geographical constraints, i.e. a virtual place. It is an impossible combination because, as Augé indicates, the non-place cannot be a no-place as it is not a valid place of communication, but rather a space of separation, isolation and loneliness; in Augé's own words (1992: 90), 'the non-place is the opposite of Utopia: it exists, and it does not contain any organic society'.

In a structure that seems to point in the direction of a never-ending, vicious circle for the story, Meg and Tom's affair ends in another non-place, Edinburgh Airport. The outcome, a brutal end put to the relationship, can be read as inevitable, as the words that are used by both characters to bridge the spatial gap and therefore invent an alternative to the ethnological place (unavailable) versus non-place (place of non-communication) dilemma gradually appear to the reader as increasingly scripted, as their love story is turned by Meg into a film script that exposes their most intimate thoughts and experiences. In the chapter entitled 'Film', which takes over the narrative to the extent that the portrayal of the break up is handed over to it, Meg, the script doctor unable to doctor her relationship, has, however, produced its virtual counterpart, its fictionalisation, its removal from the realm of the real in a manner so successful that it ironically enables her to relive the beginning of it with various Tom stand-ins whom she picks up at parties. The very last line of the novel, the words, 'It's You', spoken by Tom over the phone in an attempt to start the relationship over, is territorially ambiguous.[7] It can signal the entry of the story into the cheesy realm of romance, in a bid from the character to escape the non-place and to secure the anchoring of the relationship into the no-place of romance. This outcome is suggested by the last part of the book, 'Return', where Tom reflects upon how different the story of their relationship might have been, had it taken place several years later. But the words also signal the circularity of the process: the virtual relationship, or rather the relationship carried out in a virtual space that hovers between non-place and no-place, cannot escape the pattern it has set for himself, as is indicated by the fact that the ambivalent words ('It's You') are spoken over the phone, the space where most of the relationship has been conducted.

Morrison's first novel, *Swung*, follows another pair of lovers, David and Alice, both of whom work for Scotia TV, a local TV station which is being taken over by a large conglomerate. The merger makes David redundant, ironically so, as he is the one supposedly firing people owing to his job in human resources. He starts visiting swinging websites instead of looking for work, measuring up his own sense of isolation against the general loneliness he finds on those sites. The novel, like David, focuses on the gap separating individuals who, throughout the book, strive to achieve intimacy. In this case, the obstacle is not geographical but physiological as the main character suffers from sexual impotence, a condition which he generalises to the whole of his existence, declaring himself 'impotent. In so many ways' (S, 63). In order to stimulate him, Alice tells him 'bedtime stories' about watching people having sex in a variety of non-places such as car parks, hotels, changing-rooms in chain stores, beaches or parties. In this novel, the private, the intimate is therefore associated with non-places, the spaces of isolation and non-communication which seep into anthropological places such as homes when David watches his neighbours having sex with Alice through their window, a scene which introduces an unobtrusive but very real screen between the lovers.

If the most intimate is transferred onto a non-place, the swinging website provides the updated, electronic or virtual, therefore ubiquitous version of it, as couples log on to it to post their most intimate memories in the shape of wedding photos with the faces blanked-out.[8] In this world where relationships are 'virtualised', removed to a space that is also a non-place disguised as a no-place,[9] in spite of the frantic efforts made by all the characters who people the novel to create connections through sex, humans, like objects, are transferred onto a plane where the utopian impulse (the no-place, with its sense of community) is combined with the consumerist drive. David and Alice, an affluent couple living in Glasgow's West End, describe their living environment in words that are directly lifted from the commercial communication of such iconic retail stores as Ikea, Habitat or Homeworld, claiming that they 'need a thirty-eight-inch flat-screen digital surround-sound television' (S, 4), or referring to 'the big white kitchen slash dining room' (S, 5), or '[b]ath slash Jacuzzi unit' (S, 7). In a phenomenon that Morrison describes as 'the Ikea-fication of the world'[10] the terminology logically reaches out to infect the realm of personal relationships, as the two characters jeeringly refer to their '[neighbour's] wife slash partner', with her '[b]rown slash auburn hair' (S, 6), thereby conflating the commercial drive with the personal realm. Indeed for Morrison, swinging, only one click away from internet dating, is the perfect illustration of the consumerist approach we have of our private lives, of 'these multiple options that consumerism is giving us in terms of our sexuality'.[11] The description of the neighbours in terms borrowed from the discourse of estate agents or large retail stores turns people into signs, and it is the human itself which is abstracted into the semiotic system of consumption.

In this context, humans, like objects, become disposable as they are integrated into the short-time cycle of consumer products. The Ikea-fication process, comically – or maybe very sadly – captured in *Swung* by the sentence 'Jackson Pollock was now available in five colours of Formica. [...] Picasso really was for sale in Homeworld' (S, 23), leads to a version of the world which, in accordance with Zygmunt Bauman's definition of liquid modernity, becomes temporary. The newspeak for this world is created by Alice – Tempworld:

> Whenever I sniff Ikea, [Alice] said, I hear the word 'temp'. She'd made him read this book. Some big sociology text. The future is temporary, it said, employment, housing, relationships, marriage. The social

plan for society has collapsed. Every man for himself, till you're too old to compete [...] Hi, welcome to Tempworld. (S, 27–28)

As David discovers on being fired from his job, when his experience of isolation appears as acutely spatial, 'the mirrored walls of the elevator reflect[ing] his face into solitary infinity' (S, 25–26), Tempworld actually freezes the isolation of the individual in time but also in space. This endless duplication of the individual which is experienced metaphorically by David corresponds to the consumerist project of the mass manufacturing of individuality, a topic which is at the heart of Morrison's project:

> The old era of mass manufactured conformism ha[s] been super-ceded [sic] by the even more powerful selling strategy of associating products with unique individuality, implying that shopping is an act of self-expression – the mass manufacturing of uniqueness.[12]

In his novel, Morrison provides his reader with a reflection on the limits of consumerism, by suppressing the flimsy border between products and the human, foreshortening the process to a selling of the human directly. When what is consumed is a concept, an idea, the notion of intimacy, the relations between individuals, in short the essence of the human, then Meg's intended sarcasm in *Distance* that 'shopping is the answer to everything' takes on a new dimension, as David compulsively trawls the internet, looking to consume sex. The fact that sex is not given in exchange for money, as in a commercial relationship, paradoxically even reinforces the parallel with an exacerbated version of the consumerist ideal, as it removes all inter-mediaries and means of exchange: David and Alice, as well as their numerous swinger friends, not least of whom Dolly, the old hippy woman David nicknames 'Mother Earth' who precisely embodies this perversion of the 'free love' ideal of the 1960s by turning it into a business in which the currency is sex, remove themselves into a consumption that cannot lead to communication, because, as Jean Baudrillard showed as early as 1968 in *The System of Objects*, the semiotic contents of the act of consumption supersedes the act itself, in the process cancelling all possible relation. For Baudrillard, 'consumption is not a material practice, nor is it a phenom-enology of "affluence". [...] If it has any meaning at all, consumption means *an activity consisting of the systematic manipulation of signs*.[13] In consumption, therefore, the human relation, which becomes a relation of consumption, is abstracted from the realm of experience; it is dematerialised: '[t]he relationship is no longer directly experienced: it has become abstract, been abolished, been transformed into a sign-object, and thus consumed' (1968: 219). Baudrillard points to the fundamentally destructive power of consumption as a power which feeds off itself. For him, consumption does not lead to a state of saturation, because it is a reason for living (1968: 223), an element which is taken up again in slightly different terms by Zygmunt Bauman who points out (2000: 83) that the ever greater availability of products in supermarkets, their ability to suggest new desires, can be applied not just to products, but also to identity because identity, like consumption in the modern world, is based on the notion of desire rather than need, giving it an unlimited scope:

> The *spiritus novens* of consumer activity is no longer the measurable set of articulated needs, but *desire* – a much more volatile and ephemeral, evasive and capricious, and essentially non-referential entity than 'needs', a self-begotten and self-propelled motive that needs no other justification or 'cause'. (2000: 74)

Morrison attempts the literalisation of those postulates by transferring from the system of objects to that of human relationships. David's impotence leaves him in the space of desires which he cannot fulfil, a fact which turns him into the perfect consumer, as he very bitterly realises in a monologue that metaphorically places him in the archetypal non-place of consumption, a shopping mall:[14]

> Impotence. Like being in a land where you couldn't speak the language. Like being in a shopping mall with a maxed-out credit card. An impotent man could easily be the perfect addict. The perfect consumer. A desire which could never be fulfilled. Which left you wanting. More. More of anything. More. (*S*, 198–99)

David's realisation in this extract, with its parataxis suggestive of anger and rebellion, and the revealing correspondence established between the first and last words, 'impotence' and 'more', both being grammatically isolated from the rest of the sentence, suggests the 'perfect' vicious circle of desire, and enables him to glimpse the chasm theoretically existing between the consummation of desire and the desire of consumption. Turning consummation, the 'consummation devoutly to be wished', into consumption exposes the intimate to the semioticised realm of transactions. The symbol of that inescapable conversion is Mother Earth/Dolly, whose first name, according to David, suggests a curious mixture of 1950s culture (Dolly Parton) and scientific experiment (Dolly the sheep), and whom he aptly describes as '[s]ome weird corruption of the concept of free love' (S, 243). Dolly, an old hand at free love, has indeed become a caricature, a sort of pedlar of sex, who turns up on swingers' doorsteps with her complete kit, including Viagra, a toy-boy with a penis the size of a man's forearm, and invitations to orgies in remote places (in a parody of mildly pornographic movies). She, in fact, turns lovemaking into a perfect description of Baudrillard's definition of consumption: a subsuming of the relationship into sign: female ejaculation, double penetration, multiple coordinated orgasms, all those are but the derisory remnants of a consummation that has been engulfed by consumption. The human in that context appears as hollowed out, only delineated from the outside, from the consumption-enhanced. This is indicated at an early stage in the novel, by Alice's attempt at creating art:

> Magritte. That was the second big idea she had. [...] A picture in negative. No image, just white, framed by a border of children's wallpaper. Surrealism and Freud. We are empty, everything we will ever try to create is framed by our parents. A little po-mo. An anti-image. White square in the centre. An absence where identity should be. (S, 22)

The aptly-named 'white room' – traditionally the colour white indicates purity or the pictural equivalent of the *tabula rasa*, in this case the white canvas – in which Alice performs her 'little po-mo', 'anti-image' definition of the human, echoes the white squares on the wedding photographs posted on the swinging website, with their indication of the removal of identity,[15] and finds its counterpart in the last part of the novel, entitled 'black room'. In the black room, swingers make an ultimate attempt at connecting, by indulging in communal sex in the dark.[16] But the scene, first depicted from David's point of view then from Alice's, the latter realising that 'no matter many cocks and fingers pushed into her, she didn't feel connected in any way' (S, 326), stresses disembodiment, fragmentation, in an act which has reduced the human to a seemingly inexhaustible collection of isolated organs, mostly orifices, that interact in a mechanical, mindless manner:

> Where was she? Unless she was that hand in his hair, that mouth round his cock. Again he resisted the temptation to call her name. Fingers kneaded the muscles in his neck and his head rolled forward to find the wetness of a woman's crotch. Lips brushed his lips. And as he pushed a finger inside someone he felt a finger slowly push into his ass and his muscles tighten round it. Spit, a woman's wetness smeared into his ass. How many people were holding him? Three, four? Alice. (S, 318)

This description, turning as it does the entire scene in the black room into a grotesque body, both suggests and resists Bakhtin's grotesque, with its insistence on orifices, gaping mouths, and the allusion to his theory of the carnivalesque as an affirmative, militant and anti-authoritarian attitude to life founded upon a joyful acceptance of the materiality of the body. For Bakhtin, the body is potentially disruptive of narrative, especially when other larger narratives such as order, civilisation, progress and destiny begin to lose their authority:

> No dogma, no authoritarianism, no narrow-minded seriousness can coexist with Rabelaisian images; these images are opposed to all that is finished and polished, to all pomposity, to every ready-made solution in the sphere of thought and world outlook.[17]

The orgy in the black room, with its monstrous, grotesque body aims for the very notion of renewal:

> As opposed to artificial feast, one might say that carnival celebrates temporary liberation from the prevailing truth of the established order; it marks the suspension of all hierarchical rank, privileges,

norms and prohibitions. Carnival was the true feast of becoming, change and renewal. It was hostile to all that was immortalised and complete. (1968: 109)

But the liberation process oversteps its mark. In a hideous transformation of the real world, where the grotesque seems to seep out of its narrative containers represented by the chapter titles ('black room'; 'white room'), the characters – bodies – encountered by David, roaming the streets of Glasgow after yet another episode of sexual impotence, are evidence that the grotesque, the force of liberation from the narrative of civilisation according to Bakhtin, have been turned into the conventionally, pathetically monstrous. The parade of bodies is a parody of the body whose appearance, according to Fredric Jameson, produces 'an awakening of fresh sight', and which 'diverts a conventional narrative logic of the unfolding story in some new vertical direction'.[18] On the streets of Glasgow on a Friday night, David encounters a variety of female characters encapsulated in reductive arbitrary stereotypes – the bitch, the whore of Babylon (S, 197). The parade of desire which floats surreally in front of his eyes (to the extent that some characters, like the very big woman, belong more to the realm of hallucinations than to description) turns the grotesque back into a contemporary and mundane version of the monstrous:

> The line for the cash machine. [...] Twenty or more of them in a line. Students mostly. Three goth girls. The one in the middle wearing a corset. Her breasts E-cups at least, held rigid like a shelf on which her crucifix necklace sat. The girl next to her, fishnets and filigree. Blood red lips. Vamps and vampires. The third, thigh-high leather boots. Tattoo at the base of her spine. (S, 198)

In spite of the description's focus on the characters as grotesque bodies, what is monstrous about this description is the utter isolation of the individual and the hopelessness of the perspectives of these various caricatures of the human, whose future can only be seen as a repetition of the meaningless present. In Tempworld, the world in which, as Alice says, paraphrasing Bauman, the future is temporary (S, 31), these women have been reduced to the state of harmless caricatures, whose power to overthrow the system, hinted at with the orgiastic, grotesque body of the black room, is doomed from the start:

> See them in fifteen years' time. Partner number fifty-five, still wearing fishnets and blood red lipstick, temp jobs and one-night stands. Thinking that they've found a real connection with a man when they find out they loved the same CD from the 90s. (S, 198)

The future may be temporary, or rather, in this case, an unceasing repetition of the present in a horizontal projection that contradicts the vertical direction taken by the narrative under the impulse of the grotesque according to Jameson, but it also points to the dead-end both the white and the black rooms represent. In a similar process that curbs the subversive, the grotesque body/bodies in the black room is/are contained, its/their subversive potential lasting only as long as it/they can be safely isolated in a dark, invisible, self-contained universe. Swinging, as Alice learns at the hands of a co-worker, is not the new free love; neither, as she learns for herself, is it the carnival that has the ability to turn the social order upside down. In a total confusion of senses, organs and identities, an impossible equation in which one is desperately trying to exist in terms of another, the protagonists realise the proximity of the black room to the white room of their existence:

> He was no longer David, and Alice was no longer Alice. They were just here, bodies breathing, opening. His eyes seeing faint outlines in the dark. But as the pressure pushed deeper inside him he no longer wanted to see. With each slow thrust, each breath, in and out, deeper and deeper, he was turning inside out. Becoming body, breath, nameless. Touch is fingers, taste is mouth. Ass is taste. Taste is touch. Fingers are mouth. Mouth is ass. Touch, taste. Smell. David. Alice. Lost. (S, 319)

With the help of synecdoche and synaesthesia, this passage points to the irreversible degradation of the ideal of free love which Mother Earth falsely hangs on to. In a meeting of her TV show team on a prospective programme on swinging, which is meant to represent a sort of ultimate stage of reality TV which, if aired, will portray 'four houses. Surveillance. Four couples fucking' (S, 118), Alice realises that the old ideals have been displaced.[19] Alongside absurdly ludicrous neologisms such as 'polyamorous' (S, 292) and 'polyfidelity' (S, 294) comes for Alice the realisation that the 'gift' of fucking, given freely by people who 'don't see sex as titillation, objectification[,] [t]his whole consumerist sex-object bullshit' (S, 295), has in fact been annihilated by the very process it tries to eradicate: Alice's boss with Scotia TV, 'the head' (another synecdoche) gives over the running of the programme to Alice's friend Pauline, who is the one to laugh at the preposterous idea of free love, and who can supply a few high-profile sports celebrities to take part in the reality TV swinging show. This is a bitter fictional confirmation of Ewan Morrison's rejection of the practice of swinging when not used as an extension of feelings. In that case, it becomes 'just variety for its own sake, and has the danger of becoming an addictive behaviour that is simply postponing the lack of real contact and communication between you'.[20] Logically therefore, the reversal of the old order in *Swung* has definitely been sidelined, and the grotesque remains as a feeble sign of what might have been.

'Edinburgh city of ...': globalia, localia and the empty place

The subplot in *Distance* describes Tom's jeering comments at his own job with a PR firm, which consists in devising a corporate branding strategy to apply to the city of Edinburgh, with the goal of '[s]elling Scotland to the world' (D, 87) mostly by devising an appropriate catchphrase that can totalise the selling-power of the place. This enterprise soon reaches a dead-end as neither the professional 'creatives' nor their customers, the city council officials, manage to come up with a suitably impressive description, leaving the motto – 'Edinburgh city of ...' – unfinished for most of the narrative. This attempt, however ludicrous and however much derided by the narrator Tom, is symptomatic of the twenty-first century – of supermodernity, in Augé's terms – in that it attempts to articulate local and global, as well as physical and virtual realities. The difficulty with selling Scotland to the world is that, as only Tom seems to be aware, it has to reconcile what Claire Larsonneur, in an article about the English novelist David Mitchell, calls 'globalia' and 'localia'. She describes globalia as the phenomenon whereby places exhibit interchangeable features and an extra-territorial location, and differentiates this concept from that of non-places by stressing increased uniformity, or 'a set of standard features *systematically* reproduced in any instance of the place'.[21] Globalia is manifested in the idealised, sanitised version of Edinburgh that Tom's boss, McGregor, is trying to sell to his clients, who seem to believe that only suitably extra-territorial, globalised space can enter the global competition for economic acumen. For Morrison, globalisation is a blanket term that precisely hints at the expansion of globalia into one huge economic market driven by the forces of global capitalism, the epitome of which is suggested by Tom in his ludicrously exacerbated capitalistic bid to privatise the whole of Scotland. In the novel, the drive to level the identity of place is suggested precisely by the missing part in the slogan as well as by the fact that it can only be completed in a non-specific, rather bland way. In the reaction of one of the council officials, 'I love the European bit. European city of …' (*D*, 90), what transpires is that what matters is not identity, but rather the subsuming of the local into a vague space of 'European' – understood as other than local and therefore global – space, which has become so blank that its very definition has to rely on namelessness ('of …'). Yet at the same time the way to globalise Scotland in *Distance* is by banking on localia, that is, as defined by Larsonneur (2009: 144), 'spaces of hypertrophic geographical and historical quality'. This is represented by the corporate video that shows the Forth Bridge and the Scott Monument, both being generally considered as evidence of the historical and cultural specificity of Scotland. This paradox of stressing localia to achieve globalia leads to the result, ironically placed very early on in the narrative, that 'the world wasn't buying' (*D*, 87).

In the context meticulously delineated by *Distance*, the space of Edinburgh is therefore an impossibility, a posture, a space wedged between two contradictory drives, aiming for the global and informed by the local. It is dictated to the makers of the video by economic requirements that ruthlessly discard pertinent elements that might be selling the city to the world. This blindly homogenising policy is connected to what Eleanor Bell, borrowing Michael Billig's concept of 'banal nationalism', sees as inevitable: banal nationalism, being a dissolution of the nation-state in a movement that singles out the Unites States as the global ideal, prompts people to identify with this American-global – therefore univalent – model.[22]

In *Distance* Morrison explores how artificial, unreal and eventually damaging 'our unconscious identification with this supposed American global ideal' (Bell, 2004: 85) can be. The American ideal is represented by Meg and her walk-in New York friends who cannot make a creditable imprint upon the narrative,[23] while, back in Scotland, Tom's video empties Edinburgh's geographical and historical markers of meaning by severing their links with identity, relations and history. In so doing, he turns them into empty signs only able to make up a non-place that falls outside of the logic of identity, relation and history. When Tom says, on writing the script for the video, that he 'could write this stuff with his eyes closed' (*D*, 306), he emphasises the purely mechanical object he is thus creating and, therefore, stresses the paradox of using precisely the symbols of history and identity to construct a non-place.

But banal nationalism and the ubiquity of the American model carries its share of constraints. Tom's rant about privatising Scotland, in which he suggests cutting Edinburgh up into chunks and floating the chunks on the market, literalises the hackneyed metaphor of 'selling Edinburgh to the world' in a moment of sheer hung-over bloody-mindedness, and conjures up an absurd yet threatening vision of the marketability of everything, including the theoretically unmarketable, which comes after the marketing of human relationships and of the most intimate connection between people we see in *Swung*:

> So here's the plan. We set Edinburgh up as a company and float it on the international market. Edinburgh Inc. Everything in it, the Castle, the streets and everyone in them becomes an asset. Set up a solid border, razor wire, surveillance, the lot, charge people for admission. Privatise every blade of grass. Turn every irreversible social problem into an asset. (*D*, 235–36)

This literalisation of the idea of the commodification of everything, from history to geography, to identity or even commercially worthless items such as a blade of grass, is an exacerbated version of Guy Debord's concept of the Spectacle (evolved in 1967), which refers to 'a media and consumer society, organised around the consumption of images, commodities, and staged events.'[24] For Debord, the spectacle relies on a commodification of all the spheres of the human:

> The spectacle is the moment when the commodity has attained the *total occupation* of social life. The relation to the commodity is not only visible, but one no longer sees anything but it: the world one sees is its world. Modern economic production extends its dictatorship extensively and intensively.[25]

What Tom suggests with the privatisation of Edinburgh is that the video should aim to turn the city is into what Steven Best and Douglas Kellner call a 'megaspectacle', namely an escalation in size, range and intensity of the Debordian concept, the production of a globalised mass-culture made possible by global coverage, satellite dishes and the internet, an attempt to import and adapt worldwide phenomena such as Star Wars or Disney and apply them to Scotland. In a logical escalation, Tom suggests an extension of this concept of turning Edinburgh into a huge theme park – a megaspectacle – to the whole of Scotland, providing a method and even a logo, 'ScotLAND'. By eventually completing the motto into the cover-all and ultimately meaningless 'City of excellence',[26] Tom provides a sarcastic description of his city as a product which can only be captured in an endless repetition of buzzwords sheared of meaning and therefore of any sort of communicative potential, an insight which does not seem to be shared by any of the other characters:

> 'Yes, yes,' McGregor was saying. 'Great idea. The whole campaign can be words that start with an E – Excellence – Engineering – the Enlightenment – European!'
> Embolism. Epidural. Ecstasy. This flash through Tom's shattered mind. A billboard promoting drug use. A kid with a tab on his tongue. Edinburgh starts with an – E. (*D*, 237)

As aptly, if unwittingly, summarised by McGregor, the megaspectacle, the nonsensical city of excellence (and epidural), *is* words, a series of words with either no connections or unfortunate ones, such as the constituting of

Scotland into a huge global theme park for drug addicts, a sort of *Trainspotting* gone global. It is a Baudrillardian semiotic package in which the signs, the only objects on offer in the globalised chain of consumption, are allowed to careen freely in a (non-)space that has set them free forever. This is a vision born in the streets of the city, a macro-level equivalent of the William Wallace impersonator roaming the Royal Mile in real-life Edinburgh and charging the tourists for photographs, a character who looks not like the historical Wallace, whose statue is carved on the pillar of the Edinburgh Castle gate, but rather like the Hollywood actor Mel Gibson.[27] Divorced from the history and culture he was born in, this character is but an index of the extent of the banal nationalism which is praised in the name of globalisation.

In that context, the spectacle runs the risk of also becoming what Zygmunt Bauman, adapting a concept evolved by Claude Levi-Strauss, calls a 'phagic space', a place that devours foreign bodies to integrate them fully, to digest them into (American?) sameness, in a cannibalistic process which entails enforced assimilation, the suspension or annihilation of the other's otherness.[28] In *Swung* the others' otherness also disappears as the markers of identity and history are shown to dissolve and lose their power in the drive to turn everything into a spectacle. When David and Alice meet a swinging couple in a theme bar called 'La Revolution' packed with Stalinist kitsch and memorabilia, Alice reflects upon the annihilation of the meaning of history in the contemporary world:

> The place was supposed to be fun but it made her sad. That history was worth so little, that it had become nothing more than a backdrop to pose beside as you got drunk on vanilla vodka. Swinging and the end of communism. Some connection there. Something to do with the collapse of belief in alternatives. (S, 137)

The world of globalisation as applied to the local depicted in *Distance* provides the reader with one great phagic space: as a megaspectacle, even if only a prospective one, it both assimilates and 'globalises' the local, the individual, by turning them into semiotic objects, commodities ready for participation in the displacement, the spectacle of history and identity. The consequence is that meaning seems inevitably compromised. As Bauman indicates, the issue of making the local into a global concept defies interpretation:

> Being local in a globalised world is a sign of social deprivation and degradation. The discomforts of localised existence are compounded by the fact that with public spaces removed beyond the reaches of localised life, localities are losing their meaning-generating and meaning-negotiating capacity and are increasingly dependent on sense-giving and interpreting actions which they do not control.[29]

The gap between the reality of the city and the (aspiringly mega-)spectacle that the advertising campaign is claiming to be turning it into, is ironically made even greater than the semiotic dysfunction by the choice of a location for the shooting of the corporate video, a field of rubble – 'an area of quality Edinburgh rubble' (*D*, 308) – soon to be turned into the 'Hope Park Enterprise Zone' which may or may not become the huge corporate theme park it advertises itself as. The pathetic little council man parroting his speech on camera, repeating his single buzz word 'excellence' to a nauseating and ultimately comical degree, the discrepancy between the emptiness of the location and the overinflated discourse designed to cover the void, are underlined by Tom's jeering voice which, in the conversation he conducts with the cameraman, provides the narrative with a sustained, divergent voiceover. This effectively reduces the megaspectacle ambition to what it really is in Morrison's view: a poor attempt at keeping companies in Edinburgh for the economic survival in these times of global competition, rather than an expansion of the city. All those features underline the fact that beyond discourse, beyond the rebranding fashion, what is at stake is the way that public space has segued into distinct, increasingly disparate entities, which reflect a new, exacerbated form of social and economic segregation. For in *Distance* the emphasis is placed on the futility and ridiculousness of the attempt to go global in a gesture that owes more to banal nationalism than to an actual economic and cultural expansion.

The subversive power of empty places

As banal nationalism precludes 'the belief in alternatives', the homogenisation of the present (and of the future) is founded on a distortion, a 'banalisation' of the meaning of the past, of its ability to signify.[30] The suggestion of the distortion of the historical through commodification has two distinct but interrelated consequences. For Bauman, empty places are spaces which carry no meaning, because they are 'seen to be empty, or rather unseen':

> The maps that guide the movements of various categories of inhabitants do not overlap, but for any map to 'make sense', some areas of the city must be left out as senseless, and – as far as the sense-making is concerned – unpromising. Cutting out such places allows the rest to shine and bristle with meaning. (2000: 104)

What is described by Bauman in this extract is precisely the bet for the future of Edinburgh which is taken by the council and by Tom's PR company, I-Com, in the face of mounting evidence against the global corporate image they are trying to build from scratch. Tom, as the sole centre of consciousness of the part of the novel situated in Edinburgh, presents the reader with the return of the repressed, or rather of the empty places that he is being paid to keep out of the picture. Those places relentlessly present themselves to him in the shape of random encounters. The empty places of Edinburgh, the schemes that the council would rather forget and has in fact forgotten, seem to push their way into the narrative, against the will of the dominant discourse, the discourse of capitalist hegemony which, according to Morrison, Tom represents not only because of his job, but also through his opinions.[31] They return in a haphazard fashion, in a way that makes them appear as isolated textual spaces, short passages, vignettes: the mother from the scheme; Archie, the old Hemingway lookalike from the pub; the Ned, or his girlfriend in the white leather miniskirt, between them trace a very different map of the city (and by extension of the country), a sort of counter-map to I-Com's 'I-map', a map that forcibly reintroduces empty spaces. Tom, on the bus back from a 'corporate' meeting, encounters denizens of empty places:

> 'Mwaaa, mwaa.'
> 'Fuckin' sit still, Chelsea. Fuckin' shoosh.'
> Seven stops to go. The kid is called Chelsea, like the Clinton girl. His guess was they came from Pilton, the scheme the government had tried to forget.

THE SPACE OF FICTION

'Mwaaa, mwaa, mama.'
The kid reaches for something in her mother's bag. Mother slaps the kid's hand. Kid cries [...].
'I said no and you keep on fuckin' goin' on at me, just fuckin' shut up.' (*D*, 93)

This passage, like the description of the Ned who starts out as a solicitous enough character toward a drunk Tom on the streets, like that of the old guy in the pub, happy to chat to a stranger provided that he can cadge a drink or two off him while imparting his pragmatic wisdom, provides the narrative with the centripetal drive, a movement away from the globalising, outward-going rhetoric, and towards the minute, the most mundane and detailed, towards the empty spaces of Edinburgh, or the reality seen with the closeness of experience. This pull of the real, this mechanical movement that resists the assimilation of all into a phagic, all-encompassing, media-led space is suggested by a metaphor which captures the power of the real, the local:

You flew across the globe through day and night, through infinite skies and expansive thought, then slowly you circled your city and it pulled you down till your feet were on the ground, then it was your street, then the walk, then through the tenement door, the keys in your hand. Gravity sucking you slowly downwards. The curvature of the planet flattening. The weight increasing as the dimensions shrank. The gravity of where you came from, pulling you in, squashing you, till you fitted this tiny hole that was for a key that opened the door to your home. (*D*, 35)

What is indicated here is that there is not one continuous floating space available for any sense of place or any sense of identity. The pull of the land, of the local, is bound to reduce facts to their real proportion, the question being only one of adjusting to scale and to the distortions that fiddling with them can entail. As the character finally fits into the tiny keyhole in a way that blatantly defies verisimilitude, the text seems to predict, very early on, that making up an impossible scale ultimately does not work, no matter how much spin is put into it. The narrative is therefore submitted to those conflicting movements: one expansive, centrifugal, distributing the notion of identity towards the outside, and the other centripetal, pulling the text back to the most basic, the most elementary, a close-up on the rubble in the corner of the frame in Tom's video. But the centripetal pull of the invisible, of the empty place, the force that is associated with the gravity metaphor in the extract, is also crucially the one that is generative of words to describe the city. If the brainstorming session at I-Com's fails to come up with one single motto for Edinburgh, the characters who inhabit the empty spaces are in no short supply of words to characterise, describe, deride, therefore place 'the city of ...'. Tom, thinking about the young mother on the bus:

> He turned his head. City of self-pity. City of state dependence. Of three generations of unemployed. Grandmothers aged forty-five. He tells himself it is not just here, it is happening everywhere. [...] City of single mothers. City of lost souls. Of despair. (*D*, 93–94)

After being beaten up by the Ned:

> City of mates. City of camaraderie between the downtrodden. [...] city of strangers who went out of their way to help you. City of endless pity. City of fuck off and leave me alone. [...] City of generosity. Genero-city. Generic-city. (*D*, 224)

And lastly, in a comic scene that saves the narrative, and more particularly the treatment of the issue of empty spaces versus phagic spaces, from falling into the melodramatic, the old guys in the pub between them have a whole series of suggestions to make for the slogan:

> 'C'moan. Edinburgh, City of ...?' shouted Archie.
> 'Shite,' shouted one. 'Whisky,' another. 'The Scottish Republican Army.' 'Lapdancing!' 'Doleys.' 'Snobby English cunts.' 'Hearts!' 'Albion Rovers!' 'Shortbread.' 'Pakis.' 'Fuckin' tourists.' (*D*, 211)

The tone may vary, but the point is the same. When the zooming in has revealed 'every blade of grass' – to take up the capitalist metaphor of the privatisation of the land – what emerges is yet another concept that is evolved by Bauman in a book which focuses on the human consequences of globalisation, and in the introduction of which he states that '[a]n integral part of the globalising processes is progressive spatial segregation, separation and exclusion' (1998: 3). Bauman describes globalisation as effectively creating not just various spaces, but also two significant categories of individuals, whom he calls the tourist and the vagabond, the former living in time, which does not matter to him because he can cross both time and distance easily, while the other category is confined to space, being 'crushed under the burden of abundant, redundant and useless time they have nothing to fill with. In their time, "nothing ever happens"' (1998: 88). What the young mother and her toddler experience is this shrinking not just of space but also of their time, which is blank, with no possibility granted to them of making sense of it, of filling it with events or meaning. This is indicated by another 'conversation' between the daughter and her mother, emphasising a request for meaning that cannot be imparted:

> 'Wassa, wassa.' The little pink girl pointing out the window.
> 'Whit? Stop fuckin' gettin' in my face!'
> 'Wassa. Wassa.'
> And he sees what Chelsea is pointing at. And it takes him back to Sean, years before. Hard to describe to a child, but he would have tried with Sean. A warehouse – windows boarded up. To tell his son about post-industrial decline. The British Empire.
> 'Fuckin' sit down. Shut the fuck up. '
> The slap again, this time to the face. (*D*, 94)

What the young mother cannot realise is that the inhabitants of the empty space are also 'vagabonds' in Bauman's terminology, in the sense that they cannot exploit space and chose to move from one place to another in the way tourists do, but are condemned to stay on a piece of land, the Pilton housing scheme or the Glasgow ganglands, which can only go under erasure, with them stuck in it. City of vagabonds. City of Despair.

All of Morrison's novels focus on the vagabonds in spite of the fact that none of them are about the lower classes of society;[32] the distinction is in fact the aspect on which the plot in *Distance* is organised: Tom and Meg need to be tourists in order for their story to exist, whereas the painstaking emphasis on time that precisely cannot be cancelled, the various scenarios Tom tries to imagine in order to be freed from space, from 'distance', and live in time, the radical but manifestly inescapable solution to his problem which is delivered by the Hemingway look-alike in the pub – 'Wan of ye has tae die' (*D*, 213) – the creation of a network of connections between the poorer Edinburgh vagabonds and Tom himself (in spite of the class difference), all those signs point to the fact that his position as a vagabond cannot be exchanged for the power-wielding one of the tourist. In that sense, Morrison is tackling the question of social separation and the social situation in Scotland from a new perspective. He shows that, in a globalised capitalist world, one might have to deal with a reorganisation of the social map, with the middle classes being the vagabonds in Bauman's classification. This leaves a gapingly open blank space of nothingness for the lower classes, an empty space in both the metaphorical and literal sense of the term, in the shape of a social and economic void that leaves behind many characters, only just glanced at in *Distance* as characters who inhabit the non-space of fiction.

In this fictional universe structured by separation and isolation the result is a closing down of space and time. Both *Distance* and *Swung* are claustrophobic novels, for both strive to focus exclusively on the two protagonists' relationship. *Swung*, a novel which stresses the repeatedly failed attempts at achieving intimacy in the contemporary world, reinforces this claustrophobic feeling by alternating David's and Alice's points of view, with no possibility for the reader ever to escape into a third, less suffocating one. Both Alice and David, in spite of their multiple attempts at penetrating other people's bodies or being penetrated by strangers, attempts which are documented in the novel in surgical detail, record the desperate effort to communicate. Ironically, communication is the reason why they have chosen sex, which, according to Alice, precisely precludes objectification.[33] This effort to be in touch, in a sense that displaces the literal meaning of the sexual encounters to reach the metaphorical one, delineates a trajectory which is the exact reverse of the one suggested by Dolly's bad punning on wanting to be fulfilled, as in 'full' and 'filled', which is a movement from the metaphorical to the crudely literal. The swinging website, with its contributors who can ultimately be summed up as a collection of dicks and pussies, as the pseudonym of the first couple encountered by David and Alice,

Pussygalore, indicates, is itself a world apart. It is a sort of parallel universe to the real world which also reinforces this isolation, the novel only affording the protagonists, as a well as the reader, glimpses of the world around them. As David walks the streets of Glasgow after signing his divorce paper, '[h]e stood there at the bottom of the street and noticed that there were people everywhere. Strange that he'd walked here every day for years and never really taken any notice' (S, 283).

The emphasis is therefore not just on isolation, but also on partition, the deliberate ensconcing of individuals in their own mental, physical, but also electronic prison-house. The novel carries a representation of this compartmentalisation of (physical and novelistic) space in the shape of the revamped workspace at TV Scotia. It is a space misleadingly transparent, with glass partitions ensuring an effect of flowing circulation and communication but which in fact effectively separates the individuals. The novel therefore suggests the metaphor of the open-plan office (a version of which can be seen with the spatial organisation of the West End flats) which allows only for a system of 'sanitised' exchanges of glances, and where no real interaction can take place. As David notes, his relationships can only happen in '[f]rames within frames' (S, 54). This prompts Alice, in another compartment of her life, the swinging scene that she is part of, to yearn for a return to an antiquated form of communication, when she claims that 'she wanted to hear the voices that lived behind the white squares' of the blanked-out wedding pictures posted on the swinging site (S, 138).

In such a version of partitioned space, which promotes one sensory – in some cases sensual – form of communication over the others, it becomes unclear what status remains for David and Alice. Alice creates a parallel space of existence for David and herself which is literally a space of fiction, the space of the stories she tells David in order to induce an erection. *Swung* can therefore be seen as a dual space: a conventional space of fiction which allows the characters to exist, but which they cannot occupy because of the abstraction of this world into a po-mo world, a semiotic world that takes the postmodern postulate to its extremes by staging the fragmentation of the human and which therefore constructs a non-space of fiction, and a shadow space of fiction, the space of the stories in which one of the protagonists attempts to recreate a possible, or fictional universe for the characters to exist in. It is a world in which, in a self-reflexive movement, the characters have to re-enact the voyeuristic stance which is the basic postulate of all fiction.

In *Distance*, the immaterial space lurking behind the character's narratives takes on more definitive undertones, when Tom first undertakes, as Alice does in *Swung*, to remove himself into a shadow space of fiction, literally, in order for the story in the main ontological level to exist:

> Everything had to be 'great'. He had to buy into the dream of self-improvement. Do that impossible American thing which was to believe in yourself, even though you knew the self to be not a thing but all that was left when there was nothing left. He had to believe in himself. Make himself a character in a story. With a goal and obstacles and a happy ending with Meg. (*D*, 307)

What space remains for the characters in their private lives as well as in the public sphere therefore increasingly appears to be a scripted space, in keeping with the main metaphor in the novel, that of scripting one's life, or of living a scripted life (hence the thematic importance of Meg's job as a script doctor). But the metaphor can sometimes become threateningly close to reality, as is indicated by the 'Detox' chapter, where Tom describes himself as a character in a well-known novel:

> Take yer pick, mate! – the lady or the bottle? Choose life, chose refrigerators and DVD players and life insurance, choose walks in the country. Choose the *Trainspotting* detox. Cliché or not he had to do it. Draw up the list, like Renton did. He'd already put his hand down the shitter, like Renton did, why not go all the way? Become the cliché. (*D*, 249)

The suggestion made in this chapter in the shape of a joke is that for Tom, there is no other existence but one in which he has to 'go all the way' and 'become the cliché', namely to exist in a reality which has literally already been written, scripted, even published (and filmed). It therefore comes as no surprise to the reader that in a final narrative twist, Tom and Meg's story should be removed to the shadow land of fiction, to a scripted universe turned into a movie. This development turns the whole of the narrative from the status of primary diegetic level to that of secondary diegetic level, in the process *de facto* removing the possibility for a relationship to take place on the first level of existence. If *Swung* tentatively represents the necessity to build an imaginative version of the world in order to exist, the end of *Distance* both derides and shatters that attempt by containing the creative escape within the narrow bounds of what has already been scripted, or by upsetting the hierarchy we establish between the real and the fictional or, to adapt this dichotomy to Morrison's fiction, the real and the scripted. This shift works on Baudrillard's concept of the hyperreality of the contemporary world, which he describes as this world 'where the virtual and the real are no longer separable',[34] as applied to the creative world of fiction, and to the necessity for a creative exit to the world of liquid modernity.

The artistic dilemma

Faced with the disappearance of both the sense of place and the sense of identity in liquid modernity, Morrison turned to art to indict a world which no longer allows for true expression of the self. He chose several figures of the visual artist to make this point – Alice, and more significantly the trio of artists depicted in *Ménage*, Dorothy, Saul and Owen. While Alice, as indicated above, creates characters in the shape of blanks and therefore defined by their emptiness, in *Ménage*, Dorothy, prompted by her mentor Saul, resorts to videotaping in order to capture the banality of the real and elevate it to the status of art, as the only possible means of capturing the representation of the self. The novel clearly takes a swipe at the Young British Artists, starting as it does from the postulate that dictated their art in the first place. In *Ménage*, Saul epitomises their rebellious stance, when he says for example, '[f]uck art and turn yourself into an artwork. Steal a video camera and record yourself eating, sleeping, taking a shit!' (*M*, 29). And indeed, the intoxicating power of Saul's discourse on both Owen and Dorothy rests on the potential for freedom it contains:

> What was the point of adding more art, more reproduction of the same to the stinking stockpile of crap that was our culture? [...] Stop being creative and embrace the beauty of destruction. And in that moment of suicidal despair, reach for your first breath as a truly free soul. (*M*, 30)

But the novel's dual plot and dual temporal structure enables the reader to have access to both the young characters' acts of rebellion and the adult characters' more measured stance, as they have become absorbed in the contemporary art market – with Dorothy a successful artist leading a yuppie existence in Camden and recycling her old artwork over and over again. By turning artistic creation and individual expression, the expression of the 'truly free soul', into an endless cycle of packaging and repackaging the same pieces – which in the process have become products – for the unceasing cycle of consumption, she perpetuates a vicious circle which has forsaken both art and her capacity of expression.[35] Her art, rehashed and tamed – or at least having obtained the dubious honour of political correctness – is transmuted into a product and becomes a pale copy as well as a fake advertising of itself, as Owen notices:

> It cannot but disappoint – this expensive remake of that stoner game they'd played so many times, only Dot has filmed it and so it entered the canon of art history. The people in this remake are professional actors, their lines scripted. The lighting and production values, superb, almost Hollywood. Their faces, all different in ethnic mix, reflecting the pressure to be politically correct that Dot's work in the last few years had succumbed to. (*M*, 48)

As Dorothy's works are endlessly recycled and turned into commodities which reveal the emptiness of their own meaning, and as Saul, who bridges the gap between life and art by turning himself into a work of art, is discarded from the narrative by literally disappearing into the background only to reappear as a broken man, an empty shell without substance and even as a bitter tramp in Owen's nightmares, what surfaces from the novel is an overwhelming feeling of emptiness, as Morrison explains about Dot's artwork:

> They are empty artworks or mirrors to the culture – I had to make them like that because I wanted to show the way that Art got emptied of meaning in the 90s. We became culture addicts, consuming culture that was itself just a mirror of culture that had been made before – recycling to fill the void.[36]

The indictment applies in the novel to the inspiration and instigator of rebelliousness himself, Saul, whose philosophy of life and art appears at the end of the novel to have in fact been plagiarised, stolen from a book of quotes. Together with the empty circularity of Dot's works which feed on their own emptiness, it projects the world as a consumerist hell, a world from which no independent critical or creative discourse can emerge. This statement of the dead-end of art appears as a foregone conclusion in an early scene where Owen undergoes an epiphany simultaneously tainted by failure:

> It was then as I felt the cars push wind on my face, as I surrendered to their power, that I realised I would never escape from that voice that dared to show me the world in negative, to turn all I had known inside out, and speak to me through other people and things. In that moment all judgment fell away and I glimpsed the fatal beauty of it all. The cars were unstoppable in their force, capitalism could not be overthrown, these things were not external to me, to be critiqued, but inside me, as alive as the toxic car fumes in my lungs. I was of it, and it of me, and the headlights became stars that wept for me. I roared with laughter then and fell headlong into that scepticism that had long been brewing. I fell and all I once believed in fell away. At the end of the overpass I threw my papers to the ground and walked away. Within the week, I had said my goodbyes to Debs and my degree and I became the student of the terrifying laughing man who saw beauty in the crap of the world. (*M*, 23)

This realisation, this hope for a liberation of creativity that conjures up the possible opening up of a path of freedom is doomed from the start as Owen realises that 'these things were not external to me, to be critiqued, but inside me'. The structure of the novel also makes this clear for the reader, by starting on a piece of criticism of Dot's later work which reduces the attempts at rebellious expression depicted in the following chapters to a void of empty consumption, to the status of products that travel the world by FedEx, justifying Morrison's statement that 'the curse of contemporary art is that it is a commodity'.[37] Rebellion, independent expression, is therefore pre-empted by commodification, as the vast discourse of emptiness is being caricatured by the academic-style essays that precede each of the parts of the novel. As meaningless appraisals succeed one another – 'But the message of [Dorothy] Shears's work is a non-negative or anti-message' (*M*, 90); 'A popular interpretation of this filmed "game" is that it critiques the influence of media culture on the postmodern subject' (*M*, 131) – the value of art itself is being questioned. In that context, it is the human which seems to be contaminated by this commodification and mass marketing of what is supposedly individual, unique.[38] This issue enters the narrative in the shape of an unnamed character who makes a transient appearance and whose role in the plot is unclear as she may or may not be Dorothy's assistant or agent. As Owen puts it, '[s]he seemed like a Wall Street broker or PR girl for some transient product that was basically herself' (*M*, 100). The girl's presence in the novel can only be satisfactorily explained as a representation of Dorothy herself, the creative artist with a supposedly personal and original discourse on the world, who basically has only one product left to sell – herself.

Morrison, however, suggests an escape from this creative dead-end, or rather, to the stifling of expression by the overwhelming urge to transform everything, including oneself, into marketable products. In the last chapter the temporal and formal distance between life and art disappears as Owen, lying in a hospital bed, hears a conversation between Dorothy and Saul, who are sitting at his bedside, and simultaneously projects that conversation on a blank screen, while the scene itself is also recast in the shape of the critical essay that the reader is familiar with. This last scene, which conflates elements that were until then distributed into alternate chapters and in which all voices – artistic, narrative, exegetic – coalesce, destroys the distance between life and art for a fleeting moment. It also serves as a reminder that the novel itself is a hybrid, almost a collage, as it puts together text (both the fictional text, and the pastiche of artistic review, complete with footnotes that provide real as well as apocryphal references) and image, with the photos, the stills from Dorothy's works which are actually photographs that Morrison found on the internet. If one takes into account the fact that he also made trailers – short videos presenting/advertising the book which can be found on his website, and which also tell the story, or at least their own visual version of the story – then the novel as a whole cannot be seen as just a reflection on the emptiness of art in the 1990s. It turns into an artistic answer to that statement, by turning the whole of the 'book' or rather the artwork, if one considers its video appendages, into an installation on paper and video, which gives the reader a glimpse of itself. After the chapters consisting of the reviews, Owen's third-person narrative in the 2000s and Owen's first-person narrative in the 1990s, the making of the art object finally, and against all odds, appears in the process of being created in the last chapter, as it dawns on the reader that Owen has in fact been making the composite narrative all along. The artist becomes a synthesis of a variety of identities, setting gender and sex aside, conflating various elements of inspiration.

Thus reconsidered, *Ménage* raises the question of plagiarism, the thematic core of the novel, as a new, valid form of artistic creation, in an age that Morrison calls 'multiscreen', in the process erasing some the of the most enduring distinctions that even the postmodern era has struggled to challenge. In an article in *The Guardian* entitled 'Factual Fiction: Writing in an Information Age', Morrison takes the example of the uproar that was created in France when Michel Houellebecq cut and pasted sections of Wikipedia into his novel *The Map is Not the Territory* to predict that 'multiscreening [...] necessarily involves the collapse of a few forms that we have previously held as sacrosanct, not least the distinction between fact and fiction'.[39] One of Saul's aphorisms in *Ménage* warns us: 'I fear irony is dead. We shall be laughing ourselves into mass graves' (*M*, 99). Morrison, taking his cue from his character[40] and working against the disappearance of irony, uses it as the basis for the organisation of his novel, managing to portray the vacancy of art in the 1990s and the dead-end it led artists to, as well as to suggest a way of exploiting that meaninglessness to generate new meanings, new ways of perceiving the world we live in. This reflects the vital role to be played by irony in the literal sense of the word, the Greek sense of dissembling. If one is to draw some optimism from *Ménage*, it is to be found in the idea that art is bound to change the way we see ourselves and therefore the way we are. It empties, vacates and recycles, but also exploits this process to provide fresh ways of describing the world.

So ultimately, what Morrison is carving in his novels is a space of fiction in the vital, very literal sense of a space for art to combat the advent of a reality which, in the sweeping movement of banal nationalism, turns space into non-places, consumerises the unmarketable and threatens to disempower the human. Finally, therefore, Morrison believes both in the necessity to reconsider our definition of art, and in its capacity to shape events or to alter their course, to have an impact on the trajectory of contemporary history. Put in the aphoristic style that constitutes Saul's trademark, '[a]rt saves us from the prison of history' (*M*, 26).

Notes

1. Gallix, Andrew. 2009. 'More Thanatos than Eros: Ewan Morrison Interviewed by Andrew Gallix', First published in 3:*AM Magazine*: Friday, August 28 www.3ammagazine.com/3am/more-thanatos-than-eros/ [consulted February 2011].
2. Bauman, Zygmunt. [2000] 2012. *Liquid Modernity* (Cambridge: Polity), p. 2.
3. Holcombe, Garan. 2007. 'Author Profile – Ewan Morrison', www.contemporarywriters.com [consulted April 2009].
4. Morrison, Ewan. 2009. 'Death of a Nihilist or Obituary for a Nobody', *3AM Magazine*, July 5, www.3ammagazine.com/3am/death-of-a-nihilist-or-obituary-for-a-nobody/ [consulted November 2009].
5. Schoene, 2007, p. 15.
6. Augé, Marc. [1992] 2008. *Non-Places: An Introduction to Supermodernity* (London: Verso), pp. 63–64. Morrison engages with this notion of the non-place in all his works. *Tales from the Mall*, published by Cargo in 2012, and accompanied by internet resources in the shape of short clips both on Morrison's website at ewanmorrison.com and on YouTube, is a sort of logical conclusion to the exploration of this concept of the non-place and its consequences for human relationships.
7. The pronoun 'you' is consistently used by the two lovers throughout their affair in an ungrammatical position as both first and second person pronouns. It is therefore a byword for their love, 'it's you' indifferently meaning 'it's me' or 'it's you' only for the two of them.
8. Morrison declared in an interview that he was interested in 'people who lose themselves in different worlds when they log onto the internet'. See Gelonesi, Joe. 2005. 'Interview with Ewan Morrison', *ABC*, www.abc.net.au/rn/bookshow/stories/2007/2014517.htm [consulted August 2009].
9. As David says when he logs on, 'Goodbye world, Hello swinging-paradise' (*S*, 112).
10. Morrison, in Gelonesi. On Ikea and its eradication of the human and the individual, see Pittin-Hedon, Marie-Odile (2008), '"Learn Your Own Way to Read the Map": rôle et place du roman écossais dans le processus de dévolution', *Babel*, 17, pp. 195–210.
11. Morrison, in Gelonesi.
12. Morrison, Ewan. 2009. 'Could it be that at the age of ten I had grasped the essence of alienation?' *Scotland on Sunday*, 16 August, www.scotsman.com/ewan-morrison/Ewan-Morrison-39Could-it-be.5558233.jp [consulted October 2009].
13. Baudrillard, Jean. [1968] 1996. *The System of Objects*, trans. James Benedict (London and NY: Verso), p. 218.
14. In *Tales from the Mall* Morrison writes the story of the commodification of the human by starting precisely from the place that epitomises the process – the shopping mall. The result, a mixture of vignettes, anecdotes, short stories and fact-finding sections, can

therefore be seen as a logical follow up to *Swung* and *Distance* as it adds to the reflection a disintegration of the traditional means of telling a story. This refusal to abide by the rules separating fiction from reality is an indication of the way the commodification process is taking over our entire – *and* very real – lives.
15 This feature is repeated at a more intimate level, when Alice describes how her mother cut her father's face out of family photographs.
16 It is an ultimate attempt because it is situated at the end of the novel.
17 Bakhtin, Mikhail. 1968. *Rabelais and His World*, Trans. Helene Iswolsky (Cambridge, Mass.: MIT Press), p. 3.
18 Jameson, Fredric. 1986. 'On Magic Realism in Film', *Critical Enquiry*, vol. 12, no.2, p. 307.
19 Alice pitches the show to her boss as '*Big Brother* meets key parties meets the 60s' (*S*, 118).
20 Ross, Peter. 2007. 'Sultan of Swing', *Herald Scotland*, 7 April, www.heraldscotland.com/sultan-of-swing-1.836350 [consulted August2009].
21 Larsonneur, Claire. 2009. 'Location, location, location', *Etudes Britanniques Contemporaines*, no. 37, Décembre, p. 150. Italics mine.
22 See Bell, Eleanor. 2004. 'Postmodernism, Nationalism and the Question of Tradition', in Bell and Miller (eds), pp. 84–85.
23 See for instance the curiously autonomous story of Meg's old neighbour on Fire Island, who gives her a pair of size 10 stilettos before telling her the story of his transvestite boyfriend who died of AIDS in the 1980s, a narrative which could be read as a separate short story.
24 Best, Steven and Douglas Kellner. 1999. 'Debord, Cybersituations and the Interactive Spectacle', *SubStance*, vol. 28, no. 3, Issue 90, p. 132. Morrison both in his fiction and in interviews makes it clear that Guy Debord, and *The Society of the Spectacle* in particular, is a key influence on his work.
25 Debord, Guy. 1967. *The Society of the Spectacle*, Chapter 2, § 42, quoted in Best, p. 130.
26 As Tom scathingly remarks, 'this one word […] had been used in about fifty other campaigns for everything from men's electric razors to tampons' (*D*, 237).
27 In Edinburgh all the souvenir shops also sell little statues of a Gibson-looking Wallace, a very real sign of the phenomenon underlined in the novel.
28 See Bauman (2000: 100–04). Bauman contrasts phagic spaces with emic spaces, places which vomit, reject the individual.
29 Bauman, Zygmunt. 1998. *Globalization: The Human Consequences* (Cambridge: Polity), pp. 2–3.
30 Here we touch upon the dystopian, in a perversion of the *1984* model of erasure of the past at the hands of a totalitarian regime.
31 According to Morrison, Tom is 'pro-capitalist against the forces of Scottishness. While Meg, in contrast, is appalled at her own country, the all-American patriotism, and has a dream to escape it and be somewhere more authentic – Scotland', in Gallix.
32 In Joe Gelonesi's interview, Morrison says that he is more interested in middle-class Scottish characters, thus widening the scope of the novels' social analysis.
33 For Alice, 'Fucking was hard to objectify. There was always some kind of human contact. Not just two adverts rubbing against each other. […] There was negotiation. Empathy. Humour' (*S*, 155–56).
34 Baudrillard, quoted in Bauman (1998: 88).

35 Incidentally Dorothy's fate, her being inexorably absorbed in the cycle of consumption, could also express Morrison's own view on contemporary art and particularly the current situation of the YBAs, as the characters in the novel desacralise both the artists who desacralised art and their famous patron, by suggesting titles for Dorothy's own works such as 'Baked Hirst with the formidable formaldehyde sauce!', 'Tampon Terrine à la Emin', or 'Saucisson à la Saatchi', this last a happening which would consist in making 'Charles Saatchi eat his own intestines as a piece of performance art and make him pay for the privilege' (*M*, 205). One notes the food metaphor, which aims for the literal meaning of the word 'consumption'.
36 Gallix, p. 12.
37 Ibid., p. 10.
38 The other artistic movement *Ménage* refers to is of course Pop Art, in particular Andy Warhol's work on both repeating and recycling and on American consumer society. Warhol is actually mentioned in the book, although only in the essays' footnotes. See for example note 6, on p. 91.
39 Morrison, Ewan. 2012. 'Factual fiction: writing in an information age', *The Guardian*, Friday 2 March, www.guardian.co.uk/books/2012/mar/02/fact-fiction-writing-information-age [consulted April 2012]. It is to be noted that, in accordance with this position, Morrison conceived of *Tales from the Mall* (2012) as a 'multi-screen' art object, as the book was intended to be published by Cargo Crate as an enhanced e-book, with links to Morrison's own videos and other material from the internet. The e-book unfortunately could not be produced, but the videos are still there.
40 The distinction between himself and his character is actually very difficult to establish here, as Morrison wrote an article for *3:AM* in which he goes over the life of a supposedly dead artist friend of his who is an exact replica of/model for Saul in *Ménage*. At the end of the paper, however, Morrison confirms that 'In fact my friend didn't die. That was a lie. He never existed. Or rather he was who I used to be'. See Morrison, 'Death of a Nihilist or Obituary for a Nobody'.

6. The Confines of the Human: Shorter Fiction by Michel Faber, Des Dillon, Suhayl Saadi, Ewan Morrison and *Scotland Into The New Era*

The turn of the century has indeed been the symbolic occasion for the publication of many short stories, commissioned or otherwise, by many writers throughout the country. This last chapter aims to examine shorter fiction originating from most of the directions sketched in the preceding chapters, and will analyse stories written by some of the authors appearing in this book. It will address the 'writing Scotland' postulate, namely the connection between the national idea and literary output. Indeed, in the wake of the establishment of the Scottish Parliament and in the run up to the new millennium, Waterstone's, *The Herald* and the publisher Canongate, for example, launched a literary competition for shorter fiction which resulted in the publication by Canongate of the 2000 volume the title of which, *Scotland Into The New Era*, provides its theme. In the foreword to the volume the publisher, Jamie Byng, notes the success of the venture, with 1,251 entries for the first edition of the competition, as well as the versatility of the responses to the question of Scotland facing the new millennium. The collection contains stories by Anne Donovan, Janet Paisley, James Robertson and Dilys Rose, as well as by less established writers. This chapter will look at its particular contribution to the creative redefinition of Scotland, in connection with other 'post-millennial fables'[1] or short stories that were published during the first decade of the 2000s, namely those collected in Des Dillon's *They Scream When You Kill Them* (2006), Michel Faber's *The Fahrenheit Twins* (2005), Ewan Morrison's *The Last Book You Read* (2005) and Suhayl Saadi's *The Burning Mirror* (2001).[2] They take the reader to various locations in Scotland, both urban and rural as in Dillon's stories, back and forth across the Atlantic in Morrison's fiction or in 'Millennium Babe', Donovan's story in *Scotland Into The New Era*, to London, or the North Pole in Faber's collection, as well as Scotland and the Middle East in Saadi's stories. Between them, these collections of stories therefore map a world that is not contained within the geographical boundaries of Scotland, while describing a sense of alienation and making a plea for an increased humanity and communality.[3] Together, they seem to provide a fictional reaction not to the setting up of the Scottish parliament or to the future of Scotland after devolution, but to a more compelling issue, summed up by the comment voiced by Irvine Welsh, and addressed in different ways in the previous chapters of this book, that 'We've created a world where it's not a good time to be human'.[4]

Des Dillon's story 'Darwin the Wise Old Space Elephant', in a manner that borrows from the genre of the parable and therefore links the stories with much more universal ones, stresses the necessity to adjust to our environment and not force the environment to adjust to us, warning that, if we stop adapting, we'll spell out the extinction of our species. All the stories examined in this chapter in their own way reflect on the changed environment the characters are placed in, and the vital necessity for them to adapt, by altering the parameters of their self-definition in a globalised world. The old and the new, therefore, are considered not as a neat dichotomy, but rather in the complexity of their interaction, as is suggested by the 'old' and 'new' Glasgow ironically presented in Dillon's story with an arch-Scottish title, 'Jock Tamson's Bus'. As the passengers on a bus going through the Castlemilk area of Glasgow fearfully observe a thuggish-looking man with a scarred face and his wife, the narrator reflects on old and new Glasgow, explaining that '[t]heir mother's Glasgow's come back. Slums and razor gangs. They said it was gone. The new cosmopolitanism had wiped that out. But the man with the scar's still talking low and tickling the wane' (*SWKT*, 55).

This chapter focuses on how the stories, in their own separate ways, work towards a shift from the popular understanding of the term 'cosmopolitanism' as it is being used in this quotation, with its questionable undertones, to a more operative concept which focuses on the characters' desperate need to connect – rather than to brand or label – in all the stories.[5] The crucial question of adapting to one's environment, suggested in both this quotation and in 'Darwin the Wise Old Space Elephant', is tackled in the collections of short stories by Faber, Saadi, Morrison and Dillon, as well as the stories contained in *Scotland Into The New Era*. Between them they provide a set of examples, sometimes delivered in an essayistic manner and sometimes borrowing from fantasy or the grotesque, that combine not only to describe the adapting process but also to project the world to come. In the words of the wise elephant:

> When they had tamed the Earth they believed they had reached the end of their journey. Their final destiny. But the Divine Power is Change. Otherwise there is only stagnation. The force that drives us through the journey will not countenance stagnation. The journey is the meaning not the destination. There are no destinations, only pauses. Hiatuses. (*SWKT*, 76)

The stories are attempts to make sense of those hiatuses, of history, of personal and social relationship, of the place of the human in a capitalist society, as well as to imagine the type of communication that can be established between narrator and reader, the capacity of the story to reach out to its readers and connect what is usually regarded to be disconnected. They offer a challenging outlook on the millennial idea of renewal and progress.

A Brave New World?

As Joe, the character in 'Jock Tamson's bus' with the deep cut across his cheek, uncharacteristically takes leave of his wife in a moment of quiet domesticity, the other passengers contemplate the scene from inside the bus:

> And we're amazed at half a smile in window by passing window. The other half of his face sleeping in a palm of pain. Frame after frame our minds are changing. People even looking at each other and shaking their heads. Admitting it. For a minute, Croftfoot and Castlemilk don't exist. We're all on Jock Tamson's bus.
> As we leave Joe behind we're arranging our thoughts. As we pass over into the city, in the distance you can see the sun glinting off the new buildings right along the river. Glasgow reaches for the sky. For all we know it could be a Brave New World. (*SWKT*, 56)

This subdued epiphany hints at the possibility for a new life in newly-designed Glasgow as the passengers get a glimpse of possible felicity, communality and of an overturn of social clichés about the city.[6] Yet the reference to Huxley's novel, now integral to Western mythology, and the focus on a character whose face is quite literally split between the benign interpretation and that involving danger and pain, point to the possibility for a new, creative, conquering and communal Scotland while simultaneously branding it as confidently over-simplistic, with a hint of the pseudo-utopian turned dystopian. The epsilon characters gathered on the bus,[7] for the short period that it takes to leave Joe behind, dream themselves into a happy end, a state of community that many of the other stories in the collection, or in Faber's and Saadi's stories, undermine. In David Edwards' story 'The Sick Man of Europe', as in Des Dillon's 'The Blue Hen', 'Gold Roman Coins' and 'Jif Lemons', or in Suhayl Saadi's 'The Queens of Govan', the world depicted is one of poverty and loneliness, of violence, sectarianism, bigotry and racism where the main feature characterising the new community of Jock Tamson's bairns is their isolation and absence of communication, the side of the face 'sleeping in a palm of pain'. This is demonstrated in a paroxystic way in 'Jif Lemon', in which three 'Neds' barge upon a fishing party in the Highlands, rape a girl then appear to cut her up with a chainsaw before going after the terrorised narrator and his friend. In this story, as in many others, the ironic relationship between the story's title and its contents reinforces the discrepancy between the projected world and the persistence of the 'old' reality. This is also the case in 'Gold Roman Coins', a title evocative of wealth in a story which chronicles a tragic misunderstanding which leads to a working-class boy and his friend being stoned outside of their house which the angry neighbours have set on fire. In Edwards' story 'A sick man from Europe', the irony lies in the discrepancy between the situation – that of a man on the dole, formerly in the merchant navy who does 'the bucket round', collecting things from rubbish bins, and planning to commit suicide by jumping from the high flats – and the title, which gives the story a superficial and unexplained cosmopolitan shine. In this solipsistic narrative the choice of the first person coupled with a very natural oral style renders the external world unsuccessful at penetrating it. The narrator's only communication with the outside is through a council leaflet, the contents of which reminds the reader in a darkly comic manner of the inadequacy of the policies aimed at the poor, and therefore of the communication gap that exists in a world split along economic lines:

> I got this leaflet from the dole the other day all about good eating habits, giving up smoking and cutting back on drinking. The first thing I thought was how much it must have cost them to send out and what gave an overpaid suit the right to tell me what to do. (*SNE*, 64–65)

The notion of a split world is conveyed in Saadi's stories, by one of his 'queens' of Govan, Ruby, an 'Asian Babe' working in a kebab shop who has to come to terms with casual and aggressive racism and the lack of prospect for her life in an area where there is no escaping stereotype:[8]

> Ye couldnae hide in Govan. It wis aw pubs an carry-oots an alleyways where dogs an hookers plied their trade. Dark places, amidst the neon. It wis either wan, or the other. If ye tried tae live between the two, you would split apart like the moon. Or like Pakistan. (*BM*, 26)

The heavily accented Scottish voice coupled with the choice of simile stresses the impossible choice Ruby faces in a way that both foregrounds and sidelines the Scottish versus Asian dichotomy. In this story, as in Des Dillon's 'Echo', darkness becomes a metaphorical vehicle for the feelings of rage, guilt, and hopelessness that accompany the character's descent into social, racial and political oblivion. For Stevie in 'Echo', who leaves his drunken alcoholic brother behind in a dark close-mouth to drive his car onto the main street of his 'normal' life, there is only guilt. The feeling is a seething rage for Ruby as she can no longer isolate one particular form of oppression:

> Donners on their own were the most common order. They filled bellies which rolled wi beer an lager. Filled and neutralised the rage which simmered beneath the skins ae Govan. The rage ae the dead ships an the closed factory gates an the games lost and won; an the rage of the marchers wi their blue-an-orange banners which had been hauled, blood-spattered, fae houses ae God. An sometimes

Ruby had felt herself tae be a part of that inchoate fury but she had shied away from it because she knew that, like the great, black waters ae the Clyde River, it would sweep her away, not to the sea but to a darkness from when there would be nae return. (*BM*, 32)

In the anaphoric repetition of the word 'rage' the target is this Brave New World which, seen from the point of view of the Govan underclass, is a primitive world of darkness and fury.

Faber's own contribution to the Brave New World motif appears in 'The Eyes of the Soul', in which Jeanette, a middle-aged mother living with her son on a sink estate, acquires a contraption called an 'Outlook', a large screen that can be fitted onto her window and which reflects a pastoral scenery complete with a sloping meadows, rose bushes, a trellis of tomatoes, and geese and owls at night. On the flick of a switch, Jeanette can replace the real view from her window, which, prompted by the saleswoman, she describes as 'shite' (*FT*, 37),[9] and have access to a virtual reality that she quickly and quite simply assumes to be the stuff of real life, explaining to her amazed son that the geese 'just live here' (*FT*, 44). In this magic realist story, the intrusion of the unfamiliar into the familiar points to a very bitter conception of the world of innovation and creation symbolised in 'Jock Tamson's Bus' by the Glasgow skyline: as in Huxley's *Brave New World*, the epsilons are entertained by a new version of the flicks that can contain the dark side of their anger and manipulate them into obedience, this turning into a latter-day cynical comment on the disappearing trick performed by the councils, and more generally those in charge of social questions in the contemporary world of technology and consumerism, a theme that is also present in Morrison's stories.[10] Dillon's dystopian story also nods towards Alasdair Gray's *Lanark*, in which the 'proles' are similarly monitored and controlled, with a windscreen device that virtually transports their 'mohomes' (literally an automobile turned into a home) from the dreary line of cars parked on the curb of a side street to an idyllic garden or a breathless video-game type car race.[11] The Marxist line of criticism which features in Gray's novel is supplemented by a slogan that permeates the whole novel: 'man is the pie that bakes and eats itself and the recipe is separation' (1981: 101), pointing at a crucial theme common to the collections. The intertextual connection with Gray's novel, fittingly for Faber, who insists that he writes his stories starting from a mood rather than a theme or a thesis, bears on the reader's awareness of a discrepancy between the generic choices and their consequences. Whereas Gray uses the proles-controlling device in the fantastic part of his novel, thereby complying with the futuristic/dystopian motif, Faber, in magic realistic fashion, imports the fantastic into the realistic narrative of the here-and-now. The connection with Gray's novel therefore conveys to the reader a sense of doom, or at least of a danger which seems to be getting closer to their own reality. A brave new world seems threateningly to have mutated into a not so brave old world, a persistent world impervious to moods and fashions in criticism or sociological analysis. This re-appropriation of the dystopian in literature, which resolutely keeps the realistic in view of the fantastic, raises the issue of the respective impact of history and stories.

Choose your future

Dilys Rose's 'Out of touch' (*SNE*), an essayistic narrative about Alba, the 'old hag', points out the critical over-investment in the notion of newness when it comes to describing the future of a nation:

> It will be interesting to see what becomes acceptable terminology in the extensively revised dictionary of the new nation. The word 'new' of course, is a nonsense in this context. No nation starts from scratch. When it comes to nations, there is no such thing as new, only the old with a face-lift and slathers of make-up to mask the ravages of history, geography, religion, economics and so on. Like a bygone star whose public appearances are limited by how long the pan-stick will stay in place and cover the surgeon's scars, this revived, renovated nation poses for the world's press holding a tense, slightly startled smile. (*SNE*, 188)

This opinion of the hype that surrounds the ultimately debatable question of the 'new nation' is shared by many of the authors who contributed to the collection, amongst whom is Stephen Livingston who satirises the idea of a new era in 'Choose your Future', a pastiche of the famous 'Choose life' monologue in Irvine Welsh's 1993 *Trainspotting*. Livingston's story depicts a young narrator speaking in the second person who, while at a nightclub with his friend Tommy, passes out to experience a trance-like episode which might be described as *Alice in Wonderland* being whisked into the universe of *Trainspotting*. He finds himself in a white room with three doors, a voice telling him to choose his future in a tone that refuses to take itself seriously, 'Obi Wan Kenobi's voice [which] begin[s] a Mark Renton-from-*Trainspotting*-style rant' (*SNE*, 106). Behind the first door is Donald Dewar attired as a juggling clown and perched on a unicycle, who gives him the standard discourse on devolution, unsurprisingly claiming that 'in the realm of politics lies our future. For the first time in almost three hundred years we, the people of Scotland, have our own parliament' (*SNE*, 107). The second door opens on Dr Ian Wilmut, the scientist at the origin of the cloning of Dolly the sheep, who equally predictably advocates choosing science for a brighter future. As the reader is lulled into a sense that what he is reading is a rather conventional satire on Scotland's contemporary politics, the third door brings a new dimension to the story's title, turning it from a Renton-style sarcastic jibe on the political and scientific discourse of the country to a militant indictment of the type of society that the first two ultimately condone by ignoring the economically driven model that the modern capitalist world has created. It is a robust plea for a *meaningful* choice, a choice for a society that needs to reinvent its own bases by moving away from the economic towards the creative. The dark-suited economist behind the third door advocates such a paradigmatic shift:

> Profit, loss, buy, sell, consumer capitalism, it's all a load of horseshit. A game of monopoly made real, a stupid game for stupid people. Take the money and burn it. The way forward for mankind is through art. It is the creation of art that puts man in touch with the divinity within and allows the soul to shine free. [...] Whether it be the painter, the poet or the architect dreaming spires and towers of the glorious word in myriad hues it has always been and always will be the creative mind that leads the way. (*SNE*, 109–10)

However, as in Lewis Carroll's book, which was conceived as a temporary entertainment for young Alice Liddell, this affirmation of the supreme power of the creative, which provides the most freedom because it touches upon the metaphysical and is therefore the real choice for the future, is quickly snuffed out in 'Choose your Future'. The narrator comes back to his senses to a world of drugs and alcohol that has just cracked open to reveal the utopian choice of a future that is finally not to be and that, because of the use of the second person pronoun throughout the story, seemingly excludes the reader too. This theme is linked to Ewan Morrison's stories, which insist on the commodification of the self in a capitalist and consumerist society which turns human beings into 'crass little consumers',[12] with relationships that are consumed rather than committed to, spelling out a future marked by loneliness and vacuity.

James Robertson's own contribution to the Choose your Future theme, like Dilys Rose's, is offered in the form of an essay, 'Six Deaths, Two Funerals, a Wedding and a Divorce'. The narrator, who might be assumed to be Robertson himself, reflects on the ten high profile events in the history of contemporary Britain that have shaped the way the country defines itself, drawing for instance a parallel between Prince Charles's royal divorce and the phrase commonly used during the campaign for the first election to a Scottish parliament, the 'Anglo-Scottish divorce', or between Princess Diana's death and the deaths of Hugh MacDiarmid and John Smith. Unsurprisingly for an author who then went on to write historical novels, as well as the examination of the space of history in *And The Land Lay Still*, Robertson insists in his essay on the necessary connection with the past, as the only possibility for the present to shape the future:

> L. P. Hartley's well-worn phrase about the past being a foreign country has been rattling around in my head for years: *they do things differently there*. Seductive but misleading. Yes, they do; but *they* are also *us*, we are them. We had better not discard the past too lightly. It is all we have of ourselves. (*SNE*, 180)

What Robertson points out in this essay is the necessity first to choose one's past in order to be able to choose one's future, not in the sense of selecting or editing history, but rather in a proactive move to embrace one's past as an entity, almost a territory, as is indicated by the shift from the temporal to the spatial in this quotation. The connection that is drawn between 'them' and 'us' is also a reminder of the link between personal, individual history and the wider concept of the historical, as the narrator in Dillon's

'Nine-Eleven', going over a personal memory triggered by the 9/11 attacks, also reminds the reader, noting that 'It's funny, no matter how we try to dress it up, events are always personal' (*SWKT*, 33).

This paradigmatic link between the personal and the historical, in the sense of the first being the dimension against which the second is ultimately measured, this territorial dimension of history, is also very present in Peter Dorward's, Suhayl Saadi's and Ewan Morrison's stories. Saadi uses a geological metaphor in both 'Ninety-nine Kiss-o-grams' and 'Lughnasadh', in which the protagonists respectively feel 'as though he was sinking into the soil' (*BM*, 7) and had been 'turned into compost for the forest's avid consumption' (*BM*, 94). Both these metaphors lead back to Robertson's own version of 'the ghost of history' in *As The Land Lay Still*, returned to the earth in a very similar manner.[13] Dorward, in 'The Remains', takes the metaphor to a literal outcome by describing the fate of the only inhabitant of an Orkney island who, in the event of an excavation conducted by three paleo-anthropologists, is eerily equated with the human remains they have come to investigate. As the narrator feels that his face 'sinks slowly into mud', and that '[it] becomes harder and harder to breathe' (*SNE*, 59), he quite literally transforms his narrative of the event into a vestigial narrative, some archaeological remains for future commentators to interpret. In this story, as in Ewan Morrison's 'The Speech', it is the description of the destructive and yet constitutive power of the past which makes the narrative of the present possible. As the narrator in 'The Remains' is finally destroyed and discarded by the palaeontologists, who should preserve the remains of the past, but instead consume it to suit their own agenda, so does the narrator of 'The Speech' come to state his own inability to confront his personal history, because of his leaving 'history' in a loose sense behind, because of his refusal to choose history as one chooses one's future. Sean, a Scots immigrant to the US now with an American family and having to write the speech for his father's funeral taking place in Scotland, realises his own connection with the trauma of history:

> It was no wonder he was here now in Brooklyn. As soon as he could, he'd moved as far away from his father as possible. Got a career and put an ocean between them. When he moved and married an American, his mother cried. His father was horrified. What about

Vietnam? Bush? The religious right and the bourgeoisie? 'How could you live there, son?' But that was the point. To get away – to go, like the Pilgrim Fathers had done, escaping persecution and history. A history that was oppressive and would have destroyed you if you'd stayed. (*LBYR*, 28–29)

In the suppression of history, therefore, all Sean is left with is the sense of a void, an inability to write, encapsulated in the opening words: 'He went into Edit, clicked Select All and then hit the delete key. It wouldn't do. He'd have to start again. The cursor sat on the screen blinking at him as he rubbed his eyes' (*LBYR*, 20).

Anne Donovan and Ian Mitchell in their separate ways also tackle the notion of history as the only way of defining the future. Mitchell does that in a straightforwardly futuristic way in 'Just you Wait, You'll See' by presenting a diary of the future written by one Douglas Macdour starting in January 2049. Macdour, the embodiment of that proverbial Scottish characteristic, presents a future in which many symbols of the Scottish past and identity have been trivialised: Burns Night becomes the day for the disposal of rubbish, the derelict Parliament building drops big slabs onto the passing tourists, and Ben Lomond is being relocated five miles to the north as 'Scottish Heritage feels that they 'have no wish to be regarded as narrow-minded [...], standing in the path of progress' (*SNE*, 143). Similarly Donovan's 'Millennium Babe', the story of the spectacular rise in the world of the first baby born in the millennium, a Scottish girl, charts the possible development of Scotland in the world through this character whose name, Caledonia Scott, begs for an allegorical interpretation. Ironically Caledonia, whose mother refuses numerous offers of baby sponsorship as a way of foreclosing the consumerist galore set off by this symbolic date of birth and forms high hopes for her in the political future of Scotland, goes on twenty years later to become a very successful designer who markets the paltry remains of a commodified Scottish identity to an international consumer society. For Caledonia, as for Douglas Macdour, the Scots language, Burns, Henryson and Scottish literature in general are 'minority interests' (*SNE*, 40), and her understanding of the history of Scotland foregrounds twenty-first century global capitalism:

While I was studying it was still difficult to find markets, get capital, but since we became a fully federated member state of the Euro-American Alliance in 2021 things have really taken off. [...] what's the point of independence in the world we live in? Global markets are what's important. You can't get access to the kind of capital you need if you're a small nation. I mean we still have our identity. I'm sure part of the popularity of my work is because it's recognisably Scottish. Without the tartan motif it could be from any sophisticated European nation. (*SNE*, 39–40)

In this mindless commodification of the past in which markers of national identity such as language itself have been downgraded to the level of mere selling points, meaning starts to seep out of communication, as when Caledonia describes her artistic approach to the Scottish language as 'post-modern, post-millennium if you like; witty, ironic' (*SNE*, 41).[14] The retreat behind the meaninglessness of the 'post' prefix is set against the mother's own wishes and dreams for her daughter, which are introduced into the story in a letter she sends her on her twenty-first birthday:

Afore ye were born ah dreamed ye'd be somethin in the Parliament, the first President mibbe, but ah'm yer mither first and foremost and ah want ye tae be happy and fulfilled, so ah'm proud and pleased at the way ye're gaun on at the art school and ah've nae doots ye'll be a fine artist fur Scotland wan o these days. Keep faith in yersel and Scotland, lass. (*SNE*, 38)

In that context, the last words of the story, the interviewer's rather stereotyped thanks and good wishes, 'I'm sure that with people like you at the forefront of Scotland's business world the future of Caledonia is bright!' (*SNE*, 41) not only sound ironic, but, because of the commodification of history which has been turned into anecdotal titbits to enhance the marketing and selling of products,[15] it seems as if they are words that are pronounced over a great void, the void of the future of Scotland. This future Scotland has sunk into the lower drawers of global marketing, providing a fictional confirmation to Morrison's repeated indictment of consumer capitalism, or to Faber's comment that 'crassness and commercialism and ugliness have always been with us'.[16]

Displacing the real

In Donovan's story, the past is stripped of its historical weight to be reduced to its anecdotal, recreational value. In Des Dillon's stories, not only history, but also violence, the humiliation of human beings by other human beings, is depicted in terms of its entertaining potential. Both 'Soap Opera' and 'Jock Tamson's Bus' describe fights between people as entertainment – whether on script for a TV soap, on the streets when people queuing at a bus stop witness a heated argument between a young woman and the man who appears to be her pimp, or on the bus, between lower-class men and women. This theme of the consumption of the human in the shape of the downgrading of human life to the extent that, as Dillon's title 'Soap Opera' indicates, the reality of our lives becomes as staged and unreal as a cheap TV programme, points to the shallowness and meaninglessness of human existence when not inserted within a historical context.

For Ewan Morrison's characters, choosing their future is equally illusory. He places his protagonists in a world that has no depth, which seems to have forfeited the past in favour of a present that also commodifies the human. For Morrison, the globalised world is symbolised by global retail companies such as Ikea, which is a world that offers the consumerist illusion of possible choices and of a possible future for individuals – an illusion simultaneously contradicted, even derided, by the lack of prospects for his characters who all seem to be trapped in the commercial transaction in which the self becomes at once the product and the currency. This simultaneous entrapment and infinite multiplication of the self into myriad identical versions of itself is expressed in 'Stoop':

> Once you put this Ikea crap together, you're not really supposed to take it apart again. [...] Fucking Ikea. For the last six years, it's been buying it, having to sell it, moving, then going to another store and buying the same damn things again. Lillehammer bed. Low-to-midrange. It's the third one we've had now. [...] All our friends have them too. So, no doubt, when we're back together in London, we'll be buying another one. Walk round the megastore, like sleepwalkers.

THE CONFINES OF THE HUMAN: SHORTER FICTION

> Could do it blind now. Even though the place is like a maze, it's the same maze the world over. I remember an Ikea ad in the UK that they've never shown in the US. 'Get a divorce, buy everything again. Come to Ikea.' Funny, really fucking funny. (*LBYR*, 85)

As this extract shows, in Morrison's shorter fiction, personal crises are both underlined and generalised, as individuals increasingly evolve in a world that deprives them of the elements that precisely make their crises personal. Just as the narrator in 'Stoop' finally finds himself to be part of the Ikeafication of the world, which ultimately markets the humans to fit the 'life' suggested by their furniture, so does the rebellious narrator of the collection's eponymous story, who points to standardisation, the commodification of personal relationships.[17] Describing the world of online dating, 'The last book your read' stresses that as dating becomes more and more standardised, the human ends up being one more product that can be summed up in terms of its characteristics, and communication, the last stronghold of the human, disappears:

> We did the small talk. He asks what I'm into. The last book I bought, CDs, clubs. Are you spontaneous, romantic? What do you enjoy? Biking, movies, cooking, white-water rafting or the gym. This is what passes for dialogue in this city. (*LBYR*, 6)

As the individual becomes a standardised product, the connection with the past becomes unnecessary, an impediment even for the transaction between individuals, an idea which is captured in the phrase 'Fuck Buddy' serving as the title of one of the stories in the collection. As the narrator of 'The last book you read' (this last a standard question of online dating sites) contends 'Online dating isn't dating – it's market research into the question of whether life is worth living' (*LBYR*, 2), pointing to the fundamental despair that lies behind this transformation of the world from one in which people defined themselves through their personal and general history as well as through the connections they could establish with each other, and a timeless and spaceless universe in which we have all becomes standardised products with no past, ready to be traded on the global market of the human.

Consequently, the real as we know it becomes much more hypothetical, much less neatly separated from a general sense that everything is fictional. Many of the stories in the five collections question the border established between the real and the fictional in order to show that not only fictional worlds, but possibly also the real world is being eroded by the various attacks on the historical and on our representation of reality. This is achieved by using displaced focalisation as in Des Dillon's 'The Gift' or Michel Faber's 'The Smallness of Action', both of which play with the conventional fantastic topos of hesitation to a curious effect, or by desacralising the intertextual, as in some stories by Saadi or Dillon. In 'The Gift', a moving story of despair that cannot be alleviated by love or by attempted human interaction, the reader is led to question the validity of a world characterised by successive, problematic transfers of focalisation. The narrator makes it clear that his mother Alice is the focaliser of the story, while at the same time technically focalising it himself through the adoption of the first person and the absence of any of the discursive or semantic markers of a transfer of information from the original focaliser (the mother) to the narrator, such as free indirect style, or indications such as 'my mother told me that ...'. This displacement is in addition repeated in the story of young James, the character who tells Alice his story. The result is a narration of events in which focalisation is doubly displaced as in the passage which depicts how James's mother died when he was a child:

> —James. Come back. James – It's me. It's mammy!
> But James kept running. Tripping over the lines and getting up. Heard a train and went faster. Could be coming on any line from any direction. Flung himself onto the banked up snow. Turned in time to see sparks spraying from the wheels of the braking train. The snow vibrated and there was his mammy framed for death. Looking at James not afraid. As time crushes; emotions expand. James saw his mammy's despair that she couldn't save him. Then she was dead. (*SWKT*, 197–98)

The communication to the reader of Alice's or, as in this extract, of James's feelings and perceptions by a narrator absent from the scene and who should technically be given no access to their psyches, drives a wedge into the story as a whole, separating the psychologically plausible from the technically impossible.[18] The universe conjured up in this story is therefore a flickering one, which manages to underline the complex relationship between truth and lies, perception and reality, story and personal history. This narrative is not sufficiently stable technically to vouch for a reassuring sense of closure. It has to leave the reader on an uncertainty, the last line simply indicating that 'She never seen [sic] him again' (*SWKT*, 199).

Robertson makes a connection in his essay between empirical reality which, with hindsight, organises itself into history, and the fairly mysterious character of this organisation pattern which he sees as being related not to reality but to fiction:

> You have to reach a place, from which you can look both far enough back and far enough forward, to realise that life is more complicated than that. Maybe, for me, that place was the fortnight in September, 1997, when Diana died and Scotland voted, finally and decisively, to have its parliament back. Life on either side of that vantage point seems more complete now, it makes more sense. In fiction, it's called resolution. (*SNE*, 186)

Suhayl Saadi makes a fairly similar point in approaching terms in a story that is generically at odds with the essayistic tone of Robertson's contribution to the Canongate collection. In 'Lughnasahd', a story set in a pastoral, dreamlike setting in 'the far west of England', Fiacre, the narrator, recounts the adventures of four young friends who explore a secular and mythical version of the garden of Eden in a text which conjures up Sir James Frazer's *The Golden Bough* – actually mentioned in the story – as well as other narratives such as Neil M. Gunn's *The Green Isle of the Great Deep*. Fiacre, believing himself the least interesting character, feels it his duty to narrate the story (*BM*, 92). He paradoxically insists on the fact that his narrative does not come across to the reader as tightly organised, not because it is structured like the dream it purports to reconstruct, but because it is a journey through reality rather than fiction:

> And so, if the thought occurs that I am meandering somewhat, backtracking even, it should be remembered that this account is not

a fiction. I often think that life, unlike fiction, must build from the simple to the elaborate. There are no resolutions in life. (*BM*, 95)

Like Robertson, Saadi cites resolution as the major dividing factor between life and fiction, while contrary to Robertson, he makes this point in a fictional piece, turning it into a metafictional story. Saadi's narrative indeed reflects on the relative significance and insignificance of the characters and the narrator, the figure of the author as the main protagonist's sidekick, as well as on the way fate and fiction exist in a reversed relation. But Saadi uses metafiction to his own end, not to conduct an inquiry into the nature of writing, but rather to apply the techniques of metafiction to what the story purports to be: life itself (incidentally a postulate which is endangered by the story itself, with its setting and the magic, or at least eerie events that succeed each other). In the process, it delivers not so much a comment on the narrowing margin between life and fiction, but an investigation into the story's pressing need to regress from fact to fiction, or, to put it differently, to place fact within the realm of the idyllic, the pastoral of the story's setting, the realm of that which can be controlled, of the fictional. For Fiacre, '[o]ur journey would be a mapping of fate in reverse, a drawing from the complex down into simplicity. A search for harmony. For fiction' (*BM*, 98). In this hankering for what appears to be the security of fiction, because it can bring the resolution that life cannot guarantee,[19] Fiacre, however, does not convey the classic transcendental idea of the writer as God, but rather reaffirms the vital need for fiction if one wants to be able to measure reality and exist in it, if one wants to be able to counter history's omissions:

> But I was content to follow him, to dwell in his shadow, lest only his shadow might love me. Perhaps that is why it is I who am relating these events, and not Donal or Kaylyn. Because the writer is always merely a sidekick, at best, a trusted confidante, at worst, a despised hanger-on. Writing is the act of being outside. It is the scream of the excluded. (*BM*, 99)

In this apparent dismissal of the writer, the repetitive emphasis on his exclusion paradoxically offset by his – and his fiction's – privileged vantage point from which to reflect – scream at, or maybe scream from – reality, the conclusion affords Saadi's readers new insight on the age-old debate in Scotland on the necessary connection between creative writing and Scottish artistic as well as political identity. The creative act is a desperate act of applying the techniques of fiction-writing, the range of technical tools at the writer's disposal to express either his own tragic metaphysical exclusion from the real, or the real's escape from patterns that can easily lead to a comfortable sense of 'resolution'. Both the facts of reality and the creative artist, in other words both personal and grand history, are in fact manifestations of the more or less wide gap between ideally organised – resolved, fictionalised – events and the messy and incomplete way in which they occur.

Michel Faber and Suhayl Saadi present us with flickering ontologies which also focus on that gap. Faber makes use of the unresolved nature of the fantastic (economically summed up by Todorov as a hesitation) to account for the slippery nature of the concept of resolution itself, while Saadi relies on the desacralisation of classic texts in their intertextual evocation. In both 'The Smallness of Action' and 'All Black', Faber uses the fantastic to portray the crumbling of his protagonists' lives and sense of themselves.[20] 'All Black', which describes a bus journey home a divorced father takes with his daughter, is a sort of rewrite of the prize-winning story 'Fish'[21] in a magic-realist setting: whereas no realistic context is given in 'Fish', 'All Black' travels from a very realistic narrative covering the thoughts of the focaliser as he goes over his past and present life, to an attempt by the fantastic to cover this beginning when darkness invades the city and seems to smother all lights from inside. 'The Smallness of Action' is also a moment of hesitation as Christine, a young mother, claims to have dropped her new baby to the floor and broken it, because the narrative maintains both the possibility that she is an abusive mother and that she is suffering from hallucinations, while not entirely ruling out Christine's own fantastic version of events. In those two stories, what the narrators crave is the possibility of resolution that only fiction can bring, as they wonder about their existence in both a literal and a figurative way. For the divorced father who is in a relationship with another man, as well as for the young mother who struggles to cope with the life-changing event of a new baby, what crumbles is their sense of their own reality, their place in a world which, to follow the cue given by 'All Black', which is also confirmed by Christine's words 'I'm ceasing to exist' (*FT*, 139), is inexorably snuffing them out. The question for Faber is existential and formal. The stories point to fiction's capacity to take up a narrative when life itself leaves the characters stranded in their attempt at self-definition. In that case, the concept of resolution might more aptly be named 'continuation'.

In another attempt at providing continuation, 'Solomon's Jar' (Saadi) and 'Big Brother' (Dillon) bring classical literature into the modern world through intertextual evocation, pointing to the fact that the concept of resolution can be transferred onto the outside world of existence while desacralising the highly literary notion of intertextuality. Dillon's 'Big Brother' tells the story of Shakespeare's Iago transported into the crass, vulgar world of contemporary reality TV, while in 'Solomon's Jar', Saadi imports the classic oriental tale of the jinn in the jar into the modern world. What is striking in both these stories is the similar effort to liberate classical texts from the museums in which they are sometimes ensconced. In 'Big Brother', Iago is the focaliser and narrator and as his machinations to separate Othello from Desdemona get him nominated for eviction from the house, so is the Shakespearean classic evicted from the mausoleum of literature, set free to interact with the contemporary world. Similarly in 'Solomon's Jar', Saadi presents a highly dramatic tale in which the jinn in the jar is granted a narrative voice couched in italics, enabling the story to provide two visions of the world, depending on whether it is seen from within or without the jar. As the jinn himself explains, saying that in the jar, there is neither space nor time, the classic tale enforces a type of narrative that makes the connection with the real world difficult. The point of the story in which the curator, obsessed with the jar and engaging in a conventional master-slave relationship with the jinn inside, finally opens it to a rather formulaic pyrotechnic show of liberation is to offset its own magical postulate. The conclusion, with the curator going out into the streets to take up his mundane everyday life with relish, emphasises a liberation which, although (under-)stated in the story with the concluding words 'the Curator was free' (*BM*, 19), actually takes place at the level of the story's capacity – as with Dillon's comic rewrite of *Othello* – to conjure up a famous intertext and then downplay its impact on contemporary literary production. In both Saadi's and Dillon's cases, the narrative's capacity to liberate itself and go out into the world is depicted, therefore shifting the emphasis from fiction's necessary intervention in the definition of reality and of the place of the self in this world, to the complementary advocacy of the necessary interaction of fiction with the everyday world.

The confines of the human

Focusing on another type of interaction between the everyday world and a more fictional type of existence, Michel Faber's story 'Mouse' introduces Manny, a young man living a virtual kind of life surrounded by his computer and video games, who has to enter real life when his neighbour asks him to help her get rid of a mouse. In this story, Faber does not use the fantastic as in 'All Black' or 'Fish' to describe a place where the limit between what is real and what is virtual is fairly difficult to establish, but rather performs what could be described as linguistic blurring between the two. Not only is the choice of a mouse an obvious pun on the word to conjure up both the computer world and the world of nature (which Manny is so estranged from that he does not even know about the presence of a field behind his house), but in addition, the conclusion of the story linguistically blurs the limit between the virtual world that can be summoned by tapping a few keys and the real world: Manny has become so engrossed in the parallel world created by his computers and video games that the story itself has been contaminated by this invasion, suggesting a world that has been taken over by the virtual. It is a world where communication relies on emails and injunctions to be 'READY 2 PLAY' (*FT*, 178), where the character's mind carries a visual display, his friends are either virtual avatars in computer games or people from the other end of the world who communicate with him like a machine would,[22] and his eyes adapt to the dark in a way that suggests a computer screen. Indeed, Manny 'switched the torch off. Everything went black. He was shivering. He was blind. Then, tinge by tinge, the colours started coming through' (*FT*, 181).

Many of Morrison's stories tackle the same issue, by emphasising the lack of communication between humans and the 'virtualisation' of relationships. In his collection, the emphasis is on apathy and isolation, which Morrison relates to the general context of globalisation, claiming that '[t]he apathy-is-the-only-form-of-resistance attitude was actually a kind of mirror of globalisation'.[23] This attitude is symbolised in the collection's title story by Cassandra's profile on the dating site – a blank – which causes her to be branded as 'hopelessly empty' (*LBYR*, 5) by other users. In Morrison's stories, and on occasions in Faber's and Dillon's, the characters end up firing emails into a cybervoid; they increasingly appear to be separate entities all logging onto the same void and finally getting lost in cyberspace. Cassandra receives an avalanche of reactions to her empty profile; Jack-the-lad in 'Re: Your Ad', the provider of a cyberguide on adultery in the form of email attachments, never gets any answer from the researcher he is sending them to, in spite of his increasingly desperate, needy pleas. The virtual global space, which appears as a global void, grants the characters a virtual identity which is in fact a myriad of identities, a disintegration of the coherent idea of the self, to be replaced by constant mutations. Both Redordead, Cassandra's blind date, and Jack-the-lad in the other story disclose to their correspondents some very intimate details about who they are and then deny them, only to change their stories again. In a succession of emails, when all people need to define themselves and communicate with other beings is a series of words typed into a computer and sent off to the cybervoid, the characters place themselves under erasure several times over. They become versions, rewrites, abstractions in their own one-sided stories. Having reached the confines of the human, the characters in Morrison's, but also in Dillon's or Faber's stories seem to be condemned to isolation, separation or even virtual extinction.[24]

As an equivalent to this world of non-communication and emptiness, all three writers use madness. In Morrison's 'The Room', Jo, the manic depressive young woman who cannot get herself to communicate with the outside world, describes her condition in terms of total, almost lethal apathy – 'I want not to want' (*LBYR*, 56). Dillon's 'Heat' and Faber's 'Andy Comes Back' both use the topos of the mad character who escapes or is released from an institution, as well as an internal focalisation in order to reinforce the sense of entrapment of the self. In 'Heat', the narrator who escapes from the asylum in his pyjamas in the middle of the night ends up facing a world that is even emptier than the place he was locked up in, a city of 'neons advertising to people who weren't there', of 'interior lights on but nobody home, Like everybody had left in a hurry. Like they knew I was coming' (*SWKT*, 91). In 'Andy Comes Back' this sense of being stranded in a human desert is conveyed by the trapping of the character within his own self:

> His eyes fluttered open, and he was surprised to find himself alive. If he'd thought about himself at all in the last five years, he'd considered himself dead. Occasionally he'd peek out at the world, and for his peekhole he would use the gibbering, shrieking idiot the nursing staff called Andy. (*FT*, 25)

Although Morrison does not use the trope of the madman to connote isolation, many of his stories seem to be filtered through this constrained perspective. They appear to be narrated from a 'peekhole' that prevents the shrieking individuals from ever getting any answers, as is for instance the case with 'The Piers', 'The Speech' or 'Stoop', all stories about the individual's desperate need to come into contact with the other over their shared humanity. Schoene (2007: 15) notes of 'The Piers' that '[i]n the unstoppably increasing absence of genuine individual uniqueness, it is imperative not to lose sight of our common humanity'. Faber also makes a very similar point, saying that *The Fahrenheit Twins* 'is a journey from alienation towards a tentative connectedness',[25] but in his and in Morrison's stories, the attempt is very frustratingly unsuccessful, and the simple act of connecting is an act of regression, a shriek uttered by a madman who, recovering his sanity as in 'Andy Comes Back', is sent home only to leave it and disappear, condemned to be part of a system consisting of – as the madman in Dillon's story puts it – 'other people driving through their own nights' (*SWKT*, 91). Even sex, the most intimate of connections, cannot shake the 'gibbering shrieking idiot' loose, and gibbering and shrieking become the inarticulate noises generated by the space that has been abandoned by the human. The characters then roam a vacated space where language appears to have been discarded in the characters' incapacity to connect, or on the contrary invested, externalised as a vestigial sign of a possibility for two human beings to communicate. In Faber's 'Serious Swimmers' Gail, a reformed drug addict attempting to regain custody of her child is faced with the strangeness of words that are usually taken for granted in everyday life:

> Years of addiction had half-dissolved lots of words she'd once had no problem coming out with. They were like things you leave in a box in the garage and then when you look for them years later you find the water's got to them. (*FT*, 46)

For Gail, words have gone stale and can no longer be retrieved, while in Morrison's 'Fuck Buddy', communication has been divorced from relationship, as the occasional lovers both adopt the diary form, producing mirrored narrations – one of which the reader only gets a glimpse of at the end – that recreate two separate personal stories, the intimacy of the form unable to transfer to dialogue. As words are typed into a void, the void between the two lovers, they provide an apt representation of the virtual world that the protagonists, slipping from the status of human beings to that of nonentities, have come to inhabit, a fact also suggested by their namelessness.[26]

The lack of connection between individuals, that can be expressed either as a shortage of words with which to formulate the link, or with a wealth of words than can no longer be channelled from one individual to another but rather thrown into a void, quite logically results in some stories in the disappearance of the characters, who are actually turned into nonentities, into reflections of the emptiness which they are required to take their shape from. The narrator of Saadi's 'Lughnasadh' experiences the loss of words as a pleasurable experience of communion, a mystic experience which, however, leads him to a form of dissolution:

> I was the river. I was the heat. I was the darkness. [...] But then, I wasn't sure who I was anymore. [...] it was difficult for me to ascertain where the skin of my body ended and the water began. I just floated. I was between beats of the heart, in an ecstasy so total that I no longer had any sense of anything. [...] there were no words exchanged. Words would have been spurious. [...]
>
> The ecstasy was not one of pure happiness. Rather it was a total fusion, an omniscience, a sinking beneath walls. We were in fish time. For once, I sensed Donal's insecurity and his lack of love. The man who had been my god dissolved into the pool, leaving only the core, the essence of himself. And the heart of Donal was a wall. I sank beneath it and found ... nothing. A total emptiness. (*BM*, 103–05)

In a way that is widely different from the characters' experience in Morrison's or Faber's collections, the protagonist in Saadi's story dissolves in the absence of words and becomes an elemental life form that disappears into darkness, another kind of emptiness encountered when Fiacre attempts to get past Donal's enclosed self.

A scripted world

Faced with the abyssal blankness, with the gaping void between humans represented by the absence of words, some stories resort to borrowing others' words through the fairly conventional metaphor of the character as actor. In Morrison's 'Clean Sheets with a View of the Hudson' the adulterous couple express the failure of communication between them, the gap that opens up at the moment they should carnally and spiritually coalesce, in terms of a hackneyed theatrical metaphor – they see themselves as 'two actors without lines' (*LBYR*, 47) – and the mirrors adorning the room's walls and ceiling reflect their separate loneliness while also representing a hypothetical audience in the shape of characters, identical to them, staring at their separateness.[27] Dillon's 'Jock Tamson's Bus' mixes metaphors even though both allude to the scripted nature of the events depicted; it uses a cinematic metaphor, with the image of the bus windows providing a slow motion, frame-by-frame picture of the scene witnessed by the passengers at the end, as well as a theatrical one, when the narrator, who describes a young woman's destiny in a fairly grandiloquent manner, also stresses the idea that the 'words' of the character's life are not for her to create:

> As she talks she's taking up positions. [...] She doesn't know the name of the play she's in. Maybe it's act one of the farce of the rest of her life. Maybe it's a comedy. Or a tragedy. We'll never know till the end. And the audience are repulsed and entertained. (*SWKT*, 53)

Michel Faber takes up the idea in 'Vanila Bright like Eminem' by using the script as a form rather than a metaphor, the story reading like a synopsis. In this very sketchy, technical form, the story appears to lack the substance that precisely would make it a story. This can be seen as a sign that Faber does not deliver on this story, or that the goal behind it is precisely to evoke the emptiness, the sense of the vacuity of the events that we compile as 'our life'. This idea is reinforced by the suggestion made by Faber, as well as Dillon in 'Jock Tamson's Bus', that there are various scripts to choose from. Most of the stories in those collections bring the reader back to a foregone conclusion: we may never know till the end which script we are playing from, as the narrator in 'Jock Tamson's Bus' puts it, but we are certainly given a finite enumeration of the more predictable avenues. Dillon's 'Pink River' and 'Holy Heater' depict class prejudice in Alcoholics Anonymous meetings from the point of view of the working-class characters in a tone which makes it partly comic; Saadi's 'Ninety-Nine Kiss-o-Grams' and 'The Queens of Govan' focus on the pitfalls of multicuturalism, the inescapable racist drunks accosting the 'Asian babe' in a way that makes her describe them as 'monsters. They were indestructible. Like fear. Or hate' (*BM*, 25), or the peculiar position of those characters poised between two cultures – 'In Scola, there wus nae room fur dreams; in Pakistan, dreams were all there wus' (*BM*, 5). Like Saadi and Dillon, Faber sprinkles his narratives with the predictable scenarios which the stories are up against, and presents in 'A Hole with Two Ends' the stereotypical representation of the prejudices around English-Scottish relationships:

> 'It was nice of us to come, wasn't it?' said Sandra to Neil, as they were walking back to their car. She kept her voice low, so as not to be overheard by the woman whose horrid little cottage they'd just left.
> 'Of course it was,' sighed Neil. 'It's this little anti-English game they play – making you feel like a complete bastard even when you're bending over backwards for them.'
> [...]
> Neither of them needed to voice what had been obvious to them as soon as they'd arrived for the interview: that this latest candidate for the job was yet another Highlands loser, a waste of their valuable time. (*FT*, 119)

The characters, therefore, are part of a world which speaks for them, which utters the seemingly inescapable universal truth about them, a sort of stale, entrenched, scripted truth[28] which is itself the reason for the creative exit that all the short stories represent. This is symbolised by one of Dillon's stories, 'The Illustrated Man', a very literal presentation of the notion of creative exit. In this tragic story of poverty and institutional neglect, Stevie Maclehatton goes crazy and ends up killing his father by carving the name of his dead brother on his body, after tattooing his own body with slogans and accusations against his father. This act of turning his body into a script, literally, takes the stories out of the dead-end that is represented by the blankness that is faced by the human and the uniform blandness that the scenarios are up against. The carving of the father's body, however, reminds the reader that being turned into stories by other, stereotypical discourses is a deadly avenue.

Michel Faber, in order to offset the inexorable movement of disconnection between individuals, with its threat of dissolution and disappearance,[29] works with a reversed angle by focusing on connection both as a theme and as an extratextual goal. For him, the story starts and ends outside of the diegetic world:

> My stories always start with a feeling. A feeling that I want to evoke in the reader, a state of mind or spirit that I'd like you to be in while you're reading it and especially when you've finished it. Once I've intuited what that feeling or that spiritual state is, I then think up a plot, scenario, characters, themes, etc., to evoke it.[30]

Consequently, in order to define the 'spiritual tenor'[31] of the story and generate an array of feelings in the reader,[32] what also needs to be created is a multiplicity of very specific voices, a variety which has prompted critics to describe his fictional output as constituting 'a Babel of voices'.[33] This attempt is also in keeping with the generic multiplicity which characterises his fiction as a whole,[34] denoting a refusal on his part to be pigeonholed, but also a necessity to resort to the resources of various genres in order to create the variety of feelings that he is after. In 'Serious Swimmers' and 'Less than Perfect' which, like 'Some Rain Must Fall' in the former collection, convey a sense of poignancy, as in the title story 'The Fahrenheit Twins', the question that is raised once again has to do with identity and community, with how individuals can define themselves in connection with others around them, as well as with raising the issue of the validity of that definition. Gail in 'Serious Swimmers' has to shake off the drug addict label pinned upon her, but she does not seem to be able to know what other characteristic she could adopt for herself, as even the generic social term 'adult' does not seem to fit with her sense of herself (*FT*, 46); in 'Less than Perfect', Lachlan, a store detective, fantasises about having sex with a female customer/thief in the back office and ends up being dismissed as a 'wanker' by the woman he actually arrests, two examples that show the gap between the characters' private or fantasised version of their own identity and their social one. Beyond the emphasis on the disconnectedness of human relations, those stories point to the necessary escape from the emptiness that it leads the characters to, in a way that the author links to an endeavour to make his characters constantly redefine themselves in order to construct a new destiny for themselves. Faber explains that '[i]n all my work I've explored whether people can escape from an apparently hardwired destiny […]. I'm interested in whether there is any way out, any leeway for emotional or spiritual escape'.[35]

In spite of the great variety of voices and the competing genres which are integrated into his stories, the goal is not metatextual but rather metaphysical, almost anthropological,[36] as is made thematically obvious by 'The Fahrenheit Twins', in which Tainto'lilith and Marko'cain, the twins living with their fairly distant anthropologist parents on the Arctic island of Ostro Providenya, are placed in a situation in which the absence of any socially defined sense of their own identity in the traditional sense makes them create a value system out of the fragments which are made available to them by their own muddled sense of personal and sexual identity, their stark natural environment and the piecemeal information they can derive from their mother's erratic wisdom – 'this book was once a tree' (*FT*, 238), 'dead people don't feel anything' (*FT*, 243), 'one less clock makes no difference to the universe' (*FT*, 265) – which they have compiled in their 'Book of Knowledge'.[37] In that situation, what sense of themselves they can create verges onto a sort of mystical primitivism, as the twins perform growth-inhibiting rituals or when, at the death of their mother, they decide to 'wait for a signal from the universe as to the best thing to do with the body' (*FT*, 246). In a reversal of the earlier pattern, however, their search for signs and their performance of rituals qualifies them as anthropologists researching their own parents' civilisation. Early on in the story, the two children reverse the reader's expectations by upsetting our sense of what constitutes a primitive tribe:

> 'You think we are a tribe?'
> 'Of course we are a tribe.'
> 'Just the two of us?'

'There are more of our kind where our mother and father came from. That's our tribe.'
'Father says they are all imbeciles and back-stabbers there. And mother said once that they let the streets get dirty, and another time that the trains are always late and full of rude people who will not stand up for a lady.' (*FT*, 245–6)

Contrary to their suspicion, Tainto'lilith and Marko'cain in fact do create a tribe of two, a synthesis of their diverse and puzzling origins, and, with the animalised description of their mother's corpse, they set up a wholly new reference system for their depiction of the human. The confines of the world which they inhabit, itself a spatial equivalent for the confines of the human they embody, gives rise to a possible definition of their own and by extension the others' humanity. The story's concluding words then represent a possible blueprint for the human: 'And yes, her brother was right, they had so much to look forward to, in the big wide world down below. The Book of Knowledge had a lot of blank pages' (*FT*, 276). What is projected in this conclusion (to the story but also to the book) is finally how open-ended, paradoxically hopeful it can be to build the portrayal, past and future, of the twin's restricted and extended tribe, the human race, itself a leap of faith in a collection which, like the others examined in this chapter, foregrounds disconnectedness, isolation and lack of prospects. Faber himself points to this necessary hopefulness when he describes his novel *The Fire Gospel* in terms that could be applied to *The Fahrenheit Twins*: 'I'm focusing on those human connections that suggest we can get along, that suggest there's hope for the human race to muddle through'.[38]

Hopeful stories?

Writing in *Scotland 2020*, Marc Lambert insists, as many cultural commentators did in the aftermath of the opening of the Scottish Parliament, on what he sees as the creative drive pulling his country to a brighter future:

> I want to suggest that scenarios that will sustain us and move us forward in the future will be those scripted by our historians and writers. But ultimately I believe that fictions are a stronger means than any science because their imaginative power is non-linear

and contains, in a Whitmanesque sense, multitudes. In short, we need to develop our imaginative and critical grasp of ourselves in order to have an informed opinion about what our future might be. (2005: 129)

If we read this suggestion in connection with the stories examined in this chapter, Lambert's wish is more than fulfilled as, between them, they reflect on what an 'informed opinion' entails both in societal and artistic terms. In that respect, one might think of Saadi's story 'Solomon's Jar' as a sort a facetious and yet actual response to the claim. The jinn in the jar, desperate to be let out by the museum curator, finally ends up reversing the oriental tradition by liberating the museum curator himself. As the jinn effortlessly straddles all gaps, stating, '*I pirouette on paradox. The impossible is my domain. Thy wish is my command, Master*' (*BM*, 16), so do the stories. The jinn, as a representation of magic in stories, produces a quiet affirmation of power which ultimately not only comforts Lambert's declaration of intent, but also adds one page to the unfinished, unfinishable Book of Knowledge.

Notes

1   This phrase was used in 2005 by Greg Gordon in *The Times* to describe Morrison's collection. See Gordon, Greg. 2005. 'For Ewan the only way is up', *The Times*, 26 June, www.blackandwhitepublishing.com/chroma/ewanmorrison/ewanmorrisontimesinterview.html [consulted February 2009].
2   The collections will be quoted in the chapter as respectively *SWKT*, *FT*, *LBYR*, *BM* and *SNE*.
3   Morrison was described by Gordon in *The Times* as the 'chronicler of the broken dreams and spiritual desolation that lies beneath the surface gloss of advanced capitalistic society', while *The Fahrenheit Twins* is praised in *The Guardian* review for catching their characters 'at a moment of fracture'. (Harrison, M. John. 2005. 'The future tense', *The Guardian*, Saturday 3 September, www.guardian.co.uk/books/2005/sep/03/featuresreviews.guardianreview13 [consulted November 2008].

Those two descriptions emphasise the necessity to move away from the narrow definition of writing in Scotland as connected with national identity and the nationalist agenda. Hence my wish in this chapter to confront a collection with a clear representative goal (*Scotland Into The New Era* is indeed a programmatic title) with works that do not have a set agenda behind them. Hence also my decision to base this chapter on fiction by writers who hail from very different horizons. Des Dillon is a poet, novelist, playwright and recently a stand-up comedian, whose 1995 novel *Me and My Gal* was chosen by a poll of readers for World Book Day as the book which best 'summed up the zeitgeist' of Scotland, beating some better known literary exports. Morrison is described by Schoene (2007: 15–16) as writing books in which Scotland is not an issue, but which are 'not

THE CONFINES OF THE HUMAN: SHORTER FICTION

devoid of Scottishness', books which should be read 'ambassadorially'. Saadi's connection with Scotland is a compelling new kind of connection, as shown in the third chapter, and lastly, Michel Faber, a writer of Dutch origin who emigrated to Australia as a child before going to live in Scotland and who came to fame with the publication of his second novel, *The Crimson Petal and the White* (2002), a Victorian pastiche set in London, emphatically denies any national inspiration in his fiction, declaring in an interview with *The Barcelona Review* that he feels 'equally at home AND an outsider in each of these countries. [The Netherlands and Scotland]'. Adams, Jill. 2002. 'Interview with Michel Faber', *The Barcelona Review*, Issue 29, March-April, www.barcelonareview.com/29/e_mf_int.htm [consulted November 2008].

4   Peddie, Ian. 2007. 'Speaking Welsh: Irvine Welsh in Conversation', *Scottish Studies Review*, 8.1, p. 133.
5   On cosmopolitanism, see the introduction to this book.
6   At the beginning of the story Glasgow's status as a city of architecture is repeatedly emphasised.
7   The lower classes and underclasses are presented and subdivided into types – 'the Young Team', the 'two Spice Girls'; the 'neds and nedesses'. Those, but also a whole range of 'average', unnamed characters with a sort of choric function contained in the narrator's use of the pronoun 'we', would be epsilon types in Huxley's reference system.
8   Ruby can also be linked to the Ruby of *Psychoraag*. 'The Queen of Govan' gives the reader a glimpse of her story from her own point of view, which the novel, with its focalisation by Zaf, cannot afford. Like Faber in *The Apples*, Saadi indulges in this story in what Brian McHale (1987: 56–57) calls 'transworld identity', or more simply 'retour de personnage', as a way to create a network of characters and references that transcends the limit of any one book.
9   The story expands on this, by describing the typical squalor and violence that constitute the 'view' on a sink estate. See pp. 34–35 and 39.
10 The screen comes at a price that Jeannette cannot afford, indicating that in the story, the alleviation of poverty, squalor and human misery has been turned into a business, ironically one that thrives on those very factors and therefore would bank on their continuance. See chapter 5 on the same topic.
11 See Gray, Alasdair [1981] (1991), *Lanark: A Life in Four Books*, London: Picador pp. 446–7.
12 Morrison, *Scotland on Sunday*, June 7, 2009.
13 See chapter 3.
14 Caledonia explains that she still uses *some* Scottish words for her collections, for example marketing a 'coorie-in' or a 'Thrawn bag'.
15 Faber makes a similar point in 'Pidgin American', in which a young Polish girl has T-shirts printed with the logos of record shops' communication material with a view to selling them as Western iconography back in Poland. Donovan, reflecting upon the current trend in cinema and in the tourist industry to sell Scotland to the world in the shape of fragments from its history, goes to the logical end of this line of reasoning, by breaking up the whole of Scotland's past and future, for the benefit of the – business – world of globalisation.
16 Adams, 'Interview with Michel Faber'.

Faber even traces the origins of this contemporary Zeitgeist in his Neo-Victorian novel, as is pointed out by Georges Letissier, who notes that the novel thematically refers to the origins of the mass production of leisure and luxury products narrated through

the spectacular rise of Rackham perfumeries. Letissier links this with a wider issue, which comes up again in Faber's shorter fiction: 'Faber's fiction suggests that the very notions of origin, and originality are getting increasingly problematic as a result of mass production and commodification'. Letissier, Georges. 2009. '*The Crimson Petal and the White*: a neo-Victorian Classic?', in Georges Letissier (ed.), *Rewriting/Reprising: Plural Intertextualities*, (Newcastle: Cambridge Scholars), p. 122.
17 On this aspect see chapter 5 on Ewan Morrison.
18 The omniscient narrator, the only one technically capable of mediating all the characters' feelings, is not compatible with the postulate of who the narrator is in the story, especially with the adoption of the first person.
19 This postulate in itself deliberately ignores three decades of postmodernist writing, a strong indication that Saadi, like Robertson, is writing from a different perspective. As to *The Fahrenheit Twins*, it does not carry any explicit reference to fiction's capacity to order the real out of its chaotic pattern even though, as Letissier points out, Faber uses his Victorian novel *The Crimson Petal and the White* to reflect on the narrative's tendency to bring order to the chaos of life: 'Whereas Victorian novelists used to shape the randomness of existence through a set of coincidences connecting together apparently unrelated events, or characters, Faber suggests the defeat of narrative order, swallowed up by the anarchic historical "real"' (2009: 115).
20 'All Black' was first published in the *Edinburgh Review*, 104, 2000, pp. 103–15.
21 This story was published in Faber's first collection of stories, published in 1998, *Some Rain Must Fall* (Edinburgh: Canongate) which received the Saltire First Book of the Year award in 1999.
22 Varez, Manny's internet friend from Minnesota has achieved disembodiment to the point that he speaks like an FAQ section: 'a response from Varez. Very detailed instructions as to how to fix the minidumps. The guy clearly had an ultra-methodical mind. "Follow the instructions in the first section. If the problem is not resolved, proceed to the next section." Not exactly a buddy-buddy tone, but lucid' (*FT*, 177).
23 Gallix, Andrew. 2009. 'More Thanatos than Eros: Ewan Morrison Interviewed by Andrew Gallix', *3:AM Magazine*, Friday, August 28, www.3ammagazine.com/3am/more-thanatos-than-eros/ [consulted February 2011].
24 This explains for instance Cassandra's desperate need to speak to Redordead, to connect with her flaws, her awkwardness, which are the signs of her humanity. It also explains what Morrison describes as the 'accidental' compassion that he often met with at readings of the stories, a spontaneous reaction to the endangering of those characters' very sense of their own humanity. See the interview with Morrison on the Black and White website, www.blackandwhitepublishing.com/chroma/ewanmorrison/ewanmorrisoninterview.html
25 Lawless, Andrew. 2005. 'Spending imaginative capital – Michel Faber and *The Fahrenheit Twins*', *The Three Monkeys online*, www.threemonkeysonline.com/als/-michel-faber-interview-the-fahrenheit-twins.html [consulted February 2011].
26 The anonymous narrator even refers to her lover as 'Mister nobody' (*LBYR*, 121).
27 'They held hands and stared up at the ceiling. From above, they could see two middle-aged people under the sheets. Their faces peeking out from the covers, staring out – silent and holding hands' (*LBYR*, 50).
28 This aspect is developed in chapter 5.

29 M. John Harrison calls this 'dissociation', a phenomenon which, he concludes, 'renders [the characters] invisible to themselves and unavailable to each other'. See Harrison, 'The future tense'.
30 Adams, Jill.
31 Faber in Lawless.
32 Faber declares for example that in writing 'Fish', he wanted to create a sense of awe in his readers; for poignant, gripping 'Some Rain Must Fall' the feeling he was aiming to induce was a sense of poignancy and tenderness. See Faber in two interviews, the first by Jill Adams, and the interview in the *Scottish Review of Books* (2008), Volume 4 Issue 4, www.scottishreviewofbooks.org/index.php?option=com_content&view=article&id=65:michael-faber-the-srb-interview&catid=9:volume-4-issue-4&Itemid=51 [consulted November 2008].
33 Anonymous. 2000. 'Flesh-creeping: It is better to travel than to arrive in Michael Faber's *Under The Skin*', *The Guardian*, Sunday April 1, www.guardian.co.uk/books/2000/apr/01/fiction.reviews2 [consulted March 2005]. Faber's first collection of short stories *Some Rain Must Fall* was praised by *The Times* for the fact that 'each of the fifteen stories has such an entirely different voice that the book reads like the work of different writers', Wild, Peter. 2002. 'Snuggling up to Queen Victoria: an interview with Michel Faber', *3AM Magazine*, www.3ammagazine.com/litarchives/2002_sep/interview_michel_faber.html [consulted November 2008]. The expression 'Babel of voices' has also been used by Katherine Ashley about Saadi's peculiar linguistic mix (see chapter 4).
34 To give just a few examples, the bestseller *The Crimson Petal and the White* is a Victorian pastiche, *Under the Skin* a dark magic realist tale with a sci-fi premise which somehow manages to eschew the tropes of science-fiction, while *The Hundred and Thirty Nine Steps* hinges around a murder, but is also more complex than a crime novel in spite of the title's obvious allusion to John Buchan.
35 'Michel Faber: The SRB Interview'.
36 Faber himself is careful to reject the metatextual interpretation of his works, dismissively stating that his stories do not work in what he calls a 'clever-clever metatextual way', Ibid. See also Jill Adams, 'Interview with Michel Faber'.
37 This is one of the aspects which was emphasised in the stage adaptation by Matthew Dunster and the Told by an Idiot company shown at the Barbican Pit theatre in London in December 2009.
38 'Michel Faber: The SRB interview'.

7. Conclusion

The Tartan controversy

Voices from Scotland in a Post-devolution Age. Hopeful Stories for a northern nation. Modern Transformations: New Identities.[1] All those titles point to the inextricable connection, arguably in any context, between the literary and the extra-literary, a connection which many commentators have described as problematic in a Scottish context. The spate of critical works or histories of literature which have tried to establish the link between the literary output in Scotland after 1999 and the devolved parliament bears witness to that fact. Nevertheless, literary criticism as a whole has, in recent years, been very concerned with the pitfalls of putting a tartan badge on the literary production emanating from Scotland. The literary editor Stuart Kelly is the most openly critical of this tendency, as is shown by the title of his occasional paper for the *International Journal of Scottish Literature*, 'How Tartan is Your Text?'. In this paper he argues that what he sees as the 'deluge' of critical books on Scottish literature corresponds to a desperate need to justify its existence. For him, the how-tartan-is-your-text question has shifted in recent years to reflect a new concern, as '[a]cross all these histories [of Scottish literature], a common foundation myth appears, wrapped in the deconstruction of foundation myths: that of a polyglot diverse Scotland, a Scotland of shifting territorial or linguistic boundaries. In effect, a proto-post-colonial Scotland'.[2]

For Brown, Clancy, Manning and Pittock, the four editors of the *Edinburgh History of Scottish Literature* (Vol. 1, 2007: 10), the terms '"literature" and "Scottish" [...] need to be open to question', while for Aaron Kelly, who accuses literary critics of complacency, the recent focus on the interaction between literary production and devolution was at the expense of class antagonism. He identifies post-devolution literature, when advocated and described by such commentators as Catherine Lockerbie, as implementing 'a bourgeois narrative', a 'return to the grand narrative of yore, which postmodernism sought to undermine in the 1970s and 1980s', and comments on the generating of 'codes of historical normality' to produce that teleological narrative.[3] Kelly also sees post-nationalism as the final repression of class in its discourse of cultural difference, an issue on which the editors of the *Edinburgh History* have a different opinion:

> Scotland is often and rightly described, not only in modern times, but throughout its history, as multicultural. Given the rich ways in which such multiculturalism is at the centre of Scottish cultures and experience and the ways in which these cultures work on, with and in one another, the editors would go further and assert that Scotland is intercultural. (vol. 1, 2007: 11)

This suggestion of interculturalism could profitably be used to discuss not only the works of Suhayl Saadi, but also for instance that of Egypt-born Leila Aboulela,[4] who describes herself first as a Muslim, or of Chiew-Siah Tei, a writer of Malaysian origin who published several books in Chinese before her novel *Little Hut of Leaping Fishes* (2008), which she wrote in English. It also raises the question of delimiting the field of literary analysis, which carries with it the appended and hotly debated notion of the canon, and of the methodology adopted to define it. It certainly rests on the complex issue of the here and elsewhere, the insider/outsider debate that has long agitated the circles of literary criticism, especially in Scotland. Brown, Clancy, Manning and Pittock insist on the dialectical issue of 'understanding the importance of diaspora cultures as part of – and yet not part of – modern Scottish culture' (Vol.1, 2007: 10), while Suhayl Saadi, not a diaspora writer but an author of 'intercultural' stock, comments, both in his essays and his fiction, on the long way ahead for such writers, claiming in *The Burning Mirror* that '[w]riting is the act of being outside. It is the scream of the excluded' (2001: 99). The demarcating lines are not that clear-cut however, and one can vindicate Kelly's argument about the sidelining of class issues by quoting Kelman:

> The crucial factor is the ability to earn a living, this is what is taken from writers who work on/from the margins. [...] One side has power and authority and the other doesn't. One has the power to stop the other from earning a living. It is better to be acknowledged as a writer than have to continue proving it all the time.[5]

This statement of the capacity for the publishing establishment in effect to keep certain writing in or out of fashion (much has been said, as mentioned in chapter 4, about the appeal in recent years of boutique multiculturalism, to the detriment of other, less palatable issues) reminds us that the all-inclusive dream of the post-devolution period, even when it comes to promoting a writer whose work is perceived as belonging to the canon of modern Scottish literature such as Kelman, needs to be considered with care.[6] The same applies to the new cultural era idea which, according to both Stuart Kelly and Alex Thomson, has been overplayed in the last few years,[7] and which Kelman summarily dismisses: 'a new cultural era in Scotland ...? There is so much dishonesty around, so much humbug'.[8]

Not all writers in Scotland take the same nihilistic stance as Kelman however, and the sheer scope covered by fiction writers alone (not to mention poetry or drama) certainly allows for an optimistic appraisal of the future of literature in Scotland, an idea which, from the writers' point of view, is quite detached from the tartan controversy. If one considers for instance the work of poet and novelist John Burnside, the author of *The Dumb House* (1997), *The Mercy Boys* (1999) and *The Locust Room* (2001), which all in a different way question the notion of boundaries in literature, or novelists Rodge Glass, who plays with the genre of the family saga in *No Fireworks*,[9] and Ali Smith, whose *Hotel World* (2001) experiments with the age-old ghost narrative in a new way, one can say that the fiction that has been produced in the first decade of the millennium has started to treat the Scottishness topic as just that. Jackie Kay defines being a writer as 'observing people and observing things from really early on, and looking at the world in a certain way',[10] emphasising the human in a way that recalls Galloway's interest in the observation of events' consequences on people's psyches[11] or Michel Faber's exploration of the confines of the human, not to mention Morrison's study of how globalisation affects the individual. Moreover, a recent spate of works which, in the space of a few years, have concentrated on the genre of the autobiography indicates, if not a trend in Scottish fiction at large, at least the idea that it is acceptable for novelists to look at themselves, to write about an individual human consciousness, were it in the shape of straight autobiography – Galloway's *This is Not about Me* (2008) and its sequel *All Made Up* (2011); John Burnside's *A Lie about my Father* (2006); fictional autobiography – James Kelman's *Kieron Smith, Boy* (2008);

or letters, in Laura Hird's case her mother's letters and her own, gathered in a book entitled *Dear Laura* (2007). This is but one example of the directions that writers avail themselves of, while another very promising one has to do with the crossing not just of generic boundaries, but sometimes also of art form. Burnside, in *The Locust Room* (2001), produced a dark crime story which is not written like a crime novel;[12] Gray, who has published work across genre divisions, is now largely concentrating on his career as a visual artist; Michel Faber's fictional production is so diverse in generic terms that it has been described as potentially being produced by different artists.[13] Janice Galloway has written an opera libretto, Denise Mina and Ian Rankin have contributed to the *Hellblazer* comics series, A. L. Kennedy is also a stand-up comedian, and she and John Burnside have written two crime series for Canadian TV. Ewan Morrison, who came to writing after working and winning awards as a director in television and film for ten years, has written *Tales from the Mall* which, in addition to being a hybrid from the point of view of the organisation and contents (it mixes stories with informational and historical contents about shopping malls, as well as interviews with mall workers or customers) started its life not as a book but as a series of short videos on his website and on YouTube, originally designed to be the video contents of an interactive e-book. As such it raises the question not just of the nature of fiction and the fictional (an issue which is also at the heart of the auto-bio-fictional works mentioned above), but, famously since Morrison's paper in *The Guardian* in August 2011, of the future of the book.[14] In short, Scotland and its writers have, in the last twenty years, produced art which reaches outwith the limits of fiction, or even literature. It can now boast a wealth of creative artists who, between them, have composed, as Tom Leonard commented about Glasgow, 'an anthology of different places and contexts'.[15]

Poetry makes nothing happen

In an article about the twentieth-century writers of fiction in Britain who re-examine fictions of the past, producing what he calls 're-visionary fiction', Peter Widdowson, who cites Louise Welsh and Michel Faber as the writers of such fictions, stresses those novels' capacity to 'write back to – indeed, "rewrite" – canonic texts from the past, and hence to call to account formative narratives that have arguably been central to the construction of "our" consciousness'.[16] In a process which he describes (2006: 503) as one of 'active intertextualising', re-visionary fiction becomes a way of revising, re-examining and correcting, a way of 're-visioning' and 're-envisioning', in short of seeing in another light, potentially of 'recast[ing] and re-evaluat[ing]' the original (2006: 493).[17] This concept of looking again, of recasting, can be useful in the analysis of novels which, although intertextual to an important degree, are not properly speaking rewrites of other novels, novels such as *And The Land Lay Still*, examined in the third chapter, or Val McDermid's pastiches of the novels of Agatha Christie, mentioned in chapter two. In those novels, what is being achieved is what Widdowson describes as fiction's capacity to be 'potentially another way of writing history' (2006: 493). In this respect, the novels and short stories examined in this book, only a few examples among the wealth of creative writing produced in Scotland in the period since the devolution, do not perform, activate or induce historical event, yet they provide the theoretical projection, the possible alternative trajectories that cannot be mapped by historical or sociological records which, by definition, register only one itinerary. This is the reason why, in several of them, especially Robertson's and Saadi's, but also in Faber's stories, the recurring metaphor of the map is elevated to the rank of motif, bearing as it does not just thematic and topical connotations, but also, and maybe in the final analysis more crucially, metatextual, metafictional, and therefore theoretical and literary preoccupations. Hassan praises this unique capacity in creative writing, which can be extended to art in general – the power to suggest, not the future, but possible futures, emphasing that '[t]hinking about the future requires creativity. Analysing trends is not enough, however good the data. Imagining the future is an empowering process that opens up the possibility of action' (2005: 49).

In order to do that specifically in Scotland, one has to follow Alex Thomson's lead and look for specific features in contemporary Scottish writing that are stylistic, formal rather than systematically trying to connect those works to the political context.[18] As has been underlined in this volume, two prominent formal characteristics of contemporary Scottish fiction are its treatment of genre and the inextricable relationship between identity, artistic expression and language(s). Brown, Clancy, Manning and Pittock note that not only does Scottish literature work across genre, it also 'inflects genre in a manner distinctively its own' (Vol.1, 2007: 11). This notion of inflecting genre rather than just crossing generic borders leads to an inevitable transfer of discourses and therefore to the transformation of the initial genre that it implies, to inflecting its original discourse.[19] This characteristic brings new substance to Salman Rushdie's famous assertion that 'to see things plainly, you have to cross a frontier',[20] emphasising writers' ability to re-vision and re-envision, to borrow Widdowson's terms, as well as to imagine. The second feature, the linguistic diversity[21] and even more importantly the fictional work's propensity to metafictionally reflect on language's capacity to carry and, again, inflect the novelistic discourse, which is the one point all the chapters in this book have in common, is very often related to the external, political context, suggesting the intricate connections of the intrinsic and extrinsic approaches to literature in a Scottish context. On the occasion of the Poet Laureateship being awarded to the Scottish poet Carol Ann Duffy in 2009, poet, novelist, broadcaster and critic Clive James said on Radio 4 that 'the national memory travels in the language'.[22] True and important as a solemn affirmation of the poet's (and by extension the writer's) not only artistic, but also historical responsibility as this may be, language, 'the language' to take up James's exact words – the definite article stressing language's centrality to the issue of creativity in Scotland – cannot be reduced to a vehicular function, as carrier of the national memory, or of the national imagination. It has to be awarded a distinctive, artistic specificity. To quote another poet, John Burnside, Scotland's artists deploy 'strong words'.[23]

As early as 1983, the French philosopher and critic Paul Ricoeur was writing that 'we owe a great part of the widening of the horizons of our existence to works of fiction'.[24] This leads us to conclude that if, as the poet W. H. Auden wrote, 'Poetry makes nothing happen',[25] in other words if poetry, or fiction, does not *make* historical or social change directly, it certainly does more than record history. Fiction reflects, projects, anticipates or configures the space of our lives, the horizons of our existence. 'There are times when the world changes' is what Kelman writes in *You Have to be Careful in the Land of the Free.*[26] The many artists whose works are examined in this book, mapping for us the space of Scottish fiction, do much more than just witness or describe those changes.

Notes

1. Those are the subtitles respectively of the present monograph, Hassan, Gibb and Howland's *Scotland 2020*, and Brown, Clancy, Manning and Pittock's *Edinburgh History of Scottish Literature*.
2. Kelly, Stuart. 2009. 'How Tartan is Your Text?', *International Journal of Scottish Literature*, Issue 5, Autumn/Winter, www.ijsl.stir.ac.uk [consulted April 2010]
3. Kelly, Aaron. 2007. 'Stateless Nation/Nationless State: History, Anomaly and Devolution in Scottish and Northern Irish Writing', in *Journal of Irish Scottish Studies*, Vol. 1, Issue 1, September, respectively pp. 256 and 253–54. One must, however, avoid sweeping generalisations about the issues covered by such a diversity of writers. As seen in chapter 1 for instance, *Demo*, by Alison Miller, is very much about class consciousness and class separatism.
4. Aboulela was born in Egypt, grew up in Sudan before moving to Aberdeen with her husband as an adult. She currently lives in Doha.
5. Anderson, Darran. 2008. 'The War Against Silence: An Interview With James Kelman', *3:AM Magazine*, November 20, www.3ammagazine.com/3am/the-war-against-silence-an-interview-with-james-kelman/ [consulted 22 January 2009].
6. For Stuart Kelly's description of the proto-canon of Scottish literature, see the introduction to this book.
7. On a more political note, Alan Taylor reminds us in his editorial to the *Scottish Review of Books* in 2009 of the low level of priority for culture on the Scottish government's agenda in spite of what they proclaimed at the time of the setting up of the devolved parliament. See Taylor, Alan (May 2009), 'Editorial', *Scottish Review of Books*, 5.2, p. 3.
8. Anderson, *3:AM Magazine*.
9. *No Fireworks* (2005) is a Jewish family saga in which the paterfamilias receives letters from his dead mother, those letters being at the origin of the plot, and *Hope for the Newborns* (2008) mixes the past with the present by telling the story of a family of hairdressers, with the father living in the past, specifically the Second World War, and the son engaging in virtual connection in the dot com world via the very strange Hope for the Newborns website, while the catatonic mother is stuck in an arrested present.
10. Kay, Jackie, talking to Isobel Murray in the latter's *Scottish Writers Talking* 4, and quoted by Ali Smith in a review for *The Scottish Review of Books*. May 2009, 5.2, p. 22. Kay nevertheless also acknowledges the idea of the nation as a sort of inescapable background for all writers: 'I do believe that nations actually hand their people, particularly their imaginative, creative people, their own obsessions … a collective unconscious' (2009: 9).
11. Janice Galloway has always been clear about this aspect of her writing. For instance, she says, 'I'm interested in people's vulnerability and what they do with it. Some people can turn it into a weapon, some use it as a survival tool. [...] I'm interested in the visceral'. Galloway, Janice. May 2009. Interview in *The Scottish Review of Books*,5.2, p. 6. In the same interview Galloway, like Kay, describes the writer as an observer of the human.
12. The novel starts as a cold case kind of narrative, with a thriller structure, while the end substitutes a description of the mysterious communication between locusts and their keeper for a 'proper' resolution of the murder plot.
13. See Chapter 6.
14. Morrison, Ewan. 2011. 'Are books dead, and can authors survive?' *The Guardian*, 22 August, www.guardian.co.uk/books/2011/aug/22/are-books-dead-ewan-morrison/print

CONCLUSION

[consulted September 2011]. In this provocative article, which attracted a lot of angry reactions, Morrison raises the question of the 'end of paper' as a medium of communication for the next generation and the issue of paying for content in an age of free availability of material on the internet, which he calls 'the free revolution'. He also tackles the issue of piracy and competitive discounting, and asks the highly controversial question of whether books can in future be written in sweatshops. Morrison sets the tone with the article's opening sentence, writing that 'within twenty-five years the digital revolution will bring about the end of paper books. But more importantly, ebooks and e-publishing will mean the end of "the writer" as a profession. Ebooks, in the future, will be written by first-timers, by teams, by speciality subject enthusiasts and by those who were already established in the era of the paper book. The digital revolution will not emancipate writers or open up a new era of creativity, it will mean that writers offer up their work for next to nothing or for free. Writing, as a profession, will cease to exist'. See also Morrison, Ewan. 2012. 'Factual fiction: writing in an information age', *The Guardian*, 2 March, www.guardian.co.uk/books/2012/mar/02/fact-fiction-writing-information-age [consulted April 2012].
15 Dosa, Attila. Autumn 2004. 'Interview with Tom Leonard', *Scottish Studies Review*, 5.2, p. 71.
16 Widdowson, Peter. 2006. '"Writing back": contemporary re-visionary fiction', *Textual Practice*, 20 (3), p. 492.
17 Widdowson differentiates this re-visionary process from Genette's hypotext/hypertext dichotomy by saying that the re-visionary work is neither an imitation, nor a parody, but rather 'a two-way correspondence in which the recipient *answers* or *replies* to [...] the version of things as originally delineated' (2006: 501).
18 Alex Thomson (2007: 8) suggests that there should be a distinction between questions of identity and questions of style, a method which he sees at work in Bradford's *The Novel Now*. He advocates 'seeing the "Scottish" characteristics of a text as a stylistic question' in order to avoid the pitfall of an 'over-reliance on those mechanisms of identification' (2007: 9).
19 As already noted, Ewan Morrison's *Tales from the Mall* is a glaring example of a totally new way of defining the term 'fiction' itself. This is also the reason why I chose to include in the second chapter of this book novels which were published some years before 2000, particularly McDermid's novel, so that I could focus on genre crossing and generic redefinition (particularly with the works of Louise Welsh) in connection with one of the mistresses of the genre in the late twentieth and early twenty-first centuries.
20 Rushdie, Salman. [1991] 1992. *Imaginary Homelands: Essays and Criticism 1981-1991* (London: Granta), p. 125.
21 This feature is by no means a modern phenomenon. As the editors of the *Edinburgh History* point out, it simply expands in the contemporary period. See Brown, vol. 1, p. 11.
22 James, Clive, on Radio 4, 'A point of view', Sunday, May 10, 2009. The full quotation avers that the existence of a poet laureate is 'an acknowledgement by the state that there is something that the state can't control, which is the national memory, and that the national memory travels in the language, like an arrow-shower, as Philip Larkin said, sent out of sight, somewhere becoming rain'.
23 *Strong Words* is the title of an essay on poetry in which Burnside describes poetry as 'provisional' and as a form of alchemy. Burnside, John. 2000. 'Strong Words', in Herbert,

W. N. and Matthew Hollis (eds), *Strong Words: Modern Poets on Modern Poetry* (Highgreen, Tarset: Bloodaxe Books).
24 'C'est aux œuvres de fiction que nous devons pour une grande part l'élargissement de notre horizon d'existence', Ricoeur, Paul. 1983.*Temps et Récit* (Paris: Seuil), p. 121. My translation.
25 This line is taken from 'In memory of W. B. Yeats'.
26 Kelman, James. 2004. *You Have to be Careful in the Land of the Free* (London: Penguin), p. 90.

Bibliography

Primary Sources

Burnside, John. 2006. *A Lie about My Father* (London: Jonathan Cape)
____. 2001. *The Locust Room* (London: Jonathan Cape)
____. 2000. 'Strong Words', in Herbert, W.N. and Matthew Hollis (eds.), *Strong Words: Modern Poets on Modern Poetry* (Highgreen, Tarset: Bloodaxe Books)
____. 1999. *The Mercy Boys* (London: Jonathan Cape)
____. 1997. *The Dumb House* (London: Jonathan Cape)
Dillon, Des. 2006. *They Scream When You Kill Them* (Edinburgh: Luath Press)
Disraeli, Benjamin. [1845] 1956. *Sybil, or the Two Nations* (Oxford: Oxford U.P.)
Donovan, Anne. 2008. *Being Emily* (Edinburgh: Canongate)
____. [2003] 2004. *Buddha Da* (New York: Carroll and Graf)
____. [2001] 2004. *Hieroglyphics and Other Stories* (Edinburgh: Canongate)
Faber, Michel. [2005] 2006. *The Fahrenheit Twins* (Edinburgh: Canongate)
____. 1998. *Some Rain Must Fall* (Edinburgh: Canongate)
Galloway, Janice. 2011. *All Made Up* (London: Granta)
____. 2008. *This is Not about Me* (London: Granta)
____. [1989] (1991. *The Trick Is to Keep Breathing* (London: Minerva)
Glass, Rodge. 2008. *Hope for the Newborn* (London: Faber & Faber)
____. 2005. *No Fireworks* (London: Faber & Faber)
Gray, Alasdair. [1981] 1991. *Lanark: A Life in Four Books* (London: Picador)
____. 1992. *Poor Things* (London: Bloomsbury)
Hird, Laura. 2007. *Dear Laura* (Edinburgh: Canongate)
____. 2006. *Hope and Other Urban Tales* (Edinburgh: Canongate)
____. [1999] 2000. *Born Free* (Edinburgh: Canongate)
Kelman, James. 2008. *Kieron Smith, Boy* (London: Penguin)
____. 2004. *You Have to be Careful in the Land of the Free* (London: Penguin)
McDermid, Val. [1997] 2002. *The Wire in the Blood* (New York: St Martin's Press)
____. [1995] 2002. *The Mermaids Singing* (New York: St Martin's Press)
____. [1987] 1998. *Report for Murder* (London: The Women's Press)
Miller, Alison. 2005. *Demo* (London and New York: Penguin)
Mina, Denise. [2006] 2008. *The Dead Hour* (New York: Little Brown)
____. [2000] 2001. *Exile* (London: Bantam Books)
____. [1998] 1999. *Garnethill* (London: Bantam Books)
Morrison, Ewan. 2012. *Tales from the Mall* (Glasgow: Cargo publishing)
____. 2009. *Ménage* (London: Jonathan Cape)
____. 2008. *Distance* (London: Jonathan Cape)
____. 2007. *Swung* (London: Jonathan Cape)
____. 2005. *The Last Book You Read* (Edinburgh: Chroma)
Poe, Edgar Allan. 1845. 'The Imp of the Perverse', Electronic Text Center, University of Virginia Library, etext.virginia.edu

Robertson, James. 2010. *And the Land Lay Still* (London: Penguin)
____. 2000] 2001. *The Fanatic* (London: HarperCollins)
Rushdie, Salman. 1992. *The Satanic Verses* (Dover, Delaware: The Consortium)
____. [1983] 1984. *Shame* (London: Picador)
Saadi, Suhayl. 2009. *Joseph's Box* (Ullapool: Two Ravens)
____. 2004. *Psychoraag* (Edinburgh: Black and White)
____. 2001. *The Burning Mirror* (Edinburgh: Polygon)
Scotland Into The New Era. 2000. (Edinburgh: Canongate)
Strachan, Zoë. [2004] 2005. *Spin Cycle* (London: Picador)
____. 2002. *Negative Space* (London: Picador)
Tei, Chiew-Siah. 2008. *Little Hut of Leaping Fishes* (London: Picador)
Welsh, Irvine. 2001. *Glue* (London: Jonathan Cape)
Welsh, Louise. 2010. *Naming the Bones* (Edinburgh: Canongate)
____. 2006. *The Bullet Trick* (Edinburgh: Canongate)
____. 2004. *Tamburlaine Must Die* (Edinburgh: Canongate)
____. 2002. *The Cutting Room* (Edinburgh: Canongate)

Secondary sources

Acheson, James, and Sarah C. E. Ross (eds). 2005. *The Contemporary British Novel* (Edinburgh: Edinburgh U.P)
Adair, Tom. 2009. 'Book review: *Joseph's Box*, by Suhayl Saadi', *The Scotsman*, 15 August, living.scotsman.com/bookreviews/Book-review-Joseph39s-Box-by.5556095.jp [consulted September 2009]
Adams, Jill. April 2003. 'Interview with Laura Hird', in *The Barcelona Review*, www.barcelonareview.com/35/e_int_lh.htm [consulted December 2011]
____. (March-April 2002). 'Interview with Michel Faber', *The Barcelona Review*, Issue 29, www.barcelonareview.com/29/e_mf_int.htm [consulted November 2008]
Anderson, Benedict [1983] 2006. *Imagined Communities*, London: Verso.
____. 1998. *The Spectre of Comparisons: Nationalism, Southeast Asia and the World*, London: Verso.
Anderson, Darran. 2008. 'The War Against Silence: An Interview With James Kelman', *3:AM Magazine,* November 20, www.3ammagazine.com/3am/the-war-against-silence-an-interview-with-james-kelman/ [consulted January 2009]
Anonymous. 2003. 'Anne Donovan Interview'. *The Barcelona Review* 37, July–August, www.barcelonareview.com/37/e_ad_int.htm [consulted February 2009]
Anonymous. 1996. 'A Quick Chat with Iain M. Banks', *The Richmond Review,* www.demon.co.uk/review/features/banksint.html [consulted January 1998]
____. 2006. 'Gothic Nightmares Fuseli, Blake and the romantic imagination', www.tate.org.uk/tateetc/issue6/gothicnightmares.htm [consulted May 2008]
____. 2009. 'Ali Smith interview', *The Scottish Review of Books*, 5.2, www.scottishreviewofbooks.org/index.php/back-issues/volume-five/volume-five-issue-two/21-why-interview-writers-ali-smith [consulted May 2009]
____. 2000. 'Flesh-creeping: It is better to travel than to arrive in Michael Faber's *Under The Skin*', *The Guardian*, April 1, www.guardian.co.uk/books/2000/apr/01/fiction. reviews2 [consulted March 2005]

BIBLIOGRAPHY

____. July 2005. 'Interview with Ewan Morrison', *Arena*, www.blackandwhitepublishing.com/chroma/ewanmorrison/ewanmorrisoninterview.html [consulted February 2009]

____. 2008. 'Michel Faber: The SRB interview', *The Scottish Review of Books*, Volume 4 Issue 4, www.scottishreviewofbooks.org/index.php?option=com_content&view=article&id=65:michael-faber-the-srb-interview&catid=9:volume-4-issue4&Itemid=51 [consulted November 2008]

____. 2009. 'Suhayl Saadi Uncensored', *Kitaab*, kitaabonline.wordpress.com/2009/10/01/suhayl-saadi-uncensored/ [consulted January 2010]

____. 2006. 'Interview with James Robertson', www.scotgeog.com/interview.php [consulted June 2011]

Ashley, Katherine. 2011. '"Ae Thoosand Tongues": Language and Identity in *Psychoraag*', *IRSS* 36, 129–50.

Augé, Marc. 2010. *La Communauté Illusoire* (Paris: Payot)

____. [1992] 2008. *Non-Places: An Introduction to Supermodernity*, Trans. John Howe, (London: Verso)

Bakhtin, Mikhail. 1968. *Rabelais and His World*, Trans. Helene Iswolsky (Cambridge, Mass.: MIT Press)

Bathurst, Bella. 2010. ''And the Land Lay Still by James Robertson: An epic portrait of postindustrial Scotland is almost too painful in its accuracy', *The Observer*, August 15, www.guardian.co.uk/books/2010/aug/15/and-land-lay-still-robertson [consulted May 2011]

Baudrillard, Jean. [1968] 1996. *The System of Objects*, Trans. James Benedict (London and NY: Verso)

Bauman, Zygmunt. 1998. *Globalization: The Human Consequences* (Cambridge: Polity)

____. [2000] 2012. *Liquid Modernity* (Cambridge: Polity)

Bell, Eleanor. 2004. *Questioning Scotland: Literature, Nationalism, Postmodernism* (Basingstoke and New York: Palgrave Macmillan)

Bell, Eleanor and Gavin Miller (eds). 2004. *Scotland in Theory: Reflections on Culture and Literature* (Amsterdam and New York: Rodopi)

Bell, Ian A. (ed.). 1995. *Peripheral Visions: Images of Nationhood in Contemporary British Fiction* (Cardiff: University of Wales Press)

Best, Steven and Douglas Kellner. 1999. 'Debord, Cybersituations and the Interactive Spectacle', *SubStance*, vol. 28, no. 3, Issue 90, pp. 129–56

Bhabha, Homi K. [1994] 1997. *The Location of Culture* (London and NY: Routledge)

Bissett, Alan. May 2009. ''Damage Land' revisited: Scottish Gothic in the Noughties', *The Bottle Imp*, No. 6, asls.arts.gla.ac.uk/SWE/TBI/TBIIssue6/Bissett.html

____. 2007. 'The "New Weegies": The Glasgow Novel in the Twenty-first Century', in Berthold Schoene (ed.), *The Edinburgh Companion to Contemporary Scottish Literature* (Edinburgh: Edinburgh U.P.), pp. 59–67

____ (ed.). 2001. *Damage Land: New Scottish Gothic Fiction* (Edinburgh: Polygon)

____, 'Alison Miller Interviewed', www.laurahird.com/newreview/alisonmillerinterview.html

Boccardi, Mariadele. 2007. 'Pedlars of the nation's past: Douglas Galbraith, James Robertson and the New Historical Novel', in Berthold Schoene (ed.), *The Edinburgh Companion to Contemporary Scottish Literature* (Edinburgh: Edinburgh U.P.), pp. 97–105

Bradford, Richard. 2007. *The Novel Now* (Oxford: Blackwell Publishing)
Brown, Ian (ed.). 2007. *The Edinburgh History of Scottish Literature* (Edinburgh: Edinburgh U.P.)
Brown, Ian and Alan Riach (eds). 2009. *The Edinburgh Companion to Twentieth-century Scottish Literature* (Edinburgh: Edinburgh U.P.)
Brown, Ian and Colin Nicholson, 'The Border Crossers and Reconfiguration of the Possible: Poet-Playwright-Novelists from the mid-Twentieth century on', in Ian Brown (ed.), *The Edinburgh History of Scottish Literature*, vol. 3 (Edinburgh: Edinburgh U.P.), pp. 262–72
Burgess, Moira. 1998. *Imagine a City: Glasgow in Fiction* (Argyll: Argyll Publishing)
Calder, Angus. 2002. *Scotlands of the Mind* (Edinburgh: Luath Press Limited)
____. 2004. 'Saadi's all the rag' *The Sunday Herald*, April 25, sarmed.netfirms.com/suhayl/NEW/books/psycho/calder_review.htm [consulted March 2005]
Campbell, Angus Peter. 2009. 'The Angus Peter Campbell Interview" *Scottish Review of Books*, 5.1, www.scottishreviewofbooks.org/index.php/back-issues/volume-five/volume-five-issue-1/32-angus-peter-campbell-the-srb-interview [consulted March 2010]
Campbell, Ian. 2007. 'Disorientation of Place, Time and "Scottishness": Conan Doyle, Linklater, Gunn, Mackay Brown and Elphinstone', in Brown, Ian (ed.), *The Edinburgh History of Scottish Literature*, vol. 3 (Edinburgh: Edinburgh U.P.), pp. 106–13
Campbell, James. 2010. 'A life in writing: James Robertson', *The Guardian*, 14 August www.guardian.co.uk/books/2010/aug/14/james-robertson-land-still-profile [consulted July 2011]
Caputi, Jane. 1993. 'American Psychos: The Serial Killer in Contemporary Fiction', *Journal of American Culture*, 16/1, pp. 101–12
Carruthers, Gerald. 2009. *Scottish Literature* (Edinburgh: Edinburgh U.P.)
Carruthers, Gerald, David Goldie and Alastair Renfrew (eds). 2004. *Beyond Scotland: New Contexts for Twentieth Century Scottish Literature* (Amsterdam and New York: Rodopi)
Cartwright, Justin. 2009. 'A Week in December by Sebastian Faulks', *The Observer*, 23 August, www.guardian.co.uk/books/2009/aug/23/week-in-december-faulks [retrieved July 2011]
Christianson, Aileen and Alison Lumsden (eds). 2000. *Contemporary Scottish Women Writing* (Edinburgh: Edinburgh U.P.)
Clanfield, Peter and Christian Lloyd. 2007. 'Redevelopment Fiction: Architecture, Town-Planning and "Unhomeliness"', in Berthold Schoene (ed.), *The Edinburgh Companion to Contemporary Scottish Literature* (Edinburgh, Edinburgh U.P.), pp. 124–31
Connell, Liam. 2004. 'Scottish Nationalism and the Colonial Vision of Scotland', *Interventions: International Journal of Postcolonial Studies*, Vol. 6 (2), June, pp. 252–63
Craig, Cairns. 2006. 'No Nationality Without Literature', *GRAAT* no. 33, 79–98
____. 2001. 'Constituting Scotland', *Irish Review* 28, pp. 1–27
____. 1999. *The Modern Scottish Novel: Narrative and the National Imagination* (Edinburgh: Edinburgh U.P.)

____. 1996. *Out of History: Narrative Paradigms in Scottish and British Culture* (Edinburgh: Polygon)
____ (ed.). [1987] 1989. *The History of Scottish Literature*, Volume 4, Twentieth Century, (Aberdeen: Aberdeen U.P.)
Cranny-Francis, Anne. 1988. 'Gender and Genre: Feminist Rewritings of detective Fiction', *Women's Studies International Forum*, 11/1, pp. 69–84
Crawford, Robert. 2007. *Scotland's Books* (London: Penguin)
____. 1995. *Literature in Twentieth Century Scotland: A Select Bibliography*, (London: The British Council Literature Department)
____. 1992. *Devolving Scottish Literature* (Oxford: Clarendon)
Devine, T. M. and R. J Finlay. [1996] 2003. *Scotland in the Twentieth Century* (Edinburgh: Edinburgh U.P.)
Dosa, Attila. 2004. 'Interview with Tom Leonard', *Scottish Studies Review*, 5.2, Autumn, pp. 67–89
Edinburgh Review 100. 1999.
Edinburgh Review 102. 1999.
Erskine, Sophie. 2009. 'A New Literary Form Is Born: An Interview with Suhayl Saadi', www.3ammagazine.com/3am/a-new-literary-form-is-born-an-interview-with-suhayl-saadi/ [consulted April 2010]
Farrukhi, Asif. n.d. 'Suhayl Saadi – Life of creative tension', sarmed.netfirms.com/suhayl/NEW/books/psycho/dawn_review.htm [consulted February 2009]
Fish, Stanley. 1997. 'Boutique Multiculturalism or Why Liberals Are Incapable of Thinking about Hate Speech', *Critical Enquiry* 23/2, pp. 378-395
Forshaw, Barry. 2007. *The Rough Guide to Crime Fiction* (London: Rough Guides ltd)
Gallix, Andrew. 2009. 'More Thanatos than Eros: Ewan Morrison Interviewed by Andrew Gallix', *3:AM Magazine*: August 28, www.3ammagazine.com/3am/more-thanatos-than-eros/ [consulted February 2011]
Galloway, Janice. 2009. 'Janice Galloway – The SRB Interview, *The Scottish Review of Books* 5.2. www.scottishreviewofbooks.org/index.php/back-issues/volume-five/volume-five-issue-two/10-janice-galloway-the-srb-interview [consulted March 2010]
Galvin, Cathy. 2009. 'Sebastian Faulks on the state of the nation', *The Sunday Times*, August 23, entertainment.timesonline.co.uk/tol/arts_and_entertainment/books/fiction/article6803845.ece?token=null&offset=0&page=1 [retrieved July 2011]
Gardiner, Michael. 2009. 'Arcades – the 1980s and 1990s', in Brown, Ian and Alan Riach (eds), *The Edinburgh Companion to Twentieth-century Scottish Literature* (Edinburgh: Edinburgh U.P.), pp 181–92
____. 2006. *From Trocchi to Trainspotting: Scottish Critical Theory since 1960* (Edinburgh: Edinburgh U.P.)
____. 2005. *Modern Scottish Culture* (Edinburgh: Edinburgh U.P.)
____. 2004. '"A Light to the World?" British Devolution and the Colonial Vision', *Interventions: International Journal of Postcolonial Studies*, Vol. 6 (2), June, pp. 264–81
____. 1996. 'Democracy and Scottish Postcoloniality', *Scotlands*, 3.2, pp. 24–41
Gelonesi, Joe. 2005. 'Interview with Ewan Morrison', ABC, www.abc.net.au/rn/bookshow/stories/2007/2014517.htm [consulted August 2009]

Germana, Monica. 2009. 'Embodying the Spectral Self: the Ghost Motif on Scottish Women's Writing', *The Bottle Imp*, no.6, November, asls.arts.gla.ac.uk/SWE/TBI/TBIIssue6/Germana2.html [consulted November 2009]
Gifford, Douglas, Sarah Dunnigan and Alan MacGillivray (eds). 2002. *Scottish Literature in English and Scots* (Edinburgh: Edinburgh U.P.)
____. 1999. 'Scottish Fiction and Millenial Uncertainty', *In Scotland*, 1, Autumn, pp. 23–39
Gifford, Douglas and Dorothy McMillan (eds). 1997. *A History of Scottish Women's Writing* (Edinburgh: Edinburgh U.P.)
Glass, Rodge. 2008. *Alasdair Gray: A Secretary's Biography* (London: Bloomsbury)
Gordon, Greg. 2005. 'For Ewan the only way is up', *The Times*, 26 June, www.blackandwhitepublishing.com/chroma/ewanmorrison/ewanmorrisontimesinterview.html [consulted February 2009]
Gray, Alasdair. 2010. *Alasdair Gray: La Littérature ou le refus de l'amnésie/Literature against Amnesia* (Avignon : Editions Universitaires d'Avignon)
Hadley, Mary. 2003. 'An Interview with Val McDermid', *Storytelling*, pp. 31–45
____. 2002. *British Women Writers Mystery Writers: Six Authors of Detective Fiction with Female Sleuths* (Jefferson: McFarland)
Harrison, M. John. 2005. 'The future tense', *The Guardian*, Saturday 3 September, www.guardian.co.uk/books/2005/sep/03/featuresreviews.guardianreview13 [consulted November 2008]
Hassan, Gerry, Gibb, Eddie and Howland, Lydia (eds). 2005. *Scotland 2020: Hopeful Stories for A Northern Nation* (London: Demos)
Haywood, Ian. 1997. *Working-class Fiction: From Chartism to* Trainspotting (Plymouth: Northcote House)
Holcombe, Garan. 2007. 'Author Profile – Ewan Morrison', www.contemporarywriters.com [consulted April 2009]
Horsley, Katherine and Lee Horsley. 1999. '*Mères Fatales*: Maternal Guilt in the Noir Crime Novel', *Modern Fiction Studies*, 45/2, pp. 369–402
____. 1995. 'Body Language: Reading the Corpse in Forensic Crime Fiction', *Paradoxa* 20, pp. 7–32
Horsley, Lee. 2005. *Twentieth Century Crime Fiction* (Oxford, Oxford U.P.)
Hughes, Peggy. 2009. 'Book review: *Joseph's Box*', *The Scotsman*, 19 July, living.scotsman.com/bookreviews/Book-review-Joseph39s-Box.5472937.jp [consulted September 2009]
Hume, Samantha. 2003. '"Here's tae Us Wha's Like Us": Val McDermid's Lindsay Gordon Mysteries' in Dorothea Fisher-Hornung and Monika Mueller (eds), *Sleuthing Ethnicity: The Detective in Multiethnic Crime Fiction* (Cranbury: Associated University Presses), pp. 227–39
Hutcheon, Linda. 1988. *A Poetics of Postmodernism: History, Theory, Fiction* (London: Routledge)
Innes, Kirstin. 2007. 'Mark Renton's Bairns: Identity and Language in the Post-*Trainspotting* Novel', in Berthold Schoene (ed.), *The Edinburgh Companion to Scottish Literature*, (Edinburgh: Edinburgh U.P.), pp. 301–309
Irons, Glenwoods (ed.). 1995. *Feminism in Women's Detective Crime Fiction* (Toronto: University of Toronto Press)

BIBLIOGRAPHY

Jakeman, Jane. 2003. 'Val McDermid: The dying game', *The Independent*, Saturday, 24 May, www.independent.co.uk/arts-entertainment/books/features/val-mcdermid-the-dying-game-590995.html [Consulted May 2005]

James, Clive. 2009. 'A point of view', Radio 4, Sunday, May 10.

Jameson, Fredric. 1986. 'On Magic Realism in Film', *Critical Enquiry*, vol. 12, no.2, pp. 301–25

Jamieson, Alan Robert. 2010. 'New Publications. Book Review: *And the Land Lay Still*, by James Robertson', The *Bottle Imp*, Issue 10, www.thebottleimp. org.uk

Johnson, Dorothy. 2001. 'Laura Hird – *Born Free*', in www.spikemagazine.com/1201laurahird.php [consulted December 2011]

Johnstone, Doug. 2009. 'Suhayl Saadi', *The List*, Issue 636, edinburghfestival.list.co.uk/article/19858-suhayl-saadi/ [consulted September 2009]

Kelly, Aaron. 2007. 'Stateless Nation/Nationless State: History, Anomaly and Devolution in Scottish and Northern Irish Writing', in *Journal of Irish Scottish Studies*, Vol.1, Issue 1, September, pp. 253–69

Kelly, Stuart. 2009. 'How Tartan is Your Text?', *International Journal of Scottish Literature*, Issue 5, Autumn/Winter, www.ijsl.stir.ac.uk [consulted April 2010]

Kövesi, Simon. 2009. '*Joseph's Box, by Suhayl Saadi*', *The Independent*, Friday, 11 September, www.independent.co.uk/arts-entertainment/books/reviews/josephs-box-by-suhayl-saadi-1784898.html [consulted November 2009]

Kravitz, Peter (ed.). 1997. *The Picador Book of Contemporary Scottish Fiction* (London: Picador)

Kristeva, Julia. 1982. *Powers of Horror: An Essay on Abjection* (New York: Columbia U.P.)

Lambert, Marc. 2005. 'The Age of Capitals', in Hassan, Gerry, Eddie Gibb and Lydia Howland (eds.), *Scotland 2020: Hopeful Stories for a Northern Nation* (London: Demos), pp. 123–133

Larsonneur, Claire. 2009. 'Location, location, location', *Etudes Britanniques Contemporaines*, no. 37, Décembre, pp. 141–152

Lawless, Andrew. 2005. 'Spending imaginative capital – Michel Faber and *The Fahrenheit Twins*', *The Three Monkeys online*, October, www.threemonkeysonline.com/als/-michel-faber-interview-the-fahrenheit-twins.html [consulted February 2011]

Lawson, Mark. 2006. 'And for her next trick ..', *The Guardian*, Saturday July 22, books. guardian.co.uk/reviews/crime/0,,1826032,00.html [consulted July 2006]

Lercercle, Jean-Jacques. [1990] 1999. *The Violence of Language* (London: Routledge)

Lehner, Stephanie. 2011. *Subaltern Ethics in Contemporary Scottish and Irish Literature: Tracing Counter-Histories* (Basingstoke: Palgrave McMillan)

Letissier, Georges. 2009. 'The Crimson Petal and the White: a neo-Victorian Classic?', in Letissier, Georges (ed.), *Rewriting/Reprising: Plural Intertextualities* (Newcastle: Cambridge Scholars), pp. 113–25

Lewis, Georgie. n.d. 'Denise Mina Is a Wee Cheeky Cow!' www.powells.com/authors/mina.html [consulted March 2009]

Longley, Edna, Eamonn Hughes and Des O'Rawes (eds). 2003. *Ireland (Ulster) Scotland: Concepts, Contexts, Comparisons* (Belfast: Clo Ollscoil na Banriona)

Lyotard, Jean-François. 1973. *Des Dispositifs Pulsionnels* (Paris: UGE)

MacDonald, Kirsty. 2009. 'Scottish Gothic: Towards a Definition', *The Bottle Imp* no.6, asls.arts.gla.ac.uk/SWE/TBI/TBIIssue6/Scottish_Gothic.pdf [consulted November 2009]

MacNeil, Kevin. 2005. '100 Best Scottish Books of all Time', *The List*, January www.list.co.uk/article/2736-laura-hird-born-free-1999/ [consulted December 2011]

Maley, Willy. 2008. *Literature and Diversity: Border-crossing: New Scottish Writing*, Scottish Book Trust, online publication, www.scottishbooktrust.com/files/Border-crossing%20-%20New%20Scottish%20Writing%20by%20Willy%20Maley.pdf [consulted Sept 2009]

——. n.d. *Discovering Scottish Literature: a Contemporary Overview*, www.scottishbooktrust.com/files/Border-crossing%20-%20New%20Scottish%20Writing%20by%20Willy%20Maley.pdf [consulted December 2008]

March, Cristie L. 2002. *Rewriting Scotland: Welsh, McLean, Warner, Banks, Galloway and Kennedy* (Manchester and New York: Manchester U.P.)

Maxey, Ruth. 2012. *South Asian Atlantic Literature: 1970–2010* (Edinburgh: Edinburgh U.P.)

McDermid, Val. 2007. 'I start my day in a condition of rage', *The Guardian*, August 17, books.guardian.co.uk/departments/crime/story/0,,2150615,00.html [consulted August 2007]

McGonigal, James and Kirsten Stirling (eds). 2006. *Ethically Speaking: Voices and Values in Modern Scottish Writing* (Amsterdam and New York: Rodopi)

McHale, Brian. [1987] 1991. *Postmodernist Fiction* (London and New York: Routledge)

McNeill, Kirsty. 1989. 'Interview with James Kelman', *Chapman* 57, Summer, pp. 1–9

Miller, Alison. 2005. Interview, *BooksfromScotland.com*, www.booksfromscotland.com/Authors/Alison-Miller [consulted March 2009]

Miller, Gavin. 2006. 'Aesthetic depersonalisation in Louise Welsh's *The Cutting Room*', *Journal of Narrative Theory: JNT*, 36:1, Winter, pp. 72–89

Milton, Colin. 2007. 'Past and Present: Modern Scottish Historical Fiction' in Ian Brown (ed.), *The Edinburgh History of Scottish Literature* (Edinburgh: Edinburgh U.P.), pp. 115–29

Mina, Denise. n.d. 'the Politics of writing crime', www.britishcouncil.org/arts-literature-matters-state-mina.htm [consulted April 2009]

Mitchell W. J. T. 1995. 'Translator translated: interview with cultural theorist Homi Bhabha' *Artforum* v.33, n.7, March, pp. 80–84, prelectur.stanford.edu/lecturers/bhabha/interview.html [consulted April 2012]

Morrison, Ewan. 2012. (2012), 'Factual fiction: writing in an information age', *The Guardian*, 2 March, www.guardian.co.uk/books/2012/mar/02/fact-fiction-writing-information-age [consulted April 2012]

——. 2011. 'Are books dead, and can authors survive?', *The Guardian*, 22 August, www.guardian.co.uk/books/2011/aug/22/are-books-dead-ewan-morrison/print [consulted September 2011]

——. 2009. 'Could it be that at the age of ten I had grasped the essence of alienation?', *Scotland on Sunday*, 16 August, www.scotsman.com/ewan-morrison/Ewan-Morrison-39Could-it-be.5558233.jp [consulted October 2009]

——. 2009. 'Death of a Nihilist or Obituary for a Nobody', *3AM Magazine*, www.3ammagazine.com/3am/death-of-a-nihilist-or-obituary-for-a-nobody/ [consulted November 2009]

Morrison, Jago. 2003. *Contemporary Fiction* (London and NY: Routledge)

Moses, David. 2004. '*Buddha Da*. By Anne Donovan', in *Scottish Studies Review*, 5.1, Spring, pp. 130-32
Munt, Sally R. 1994. *Murder by the book?: Feminism and the Crime Novel* (London: Routledge)
Nairn, Tom. 2004. 'Break-Up: Twenty-Five Years On', in Bell, Eleanor and Gavin Miller (eds), *Scotland in Theory: Reflections on Culture and Literature* (Amsterdam and New York: Rodopi), pp. 17-34
Neubauer, Jürgen. 1999. *Literature as Intervention: Struggles over Cultural Identity in Contemporary Scottish Fiction* (Marburg: Textum Verlag)
Norquay, Glenda and Gerry Smyth (eds). 2002. *Across the Margins: Cultural Identity and Change in the Atlantic Archipelago* (Manchester and New York: Manchester U.P.)
____ (eds). 1997. *Space and Place: The Geographies of Literature* (Liverpool: John Moore U.P.)
O'Connor, Edmund. 2007. 'Tartan Noir', *Chapman* 108, pp. 50-58
O'Rourke, Donny. 2011. '*And the Land Lay Still* - James Robertson', *Scottish Left Review*, 63, March-April, pp. 26-7, www.scottishleftreview.org/li/images/stories/pdf/i63.pdf [consulted July 2011]
Peddie, Ian. 2007. 'Speaking Welsh: Irvine Welsh in Conversation', *Scottish Studies Review* 8.1, pp. 130-39
Phillips, Richard. 1997. *Mapping Men and Empire: A Geography of Adventure* (London: Routledge)
Pittin-Hedon, Marie-Odile. 2009. 'Scottish Contemporary Popular and Genre fiction', in Ian Brown and Riach, Alan (eds), *The Edinburgh Companion to Twentieth-century Scottish Literature* (Edinburgh, Edinburgh U.P.), pp. 193-203
____. 2008. '"Learn Your Own Way to Read the Map": rôle et place du roman écossais dans le processus de devolution', *Babel*, 17, pp. 195-210
Plain, Gill. 2007. 'Concepts of Corruption: Crime Fiction and the Scottish "State"', in Berthold Schoene (ed.), *The Edinburgh Companion to Contemporary Scottish Literature* (Edinburgh: Edinburgh U.P.), pp. 132-40
____. 2001. *Twentieth Century Crime Fiction: Gender, Sexuality and the Body* (Edinburgh: Edinburgh U.P.)
Priestman, Martin (ed.). 2003. *The Cambridge Companion to Crime Fiction* (Cambridge: Cambridge U.P.)
____. 1998. *Crime Fiction: From Poe to the Present* (Plymouth: Northcote House)
Rankin, Ian. 2007. 'Foreword', in Barry Forshaw, *The Rough Guide to Crime Fiction*, (London: Rough Guides ltd), pp. vi-vii
____. 1999. 'Why Crime Fiction is good for you', *Edinburgh Review* 102, pp. 9-16
Rawlinson, Zsuzsa. n.d. 'Zoë Strachan interview', www.britishcouncil.org/hungary-arts-literature-strachan.htm [consulted June 2010]
Reder, Michael (ed.). 2000. *Conversations with Salman Rushdie* (Jackson: University Press of Mississipi)
Renton, Jennie. 2006. 'Death and Literature' *Textualities* (online magazine), textualities.net/writers/features-n-z/welshlo1.php [consulted March 2007]
Riach, Alan. 2005. *Representing Scotland in Literature, Popular Culture and Iconography: The Masks of the Modern Nation* (London: Palgrave Macmillan)
Ricoeur, Paul. 1983. *Temps et Récit* (Paris: Seuil)

Ross, Peter. 2007. 'Sultan of Swing', *Herald Scotland*, 7 April, www.heraldscotland.com/sultan-of-swing-1.836350 [consulted August 2009]
Rowland, Susan. 2001. *From Agatha Christie to Ruth Rendell: British Women Writers in Detective and Crime Fiction* (Basingstoke: Palgrave)
Rushdie, Salman. [1991] 1992. *Imaginary Homelands: Essays and Criticism 1981–1991* (London: Granta)
Saadi, Suhayl. 2007. 'In Tom Paine's Kitchen', in Berthold Schoene (ed.), *The Edinburgh Companion to Contemporary Scottish Literature* (Edinburgh: Edinburgh U.P.), pp. 28–33
———. 2006. '*Psychoraag*: The Gods Of The Door', *Spike Magazine*, www.spikemagazine.com/0206-suhayl-saadi-censorship-in-the-uk.php [consulted March 2007]
———. 2006. 'Songs of the Village Idiot: Ethnicity, Writing and Identity', in McGonigal, James and Kirsten Stirling (eds), *Ethically speaking: voice and values in modern Scottish writing* (Amsterdam and New York: Rodopi), pp. 117–138
———. 2000. 'Infinite Diversity in New Scottish Writing', asls.arts.gla.ac.uk/SSaadi.html [consulted February 2011]
Sardar, Ziauddin. 2008. *Balti Britain: A Journey through the British Asian Experience* (London: Granta)
Shaikh, Farhana (ed.). 2010. *Happy Birthday to Me: A Collection of Contemporary Asian Writing* (Leicester: Dahlia Publishing)
Schoene, Berthold. 2008. 'Cosmopolitan Scots', *The Scottish Studies Review*, 9, 2, Autumn, pp. 71–92
——— (ed.). 2007. *The Edinburgh Companion to Contemporary Scottish Literature* (Edinburgh: Edinburgh U.P.)
———. 2007. 'Going Cosmopolitan: Reconstituting "Scottishness" in Post-devolution Criticism', in Berthold Schoene (ed.), *The Edinburgh Companion to Contemporary Scottish Literature* (Edinburgh: Edinburgh U.P.) pp. 7–16
———. 1995. 'A Passage to Scotland: Scottish Literature and the British Postcolonial Condition', *Scotlands*, 2.1, pp. 107–22
Scott, Jeremy. 2009. *The Demotic Voice in Contemporary British Fiction* (Basingstoke and New York: Palgrave MacMillan)
Scott, Maggie. 2008. 'Voices from Modern Literary Glasgow: *Buddha Da* and *Psychoraag*', *The Bottle Imp*, Issue 3, May, asls.arts.gla.ac.uk/SWE/TBI/TBIIssue3/Voices.pdf
Searle, Adrian. 2008. 'Anne Donovan Interview', glasgowwriters.wordpress.com/featured-writers/anne-donovan/ February 2008, [consulted March 2009]
Smith, Ali. 2009. 'Why Interview Writers?', *Scottish Review of Books*, 5.2, www.scottishreviewofbooks.org/index.php/back-issues/volume-five/volume-five-issue-two/21-why-interview-writers-ali-smith [consulted March 2010]
———. 2004. 'Life Beyond the M25: Ali Smith enjoys new fiction from Scotland and Wales', *The Guardian*, 18 December, www.guardian.co.uk/books/2004/dec/18/fiction.alismith [consulted November 2009]
Stevenson, Randall. 2011.'*And the Land Lay Still*', in *Edinburgh Review*, 131, pp. 98–99
Stotesbury, John A. 2010. 'Language and identity in the narration of Suhayl Saadi's Glasgow fiction', in Georgieva, Maria and Allan James (eds), *Globalization in English Studies* (Newcastle: Cambridge Scholars)

Strachan, Zoë. 2007. 'Is that a Scot or am Ah Wrang?' in Berthold Schoene (ed.), *The Edinburgh Companion to Contemporary Scottish Literature*, Edinburgh: Edinburgh U.P.), pp. 51–58
Taylor, Alan. 2009. 'Editorial', *Scottish Review of Books*, 5.2, May; p. 3, www.scottishreviewofbooks.org/index.php/back-issues/volume-five/volume-five-issue-two/8-editorial-volume-5-issue-2 [consulted March 2010]
____. 2004. 'Fable bodied: Born in England to Pakistani parents, and now working', *The Sunday Herald*, April 4, findarticles.com/p/articles/mi_qn4156/is_20040404/ ai_n12587975/ [consulted August 2009]
Taylor, Diana. 1991. 'Transculturating Transculturation', in Marranca, Bonnie and Gautam Dasgupta (eds.), *Interculturalism and Performance* (New York: PAJ Publications), pp. 60–74
The Scottish Review of Books 5.2. May 2009, www.scottishreviewofbooks.org/index.php/back-issues/volume-five/volume-five-issue-two/8-editorial-volume-5-issue-2
Thomson, Alex. 2007. '"You can't get there from here": Devolution and Scottish literary history', *International Journal of Scottish Literature*, Issue 3, Autumn/Winter, www.ijsl.stir.ac.uk [consulted April 2010]
____. 1999. 'Editorial', *Edinburgh Review* 102, p. 3
Turton-Smith, Ian. 2010. 'Is this a Novel I See Before Me? James Robertson's *And the Land Lay Still*', *Scottish Review of Books*, Volume 6, Issue 3, www.scottishreviewofbooks.org/index.php?option=comcontent&view=article&id=348:is-this-a-novel-i-see-before-me-james-robertsons-and-the-land-lay-still-ian-bell&catid=36:volume-6-issue-3-2010&Itemid=85 [retrieved July 2011]
Upstone Sarah. 2010. *British Asian Fiction: Twenty-First Century Voices* (Manchester: Manchester U.P.)
Wallace, Gavin and Randall Stevenson (eds). [1993] 1994. *The Scottish Novel since the Seventies: New Visions, Old Dreams* (Edinburgh: Edinburgh U.P.)
Waters, Colin. 2010. 'Scotland is the subject of a state-of-the-nation novel with a Dickensian scope', *The Herald*, August, www.heraldscotland.com/arts-ents/fiction-reviews/james-robertson-and-the-land-lay-still-hamish-hamilton-18-99-1.1045894?50883 [retrieved July 2011]
Watson, Roderick. [1984] 2007. *The Literature of Scotland II: The Twentieth Century* (New York and London: Palgrave Macmillan)
____. 1998. 'Postcolonial Subject?: Language, Narrative Authority and Class in Contemporary Scottish Culture', *The European English Messenger*, 7:1, pp. 21–31
Welleck, René and Austin Warren. [1949] 1963. *Theory of Literature* (Harmondsworth: Penguin)
Welsh, Irvine. 2010. '*And the Land Lay Still* by James Robertson. Irvine Welsh enjoys a sweeping look through a Scottish lens at a turbulent era', *The Guardian*, 24 July www.guardian.co.uk/books/2010/jul/24/land-lay-still-james-robertson [consulted May 2011]
Widdowson, Peter. 2006. '"Writing back": contemporary re-visionary fiction', *Textual Practice*, 20 (3), pp. 491–507
Wild, Peter. 2002. 'Snuggling up to Queen Victoria: an interview with Michel Faber', *3AM Magazine*, www.3ammagazine.com/litarchives/2002_sep/interview_michel_faber.html [consulted November 2008]

Woodward, Catherine. 2008–9. 'Joseph's Box by Suhayl Saadi', The Glasgow Review, www.glasgowreview.co.uk/ [consulted March 2011]

Wright, Jude.2000. 'A Glasgow kiss for legal lads', The Independent, 19 August, www.independent.co.uk/arts-entertainment/books/features/a-glasgow-kiss-for-legal-lads-697303.html [consulted September 2009]

Websites

The Association for Scottish Literary Studies: www.asls.org.uk
The Bottle Imp: www.thebottleimp.org.uk
Ewan Morrison's website: www.ewanmorrison.com
International Journal of Scottish Literature: www.ijsl.stir.ac.uk
Joseph Box's website: www.josephsbox.co.uk
Laura Hird's website: www.laurahird.com
Scottish Review of Books: www.scottishreviewofbooks.org
Scottish Writing: www.scottishwriting.org.uk

List of abbreviations

The following abbreviations refer to the novels or short story collections examined in this book. The editions used are those indicated in the bibliography:

ALLS: And the Land Lay Still
BD: Buddha Da
BE: Being Emily
BF: Born Free
BM: The Burning Mirror
BT: The Bullet Trick
CR: The Cutting Room
D: Distance
DE: Demo
DH: The Dead Hour
E: Exile
F: The Fanatic
FT: The Fahrenheit Twins
H: Hieroglyphics
HO: Hope and Other Urban Tales
JB: Joseph's Box
LBYR: The Last Book You Read
M: Ménage
MS: The Mermaids Singing
NS: Negative Space
P: Psychoraag
RM: Report for Murder
S: Swung
SC: Spin Cycle
SNE: Scotland Into The New Era
SWKT: They Scream When You Kill Them
TMD: Tamburlaine Must Die
WB: The Wire in the Blood

Index

Aboulela, Leila, 183
a-heroic noir, 42, 45
Anderson, Benedict, 59, 65
anti-fairy tale, 15
articulation, 87, 96–97, 109
Auden, W. H., 187
Augé, Marc, xviii, 110, 118–20, 129
Bakhtin, Mikhail, 23, 126–27
Banks, Iain, viii
Baudrillard, Jean, 118, 123–25, 133, 142
Bauman, Zygmunt, xix, 117–18, 122, 127, 133–35, 138–39
   Globalization: the Human Consequences, 134, 138
   Liquid Modernity, 124, 133, 135
Bell, Eleanor, vii, xii–xiii, 60, 62, 130–31
   Questioning Scotland: Literature, Nationalism, Postmodernism, 60, 62, 131
   and Gavin Miller, *Scotland in Theory* vii, xii–xiii, 130
Benjamin, Walter, 102
Best, Steven, 132
Bhabha, Homi, 81, 83, 87, 96, 101–02, 104, 110
Billig, Michael, 130
Bissett, Alan, xi–xii, xvi–xvii, 3, 13–15, 94, 101
Boccardi, Mariadele, 59–60
Bradford, Richard, vii, 186 n.18
Brookmyre, Christopher, 33, 37
Brown, Ian, xi, xv, 182–83, 186
Burgess, Moira, 3
Burnside, John, 184–85, 187
Calder, Angus, viii, xiii, xv, 28
   Scotland of the Mind, viii, xv, 81 n.3
Campbell, Angus Peter, xvi
Campbell, Ian, 33
carnivalesque, 126–28
Carrol, Lewis 107, 157
Carter, Angela, 84
Chandler, Raymond, 33–34, 36, 37 n.14
Christianson, Aileen, 1
Christie, Agatha, 33–34, 37 n.14, 49, 186
Clancy, Thomas, 182–83, 186
Conan Doyle, Arthur, 33
Cornwell, Patricia, 39
cosmopolitanism, xii–xx, 8, 10, 20–21, 28, 151, 153
Craig, Cairns, vii–viii, xiii, 58–60, 63–64
Crawford, Robert, *Scotland's Books*, xiii
cybercommunication, xix, 119, 170
Debord, Guy, 118, 131–32

devolution/devolved Scotland, vii–viii, xii, xv, 37, 56, 58, 62, 75, 151, 157, 182, 186
Dillon, Des, xix, 150–55, 158–59, 162, 164, 168–71, 173–75
Disraeli, Benjamin, 61–62
Donald, Jason, *Choke Chain*, xii
Donovan, Anne x–xi, xvi–xvii, xx, 1–3, 6, 8–11, 15, 22–29, 33, 81, 150, 160–62
   Being Emily, 8–10, 22, 25
   Buddha Da, x, 2, 11, 15, 22–29
   Hieroglyphics, 22–25
   'Millennium Babe', 150, 160–62
Dorward, Peter, 159
Duffy, Carol Ann, 187
Dunant, Sarah, 43
Edwards, David, 153–54
Ellroy, James, 34
Faber, Michel, xi, xvi, xix, 150–51, 153, 155–56, 162, 164, 167–77, 184–86
Fagan, Jenni, xii, 33
feminism, 16, 38–40, 49, 60
Fish, Stanley, 82
Frazer, James, 165
Gaboriau, Emile, 33
Galloway, Janice, viii–ix, xi, xiv–xv, xvii, 1–2, 6, 8, 14–17, 25, 33, 184–85
Gardiner, Michael, 69
generic crossing, xi, xvi–xviii, 33–34, 58, 65, 68–69, 106, 117, 156, 175, 184–87
Gifford, Douglas, xv, 1
   A History of Scottish Women's Writing, 1, 14 n.29
Glass, Rodge, xi, 184
globalisation, xii–xvi, xviii–xx, 3, 27, 94, 117, 130–34, 136–39, 162, 169–70, 184
gothic, xvii, 13–14, 34–35, 50–51
Gramsci, Antonio, 14
Grassic Gibbon, Lewis, 71, 76
Gray, Alasdair, ix–xi, 10–11, 14, 59, 61, 94, 155–56, 185
grotesque, 126–29, 152
Gunn, Neil M., 165
Habermas, Jürgen, xii, 81
Hammett, Dashiell, 33–34
Harvie, Christopher, vii
Hassan, Gerry, *Scotland 2020*, xv–xvi, 186
Hird, Laura, xvii, 2–3, 10–16, 29, 33, 185
   Born Free, 2–3, 10–16
   'Castle Terrace Car Park', 12
   Hope, And Other Urban Tales, 2, 14
Hogg, James, 34, 76

INDEX

Holcombe, Garan, 118
Horsley, Lee, 36, 42
Horsley, Lee and Katherine, 42,
Houellebecq, Michel, 146
Hrushovski, Benjamin, 74
Huxley, Aldous, 153, 155
Innes, Kirstin, 1–2, 16
James, Clive, 187
Jameson, Fredric, 127–28
Johnston, Paul, 33
Joyce, James, 84
Kay, Jackie, xi n.16, 6, 184
Kearney, Richard, xii
Kellner, Douglas, 132
Kelly, Stuart, xvii n.32, 182–84
Kelman, James, x–xi, xiv, xvi–xviii, 2–3, 5–6, 11, 13–15, 23, 183–84, 187
   You Have to be Careful in the Land of the Free, xiv, 187
Kennedy, A.L., xi, xvi–xvii, 1–2, 14, 33, 185
Kristeva, Julia, 44
Lambert, Marc, xiii, 177–78
language, xi–xii, xvi–xviii, 1, 6–8, 11–12, 16, 18, 22–29, 87–89, 92–101, 105, 107, 109–11, 160–61, 171, 186–87
Larsonneur, Claire, 129–30
Lecercle, Jean-Jacques, 92
Legge, Gordon, 2
Lehner, Stephanie, xvii, 14–15, 16 n.38
Leonard, Tom, viii, x, 5, 185
Letissier, Georges, 162 n.16
Livingston, Stephen, 156–57
Lockerbie, Catherine, 182
Lumsden, Alison, 1
Lyotard, Jean-François, 77
McBride, Stuart, 33
McCall Smith, Alexander, 33
McDermid, Val, xvii, 33–34, 36–40, 42–45, 47–50, 53, 81, 186
   The Mermaids Singing, 40, 43, 45, 48–49
   The Wire in the Blood, 43–45, 48
   Report for Murder, 49
MacDiarmid, Hugh, xv, 34, 63, 74, 77, 158
McGovan, James, 33
McHale, Brian, 74, 154 n.8
McIlvanney, William, xv, 12, 14, 37
McLean, Duncan, viii, 2
McLevy, James, 33
McMillan, Dorothy, xv, 1
   A History of Scottish Women's Writing, 1, 14 n.29

MacNeil, Kevin, 10–11, 14–15
McNicoll, Andrea, xii
Maley, Willy, xi, 58, 67
Manning, Susan, 182–83, 186
March, Cristie, 15, 17
Meek, James, 2
metafiction, 93–94, 98, 110 n.83, 166, 186–87
Miller, Alison, x, xvii, 2–8, 10, 11 n.19, 29, 33, 183 n.3
   Demo, x, 2–8, 183 n.3
Milton, Colin, 57
Mina, Denise, xvii, xx, 33–34, 36–42, 44–49, 53, 185
   The Dead Hour, 41–42, 45, 47
   Exile, 40–42, 45–46
Mitchell, Ian, 160
Morgan, Edwin, xi n.16, xvii n.32, 56
Morrison, Ewan, x–xi, xiv–xv, xviii–xx, 97 n.54, 117–47, 150–51, 155, 158–64, 169–73, 184–85, 187 n.19
   Distance, x, xiv, xviii, 117–21, 123, 129–39, 141–42
   The Last Book You Read, x–xi, 117, 150, 159–60, 162–63, 169–70, 173
   Ménage, xviii, 117, 142–47
   Swung, x–xi, xviii, 117, 121–29, 131, 133, 139–42
multiculturalism, xv, xviii–xix, 3, 7, 23, 27–28, 81–83, 88, 102, 110, 183–84
   'boutique multiculturalism', 82–83, 184
Nairn, Tom, vii, xiii, 59–60, 67–68
   The Break-up of Britain, vii, 59–60
national imagination, vii, 58–60, 64, 187
Neubauer, Jürgen, xii–xiii, 81
Nicholson, Colin, xi, xv
non-place, xviii, 118–24, 130–35, 146–47
O'Connor, Edmund, 34
O'Rourke, Donny, 59, 68–69
orientalism, 82
Ortiz, Fernando, 83
overdetermination, 60–62
Paisley, Janet, 150
Paretski, Sarah, 34
Pittin-Hedon, Marie-Odile, 35 n.10, 46 n.37, 67 n.24, 122 n.10
Pittock, Murray, 182–83, 186
Plain, Gill, xviii, 34–37, 50
Poe, Edgar Allan, 51–52
polyphony, 3, 28, 87–88
post-devolution writing, xii–xiii, xv–xvi, xviii, 37, 151, 182, 184, 186
postmodernity/postmodernism, xii–xiii, xvi, 11, 62, 74, 98, 140, 145–46, 161, 182

INDEX

'postnational constellation', xii–xiii, 81, 117
post-nationalism, xii–xiii, xix, 3, 81, 183
Priestman, Martin, 36
Rankin, Ian, x, 33–38, 44, 185
Ricoeur, Paul, 187
Robertson, James, xi, xviii, xx, 56–78, 81, 84, 117, 150, 158–59, 165–66, 186
   And the Land Lay Still, xviii, 56–78, 84, 158–59, 186
   The Fanatic, 63, 71, 74–75, 77
   Joseph Knight, 57
   'Six Deaths, Two Funerals, a Wedding and a Divorce', 158–59, 165
   The Testament of Gideon Mack, 76
Rose, Dilys, 150, 156, 158
Rowling, J. K., xii
Rushdie, Salman, 81, 90–91, 106, 106 n.73, 187
   The Satanic Verses, 87
   Shame, 90–91
Saadi, Suhayl, xi, xvi, xviii–xx, 2, 28, 81–111, 150–51, 153–55, 159, 164–69, 172–74, 178, 183, 186
   The Burning Mirror, 150, 154–55, 159, 165–68, 172–74, 178, 183
   Joseph's Box, xi, 82–86, 94–100, 103–11
   Psychoraag, xi, 28, 81–111, 154 n.8
   'Songs of the Village Idiot', 82 n.7, 88 n.30, 98 n.57, 110 n.85
Said, Edward, 15 n.32, 82
Sayers, Dorothy L., 33–34
Schoene, Berthold, xiii–xv, 8, 10, 18 n.10, 117–18, 151 n.3, 171
Scott, Jeremy, xvii, 2, 22–23
Smith, Ali, x, 85–86, 184
spectacle/megaspectacle, 131–34
Stevenson, Randall, 70 n.31, 71
Stevenson, Robert Louis, 34
Stonesbury, John, 93
Strachan, Zoë, x–xi, xvii, 2–3, 15–22, 28–29, 33, 81
   Negative Space, 2, 15–21
   Spin Cycle, 2–3, 15–22
subalternity, xvii, 10–15
Tartan Noir, 34–38
Taylor, Alan, 86–87, 184 n.7
Taylor, Diana, 83 n.11
Tei, Chiew-Siah, 183
third space, 81, 100–111
Thomson, Alex, ix, 37, 39, 45, 184, 186
Todorov, Tzvetan, 167
transculturation, 83, 89, 101–02, 110

Upstone, Sarah, 82, 84–85, 88
   'civic nationalism', 84–85, 88
urban Kailyard, 12
Virilio, Paul, 119
Warner, Alan, xi, 3 n.6
Welleck, René and Austin Warren, *Theory of Literature*, ix
Welsh, Irvine, vii, xi, xiv, xvii, 2–3, 11–12, 14, 59, 81, 151, 156
   Trainspotting, vii, 133, 141, 156–57
Welsh, Louise, x, xvii, xx, 33–34, 36–39, 42, 46–47, 49–53, 185, 187 n.19
   The Bullet Trick, 34, 46, 51 n.46, 51–52
   The Cutting Room, 34, 37–38, 42, 45–47, 50, 51 n.46, 52
   Naming the Bones, 38
   Tamburlaine Must Die, 38, 50–51
Widdowson, Peter, 185–87
Williamson, Kevin, 2
Woodward, Catherine, 85

www.ingramcontent.com/pod-product-compliance
Lightning Source LLC
Chambersburg PA
CBHW050243170426
43202CB00015B/2895